Rethinking Genesis

Rethinking Genesis

The Sources and Authorship of the First Book of the Pentateuch

Duane A. Garrett

BAKER BOOK HOUSE
Grand Rapids, Michigan 49516

Printed in the United States of America

Library of Congress Cataloging-in-Publication Data

Garrett, Duane A.
Rethinking Genesis: the sources and authorship of the first book of the Pentateuch /
Duane A. Garrett.
p. cm.
Includes index.
ISBN 0-8010-3837-5
1. Bible. O.T. Genesis—Sources. 2. Bible. O. T. Genesis—Authorship. 3. Bible. O.T.
Genesis—Criticism, interpretation, etc. I. Title.
BS1235.5.G32 1991
222'.11066—dc20
91-2008
CIP

The author wishes to acknowledge permission to reprint material from
J. B. Pritchard, ed., *Ancient Near Eastern Texts: Relating to the Old Testament*,
3d ed. with Supplement. Copyright (c) 1969 by Princeton University Press.

Contents

List of Abbreviations

AB	Anchor Bible
AcOr	*Acta orientalia*
ANET	*Ancient Near Easter Texts,* ed. J. B. Pritchard
BA	*Biblical Archaeologist*
Bib	*Biblica*
BZAW	*Beihefte zur Zeitschrift für die alttestamentliche Wissenschaft*
Cal Th J	*Calvin Theological Journal*
Ev Q	*Evangelical Quarterly*
HSS	Harvard Semitic Series
ICC	International Critical Commentary
Interp	*Interpretation*
ISBE	*International Standard Bible Encyclopedia* (rev. ed.), ed. G. W. Bromiley
JAOS	*Journal of the American Oriental Society*
JBL	*Journal of Biblical Literature*
JCS	*Journal of Cuneiform Studies*
JETS	*Journal of the Evangelical Theological Society*
JNES	*Journal of Near Eastern Studies*
JSOT	*Journal for the Study of the Old Testament*
JSOTSS	JSOT Supplement Series
MT	Masoretic Text
NASB	New American Standard Bible
NEB	New English Bible
NICOT	New International Commentary on the Old Testament
NIV	New International Version
OTL	Old Testament Library
OTS	*Oudtestamentische Studiën*
RSV	Revised Standard Version
St Bib	*Studia Biblica*
ST	*Studia theologica*
TOTC	Tyndale Old Testament Commentary
VT	*Vetus Testamentum*
WBC	Word Biblical Commentary
ZAW	*Zeitschrift für die alttestamentliche Wissenschaft*

List of Figures

Preface

I t is said that fools rush in where angels fear to tread. However much this axiom may apply to other endeavors, it is at least partially true of those who attempt to discover the literary background of the Book of Genesis. In addition to the problem that the book never alludes to any sources, it is also anonymous. Who wrote it? When was it written? What are its sources? Genesis directly addresses none of these questions.

The history of the study of Genesis is strewn with the wrecks of earlier literary theories. The very idea of a consensus among biblical scholars on Genesis has become something of a joke. One writer, addressing this issue, has stated that if historical-critical biblical studies were a parliament, a government could never be formed.[1] With astonishing rapidity, previously held "assured results" and seemingly invulnerable positions are being not modified but abandoned altogether. Widely practiced methods of analysis, indeed methods which are currently being taught, are falling from favor as scholars on the leading edge of research pronounce them to be presumptuous or even useless.

This is not to say that an older view like the Documentary Hypothesis is now a mere relic; it continues to be taught in schools all over the theological world and scholars continue to publish papers and studies founded upon it. Nevertheless, the continued "dominance" of the hypothesis is a result more of the present confusion and flux in biblical studies than of any dynamic within the hypothesis itself.

Precisely for these reasons the evangelical community of biblical scholars must readdress these issues. For the past 100 years, "conser-

---

1. Thomas L. Thompson, *The Origin Tradition of Ancient Israel,* JSOTSS 55 (Sheffield: JSOT Press, 1987), 201.

vatives," up against a near monolithic critical consensus, have been locked in a battle with "liberal" scholarship. All attention in the evangelical camp was focused on apologetic studies. The Mosaic authorship of Genesis was stoutly defended, the arguments for the Documentary Hypothesis were assailed, and archaeology was employed in the defense of the historicity of the text. Much was accomplished here. Many conservatives, both Christian and Jewish, were pointing to the deficiencies in the standard critical arguments long ago, and it is a testimony to the validity of their studies that modern scholars who cannot in any sense be called conservative are now using those same arguments as they jettison the orthodoxy of higher criticism.

It would be a grave mistake, however, to suppose that biblical scholarship is now moving in a more conservative direction. It is, to the contrary, moving in *every* direction. It would seem that every writer who addresses these issues has a new theory of Pentateuchal origin or of the composition and redaction of Genesis. This is not at all a bad thing (I am myself adding another hypothesis). Old Testament studies have been opened afresh as scholars return to the texts to seek answers to questions that were once thought settled. A new vigor has entered biblical studies. For this reason the older conservative defenses of Genesis against the older critical consensus are no longer adequate: the "consensus" no longer exists.

It is against this environment that I have attempted to address the issues of the origin and intention of Genesis. Therefore, although I approach the question from an evangelical perspective, I undertake to address questions that earlier conservatives did not. Specifically, I endeavor to demonstrate that formal patterns are present in the text of Genesis which point back to the sources of Genesis. From these hypothetical sources, I attempt to set forth the original setting and intention of Genesis.

The first three chapters of this book are preliminary. In them, I set forth the three major assumptions behind the program of this book. The first is that the Documentary Hypothesis can no longer be regarded as valid in any sense, the second is that the attempt to find long streams of oral tradition behind Genesis is both futile and misleading, and the third is that an early date for Genesis and indeed Mosaic authorship are reasonable working "hypotheses" for a new look at Genesis.

Chapters 4 to 9 make up the heart of this study. Here, I attempt to show what is the structure of Genesis and also what may have been the sources that lay behind this structure. I also make preliminary statements on the intentions and interpretations of these texts and on what may have been their settings.

In chapters 10 through 12, I attempt to draw together reasonable conclusions from the earlier analysis. Specifically, I point out what may be indications of authorship in the text, who may have transmitted and preserved the sources of Genesis, and what may have been the occasion and setting for drawing these sources together into the Book of Genesis.

In order to make this book more accessible to the nonspecialist, I have avoided the use of Hebrew wherever possible. I have found it necessary to use Hebrew characters only in chapter 1. Elsewhere, I have used simplified transliteration when referring to a Hebrew text.

In any endeavor such as this, thanks is owed to many people. I specifically would like to thank Dr. Clint Ashley, President of the Canadian Southern Baptist Seminary, for his encouragement. I would also like to thank my colleague Dr. Robert Tucker and my student Mr. Frank Stirk, each of whom laboriously read and corrected the early draft. Above all, I owe a great debt to my wife, Patricia Garrett, who has supported me and gone with me around the world and who has never been jealous of the many hours I have spent with the Book of Genesis.

Duane A. Garrett
Canadian Southern Baptist Seminary
Alberta, Canada

ONE

The Higher Criticism of Genesis

1

The Documentary Hypothesis

The time has long passed for scholars of every theological persuasion to recognize that the Graf-Wellhausen theory, as a starting point for continued research, is dead. The Documentary Hypothesis and the arguments that support it have been effectively demolished by scholars from many different theological perspectives and areas of expertise. Even so, the ghost of Wellhausen hovers over Old Testament studies and symposiums like a thick fog, adding nothing of substance but effectively obscuring vision. Although actually incompatible with form-critical and archaeology-based studies, the Documentary Hypothesis has managed to remain the mainstay of critical orthodoxy.[1] One wonders if we will ever return to the day when discussions of Genesis will not be stilted by interminable references to P and J. There are indications that such a day is coming. Many scholars are exploring the inadequacies of the Documentary

1. The amount of literature on the Documentary Hypothesis and the number of scholars who support it are enormous. A few of the major works, with particular reference to Genesis, are S. R. Driver, *An Introduction to the Literature of the Old Testament* (1897; reprint, Gloucester, Mass.: Peter Smith, 1972); John Skinner, *A Critical and Exegetical Commentary on Genesis,* 2d ed., ICC (Edinburgh: T. and T. Clark, 1930); Robert H. Pfeiffer, *Introduction to the Old Testament* (New York: Harper and Brothers, 1941); Gerhard von Rad, *Genesis,* trans. John H. Marks (Philadelphia: Westminster, 1961); E. A. Speiser, *Genesis,* AB (New York: Doubleday, 1964); Otto Eissfeldt, *The Old Testament: An Introduction,* trans. Peter Ackroyd (New York: Harper and Row, 1965); Georg Fohrer, *Introduction to the Old Testament,* trans. David E. Green (Nashville: Abingdon, 1968); J. Alberto Soggin, *Introduction to the Old Testament,* OTL

Hypothesis and looking toward new models for explaining the
Pentateuch.[2]

The History and Salient Points
of the Documentary Hypothesis

The Documentary Hypothesis began when Jean Astruc (1684–1766)
came to believe that he could uncover the sources of the Pentateuch by
using the divine names *Yahweh* and *Elohim* as a guide. He placed passages that use the name *Elohim* in one column (A), those that use
Yahweh in another (B), and passages with "repetitions" (C) and inter-
polations (D) in a third and a fourth column. From this simple, if not
facile, beginning originated the road to the Documentary Hypothesis.
Along the way came a "fragmentary hypothesis" (which asserts that the
Pentateuch was compiled from a mass of fragmentary sources) and a
"supplemental hypothesis" (which asserts that a single, unified document lies at the core of the Pentateuch, but that many fragmentary
sources have been added to it). But the triumphant theory of
Pentateuchal origins was the Documentary Hypothesis, often called the
Graf-Wellhausen hypothesis after the two men, K. H. Graf and Julius
Wellhausen, who gave it its classic expression.[3]

The theory, in its most basic form, is easy enough to grasp: Behind
the Pentateuch are four source documents, called J (Yahwist), E
(Elohist), D (Deuteronomist), and P (Priestly Code).

J, the oldest, begins at Genesis 2:4b and includes large portions of
Genesis as well as portions of Exodus and Numbers and a few short

---

(Philadelphia: Westminster, 1976); George W. Coats, *Genesis: With an Introduction to
Narrative Literature*, FOTL (Grand Rapids: Eerdmans, 1984); Claus Westermann,
Genesis 1–11, trans. John J. Scullion (Minneapolis: Augsburg/Fortress, 1984); Werner
H. Schmidt, *Introduction to the Old Testament*, trans. Matthew J. O'Connell (London:
SCM, 1984).

2. R. N. Whybray, *The Making of the Pentateuch* (Sheffield: JSOT Press, 1987), is a
major critique. A significant assessment from the traditio-historical camp is Rolf
Rendtorff, *Das überlieferungsgeschichtliche Problem des Pentateuch*, BZAW 147 (Berlin:
de Gruyter, 1977). Cf. Brevard S. Childs, *Introduction to the Old Testament as Scripture*
(Philadelphia: Fortress, 1979), 119ff., and Gordon J. Wenham, *Genesis 1–15*, WBC
(Waco: Word, 1987), xxxiv–xxxv.

3. For a history of Old Testament criticism, see R. K. Harrison, *Introduction to the
Old Testament* (Grand Rapids: Eerdmans, 1969), 3–82. See also R. J. Thompson, *Moses
and the Law in a Century of Criticism Since Graf* (Leiden: Brill, 1970); also Fohrer,
Introduction, 23–32, 106–13; and Soggin, *Introduction*, 79–98.

texts in Deuteronomy. It may be dated to the early monarchy (Solomonic?) period. In Genesis, J refers to God as Yahweh, for, according to the hypothesis, people began using the name *Yahweh* early in the antediluvian period (Gen. 4:26, a J text). As a theological statement, J is often regarded as the work of a great, original thinker who gave shape to the Old Testament idea of the history of salvation.

E is somewhat later than J but follows the same basic story line as J. Genesis 15 is the earliest extant E text. E's provenance is the northern kingdom. In Genesis, E refers to God as Elohim rather than Yahweh, for, according to E, the name *Yahweh* was not revealed until the exodus period (Exod. 3:15, an E text). E is more sensitive to moral issues than J, but it views God as somewhat more distant from man. J and E were subsequently redacted into a single document by R^JE (R = redactor). In the course of redaction, much of the E material was edited out and thus lost to posterity.

D was produced at the time of the Josianic reformation (2 Kings 22) and is essentially the Book of Deuteronomy. D does not have a characteristic divine name since it has little if any representation in Genesis. R^D subsequently combined the texts JE and D.

P was produced last, in the exilic period. It begins at Genesis 1:1 and includes large portions of Genesis, Exodus, and Numbers and all of Leviticus. In Genesis, P refers to God as Elohim since, like E, it assumes that the divine name *Yahweh* was first revealed at the exodus (Exod. 6:3, a P text). It is dominated by genealogies, priestly regulations, and a highly stylized manner of narration. P was soon redacted into JED by R^P . The Pentateuch was thus formed.

A few fragments not related to any of the four source documents (e.g., Gen. 14) are also to be found in the Pentateuch.[4]

Presuppositions of the Documentary Hypothesis

R. N. Whybray (and before him other scholars as well) has pointed out that the Documentary Hypothesis is founded on four presuppositions:[5]

4. See also the summary in Whybray, *Pentateuch*, 20–21. For a detailed presentation of the classic form of the hypothesis, see Driver, *Introduction*, 1–159. For a presentation of the hypothesis in a more complex, evolved form, see Fohrer, *Introduction*, 120–95. For a survey of the hypothesis in the context of some more recent developments, see Soggin, *Introduction*, 99–160, and Wenham, *Genesis 1–15*, xxv–xlv.

5. *Pentateuch*, 43–55. I here basically follow Whybray's outline but use some different terminology.

An evolutionary, unilinear approach to Israelite history. It has long been recognized that Wellhausen built his theory on a now-discredited evolutionary philosophy with its roots in the thought of G. W. F. Hegel. Of course, it is not enough to say that Hegelianism is discredited and therefore Wellhausen is wrong. On the other hand, it is certain that the history of Israelite religion cannot be portrayed in the simple, highly evolutionary manner that Wellhausen thought possible.[6]

The possibility of dividing the Pentateuchal texts on the basis of stylistic criteria. Early advocates of the Documentary Hypothesis felt they could easily separate one text from another on the basis of style. In fact, the whole Pentateuch is in standard biblical Hebrew. The only way a single style could be found for each document would be if each one monotonously and rigorously maintained a highly idiosyncratic style.

A simple conflation of documents by redactors. According to the theory, the redactors simply conflated the texts at hand by the "scissors-and-paste" method of cutting up each document and then joining the whole into a continuous narrative. No true analogy to this somewhat bizarre editorial procedure is available.[7]

Easy determination of the purposes and methods behind the documents and redactions. The early framers of the Documentary Hypothesis thought they could deduce the purposes and methods of the redactors, despite the fact that enormous cultural differences existed between the scholars who studied Genesis and the men who wrote it. More than that, scholars came to have strange perceptions of the writers of the documents over against the redactors. In particular, it was assumed that each writer aimed to produce a single, continuous history but would tolerate no inconsistency, repetition, or narrative digressions. The redactors, on the other hand, were said to be utterly oblivious to every kind of contradiction and repetition.[8]

6. See K. A. Kitchen, *Ancient Orient and Old Testament* (Chicago: Inter-Varsity, 1966), 113–14.

7. It is true that writers and editors frequently cut or rearrange material in a single document as part of the writing process, but this is not what the Documentary Hypothesis implies. A more accurate analogy would be if an editor were to take Homer's *Iliad* and *Odyssey, The Trojan Women* of Euripides, and Vergil's *Aeneid,* cut up the manuscripts, and then rearrange all the pieces into a single work on the Trojan War. The product of such an endeavor not only would be unintelligible, but also would have none of the literary power of the original works. See the discussion in Whybray, *Pentateuch,* 45–46.

8. Ibid., 49.

The Arguments for the Documentary Hypothesis

It is critical to recognize that according to this theory the four documents were first composed as continuous, single narratives and only later were brought together and edited into the present work. As scholars continued to study the hypothesis, many modifications were proposed. Some scholars tended to make the theory more complex by dividing the four sources into even smaller sources (e.g., J^1 and J^2), whereas others reduced the number of sources, questioning the existence of E altogether. Further developments came out of the application of form-criticism to the documents.[9] Nevertheless, the basic Documentary Hypothesis from which all refinements come is the simplest place at which the theory can be analyzed. The central arguments for the hypothesis are as follows:

Some texts in Genesis refer to God as Yahweh, whereas others call him Elohim. Those texts that call him Yahweh may be assigned to J, who thought the name *Yahweh* was revealed to humanity well before the patriarchal age began. Those texts that refer to God as Elohim may be assigned to E or P, both of whom thought the name *Yahweh* was not revealed until the exodus.

Genesis contains some duplicate stories and repetitions. This is because each of the two source documents contained its own version of a single tradition. Thus 12:10–20 (J) and 20:1–18 (E) are variants of a single tradition.[10] Sometimes the two variant versions were redacted into a single narrative, yet the documents behind the single redaction are still apparent. J and P each had a version of the flood story, for example, but these have been combined in the present text.

Contradictions within Genesis indicate the existence of the separate documents. The implication is that one document had one tradition, but a second had another.

The language and style of the documents vary. J is said to have been a masterful storyteller, but P is prosaic and wordy. Each document also has its own preferred vocabulary. For the English "begot," J prefers the G stem יָלַד, but P uses the H stem הוֹלִיד.

Each document, when extracted from the present text of Genesis, shows itself to have been a continuous, meaningful piece of literature.

9. For a good survey of developments since Wellhausen, see ibid., 31–43.
10. See Speiser, *Genesis*, 150–52.

In particular, it is possible to see a specific literary and theological purpose behind each.[11] This validates the method.

Even on a superficial reading, some texts obviously involve more than one source. The best example is Genesis 1–2, which can hardly come from a single source. Instead, Genesis 1:1–2:3 and Genesis 2:4ff. must be regarded as separate works.[12] The presence of obvious examples of separate sources in a text validates the principles of the Documentary Hypothesis, which may then be applied to texts where the source division is not obvious.

The confused history of the Israelite priesthood found in the Pentateuch is best explained by the Documentary Hypothesis. In some texts (e.g., Deuteronomy), all Levites are priests. In other texts, (the P portions of Exodus and Leviticus), only the Aaronites are priests and the rest of the Levites are mere hierodules—workers in the temple without priestly privileges. The Pentateuch, therefore, cannot be a unified work from a single hand. Rather, documents D and P come from different perspectives and different ages.

Analysis of the Arguments for the Documentary Hypothesis

The Names of God

The criterion of the divine names for source analysis has been challenged from several directions. First, the criterion cannot be applied consistently. For example, Genesis 22:11, an E text, uses the name *Yahweh*. Indeed, at the very beginning of the Pentateuch we read not simply Yahweh in the J source (Gen. 2–4) but the unusual Yahweh Elohim. In addition, M. H. Segal notes that the divine names are used interchangeably in texts that cannot have different sources, which begs the question of why Genesis should be treated exceptionally.[13]

Second, the editorial rationale for the avoidance of Yahweh in E and P sources in Genesis is specious. Even if the E and P writers thought that the Israelites did not know of the divine name *Yahweh* until the time of Moses, there is no reason for them to avoid using the

11. For a detailed presentation, see Walter Brueggemann and Hans Walter Wolff, *The Vitality of Old Testament Traditions* (Atlanta: John Knox, 1975).

12. At this point, we are not concerned about the position of 2:4a. This issue is taken up in chap. 4.

13. *The Pentateuch: Its Composition and Authorship* (Jerusalem: Magnes, 1967), 11–14.

name in patriarchal stories unless they are directly quoting a character.[14] For that matter, there is absolutely no reason that J should avoid Elohim.

Third, the phenomenon of the interchange of Yahweh and Elohim can be explained far more satisfactorily and simply without resort to source criticism. Umberto Cassuto makes the point that the two names bring out different aspects of the character of God. Yahweh is the covenant name of God, which emphasizes his special relationship to Israel. Elohim speaks of God's universality as God of all earth.[15] To put it simply, Elohim is what God is and Yahweh is who he is. It is true that Cassuto exploits this distinction too rigorously and goes beyond what the text intends at some points,[16] but the distinction is valid.

In addition, Segal points out that the interchange of the divine names is often for the sake of variety or reflects popular usage.[17] Whybray adds to this that the alternation of names may be unconscious because of the identity of the two names.[18]

Perhaps it is best to speak of Yahweh and Elohim having semantic overlap. In a context that emphasizes God as universal deity (e.g., Gen. 1), Elohim is used. In a text that speaks more of God as covenant savior (Exod. 6), Yahweh is more likely to be utilized. In other cases, in which neither aspect is particularly stressed, the names may be alternated for variety or indeed for no specific reason.

Fourth, the assumption that the J text thought the patriarchs knew the name *Yahweh* but that E and P texts claim they did not is based on faulty exegesis. Genesis 4:26, "Then people began to call on the name of Yahweh," is often taken as an assertion by J that the name *Yahweh* was revealed at this moment in history. Thus, it is claimed that J believed the patriarchs knew their God as Yahweh. E and P, on the other hand, are said to have believed that the name *Yahweh* was first revealed in the period of the exodus. The relevant texts are Exodus 3:13–15 (E) and Exodus 6:2–8 (P).

Genesis 4:26 has nothing to do with the question of when Yahwism began. Even Claus Westermann, who considers this a J text, notes that it has been misunderstood. He comments, "When he [J] uses 'Yahweh' here, he is only saying that, despite the variety of religions, the creator of humankind can only be one. He could not say אלהים, which would

14. Whybray, *Pentateuch*, 64–65.

15. Umberto Cassuto, *The Documentary Hypothesis and the Composition of the Pentateuch*, trans. Israel Abrahams (Jerusalem: Magnes, 1941), 15–41.

16. Cf. Whybray, *Pentateuch*, 71.

17. *Pentateuch*, 13–14.

18. *Pentateuch*, 72.

be clearer for the modern reader, because he is speaking of the very same God who already has been mentioned in 4:1, 6."[19] The author thus gives an optimistic closure to the sad history of Genesis 3–4[20] and says that the God his readers know as Yahweh is the one true God whom people have worshiped from earliest times.

In Exodus 3:13–15, Moses asks God his name, and is told first that God is the "I am," and then that he should tell the Israelites that Yahweh, the God of their fathers, sent Moses to them. God adds that Yahweh is the name by which he is to be worshiped forever. The text hardly says that no one had ever heard the name *Yahweh* before this time. If that were the intention, one would find something like, "No longer will you call me the God of your fathers; from now on my name is Yahweh," similar to Genesis 17:5, 15. Rather, the text asserts that the name *Yahweh* will have new significance because of the mighty act of the exodus. The people will now see that Yahweh is present with them.[21]

Exodus 6:2c–3 appears to be a straightforward assertion that the patriarchs did not know the name *Yahweh*. Most translations are similar to the following: "I am Yahweh. I appeared to Abraham, and to Isaac, and to Jacob as God Almighty, but by my name Yahweh I did not make myself known to them."

But the Hebrew text, as Francis I. Andersen points out, contains a case of noncontiguous parallelism that translators have not recognized: וּשְׁמִי יהוה . . . אֲנִי יהוה ("I am Yahweh . . . and my name is Yahweh"). The לֹא ("not") is therefore assertative in a rhetorical question rather than a simple negative, and it should not be connected to what precedes it.[22] In fact, the whole text is set in a poetic, parallel structure beyond what Andersen notes (see fig. 1.1).

The text does not assert that the patriarchs had never heard of Yahweh or only knew of El Shaddai, although it does say that God showed them the meaning of his name *El Shaddai*. El Shaddai is preceded by the בּ *essentiae*,[23] which implies that God filled the name with special significance for them when he made a covenant with them and promised the land of Canaan as their inheritance (v. 4). Now he is going to fill the name *Yahweh* with significance ("And my name is Yahweh")

---

19. *Genesis 1–11,* 340.

20. See the discussion in chap. 10.

21. Cf. John I. Durham, *Exodus,* WBC (Waco: Word, 1987), 39–41.

22. Francis I. Andersen, *The Sentence in Biblical Hebrew* (The Hague: Mouton, 1974), 102.

23. See J. A. Motyer, *The Revelation of the Divine Name* (London: Tyndale, 1959), 11ff.

Figure 1.1

The Structure of Exodus 6:2c–3

A אֲנִי יהוה

B וָאֵרָא אֶל־אַבְרָהָם אֶל־יִצְחָק וְאֶל־יַעֲקֹב בְּאֵל שַׁדָּי

A' וּשְׁמִי יהוה

B' לֹא נוֹדַעְתִּי לָהֶם

A I am Yahweh.

B And I made myself known to Abraham, to Isaac, and to Jacob as El Shaddai.

A' And my name is Yahweh;

B' Did I not make myself known to them?

in the even greater deliverance of the exodus (v. 5). Even so, the text stresses the continuity between the revelation to the patriarchs and the revelation of the exodus rather than any discontinuity ("Did I not make myself known to them?"). Andersen's comments are to the point: "There is no hint in Exodus that Yahweh was a new name revealed first to Moses. On the contrary, the success of his mission depended on the use of the familiar name for validation by the Israelites."[24]

Fifth, use of the divine names as a source criterion is contrary to all ancient Near Eastern analogies. K. A. Kitchen documents many examples from Egyptian and Mesopotamian sources of a single god being called by several names in a single text. He adds that no Egyptologist would ever use divine names for source criticism.[25]

In short, the criterion of divine names, the historical and evidential starting point for the Documentary Hypothesis, is without foun-

24. *Sentence*, 102. The traditional translation (represented by the NIV, NEB, RSV, etc.) is impossible on other grounds as well. First, this translation must assume that the ב in בְּאֵל שַׁדָּי does double duty and also governs וּשְׁמִי יהוה. But this is impossible, for the two phrases are in separate clauses even in the traditional translation. Second, the N stem of ידע cannot take a direct object (וּשְׁמִי יהוה) because it is reflexive. Third, it is unusual for a subordinate phrase in Hebrew to precede לֹא, because לֹא is normally the first word in a sentence in which it occurs. See C. L. Seow, *A Grammar for Biblical Hebrew* (Nashville: Abingdon, 1987), 94. Disrupted word order is possible, but, in light of the structure of the text as described, there is no reason to think this is the case here.

25. *Ancient Orient*, 121–23.

dation. It is based on misinterpretation, mistranslation, and lack of attention to extrabiblical sources.

Repetition, Parallel Accounts (Doublets), and Redundancy

The use of doublets and repetition as evidence for multiple documents in Genesis is perhaps of all the arguments the most persuasive for the modern student, while in fact being the most spurious and abused piece of evidence. Thus it seems to the modern reader that Genesis 12:10–20 and 20:1–18 must be variants of a single tradition.[26] How else could one explain the presence of two stories that seem so remarkably similar? Surely, the modern reader thinks, the variants (e.g., Pharaoh's house in Gen. 12, Abimelech's house in Gen. 20) are simply examples of how a single tradition has been handed down in different forms in different communities.

The assumption appears reasonable, but it is altogether a fallacy. It is an entirely modern reading of the text and ignores ancient rhetorical concepts. In an ancient text, there is no stronger indication that only a single document is present than parallel accounts. Doublets, that is, two separate stories that closely parallel one another, are the very stuff of ancient narrative.[27] They are what the discriminating audience sought in a story.

Simple repetition, first of all, is common in ancient Near Eastern literature. In the Ugaritic Epic of Keret, for example, King Keret is in distress because his entire family has been killed in a series of disasters. In a dream, he receives instruction from El concerning what he should do. El's instructions, which occupy lines 60–153, say that he should make a sacrifice, muster his people for a military campaign, and go to the land of Udum, ruled by King Pabil. There he is to demand the daughter of Pabil, Hurriya, for his wife. Keret awakens and carries out the instructions. In describing how Keret obeyed El's

26. For the present purposes it is not necessary to deal with the third parallel in Gen. 26. See chap. 6 for a full treatment.

27. Cf. Thomas L. Thompson, *The Origin Tradition of Ancient Israel*, JSOTSS 55 (Sheffield: JSOT Press, 1987), 59: "This time-worn effort to relate parallel traditions and units of traditions, which has been a fundamental first step into the history of traditions, needs to be radically questioned. We have neither the number nor the variety of tale-types in the Bible with which one might reasonably analyze their interrelatedness. Moreover, the existence of doublets is definitely not a criterion with which we can demonstrate a separateness in the traditions or in the complex sources of traditions. Doublet and triplet stories can and do exist within the same traditions. . . ."

command, lines 156ff. are for the most part a verbatim repetition of lines 60–153 (albeit from a different perspective). This narrative technique is employed in the Bible as well. In Genesis 24, the text tells how Abraham's servant, after a prayer for divine guidance, meets the future wife of Isaac at a well (vv. 12–27). Then it gives the servant's account of all of this to Laban, but again quotes almost verbatim the previous material (vv. 34–48; with adjustments for the difference of perspective). Acts, similarly, gives three complete accounts of Paul's vision on the way to Damascus (9:1–19; 22:3–16; 26:9–18).

In an analogous manner, if two or more separate events were perceived to be similar to one another, ancient writers tend to give accounts of the events in parallel fashion. In the course of doing this, the narrator might put all the accounts in the same form. As he tells his story, he will select especially material that fits the formal, parallel pattern. For this reason the author of the Book of Kings, in summarizing the reigns of each king of Israel and Judah, tends to employ a number of formulas. He gives the date a king came into power, the length of his reign, an evaluation ("he did evil/good in the sight of the Lord"), a reference indicating where the reader can find more information, and a statement of the king's death and burial. By employing this technique, he emphasizes the evil done by the kings by the frequent repetition of "and he did evil in the sight of the Lord." A modern writer, even one with the same theological point to make, would never employ this technique. He would instead say, "The vast majority of the kings of Israel and Judah were evil," and proceed to give specific examples.

Employment of the technique of parallel accounts survived even into the Greco-Roman period, albeit in a less stylized format. Plutarch's *Lives* sets the biographies of famous Greeks alongside those of famous Romans (for example, the life of Demosthenes is set in parallel to that of Cicero). Luke's account of the ministry of Peter to some degree parallels his account of the life of Paul. The interest in parallel events and lives still continued, but in the earlier literature the technique is far more deliberate and formulaic (and thus more obvious). Simply put, the parallels between Genesis 12:10–20 and 20:1–18, when analyzed by ancient rather than modern literary standards, strongly indicate that the two accounts are from the same source.

In light of the love for repetition and parallelism in Hebrew narrative and poetry, it is not surprising that Hebrew narrative is sometimes redundant even within a single story. To be sure, this "redundancy" is

Figure 1.2

The Structure of Genesis 7:21–22

A They perished (וַיִּגְוַע)

   B Every living thing that moves on earth . . .

   B' Everything that has the breath of the living spirit . . .

A' They died (מֵתוּ)

---

never pointless repetition. At times a summary statement is followed by a more detailed account. This is in fact the case in Genesis 1:1ff., where 1:1 is a summary statement and 1:2–2:3 is a more detailed description. Other ancient literature employs this technique as well.[28] At other times, the redundant style is for dramatic effect, as in 1 Samuel 3:4–10.

The flood narrative, according to the Documentary Hypothesis, is a classic example of two accounts having been conflated. As evidence for the conflation, advocates of the hypothesis cite the redundancies and argue that a single author would not have repeated himself so much. Thus, for example, Genesis 6:9–22 is P but 7:1–5 is J.

As the text reads, however, the two passages are not redundant but consecutive. The P material is prior to the building of the ark and the J material is a speech of God after its completion but just prior to the beginning of the flood. The repetition heightens the dramatic anticipation of the deluge to follow.

Careful examination of a "redundancy" in the flood narrative often shows it to be a carefully constructed single unit. Genesis 7:21–22 is such an example. The Documentary Hypothesis assigns verse 21 to P and verse 22 to J,[29] but Andersen has shown that the two verses are chiastic (fig. 1.2). This text is in fact the fulfillment report of a similar chiasmus in 6:17.[30]

Andersen himself is not hesitant to point out the implications of this for documentary analysis. He concludes that when the text is left

---

28. See Kitchen, *Ancient Orient,* 117.

29. Thus Speiser, *Genesis,* 49; Skinner, *Genesis,* 153, 165.

30. Andersen, *Sentence,* 39–40. J. A. Emerton, "An Examination of Some Attempts to Defend the Unity of the Flood Narrative in Genesis. Part II," *VT* 38 (1988): 2–3, is unimpressed by this and remarks that a link between 6:17 and 7:21 is not surprising since both are in P. What Emerton fails to note, however, is that 7:21b–22a contains an expansion of 6:17. 6:17 speaks of God's determination to destroy כל־בשר אשר־בו רוח חיים, whereas 7:21b–22a tells of the death of כל־בשר . . . נשמת־רוח חיים באפיו. And yet 7:22 is said to be a J text. Andersen's point stands.

as it stands rather than arbitrarily divided into sources and doublets, the artistic unity and solemnity of the whole, from the standpoint of discourse grammar, gives the impression of having been formed as a single, unified narration.[31]

Another significant issue that relates to the story of the flood is the matter of contradictions in the text, a problem to which we now turn.

Contradictions in the Text

Apparent contradictions in Genesis are often cited as markers to the different documents behind the text. In the flood account, the two most frequently cited contradictions are in regard to the number of animals to be brought on board the ark (6:20 says to bring one pair of every kind of animal, but 7:2 says to bring seven pairs of clean animals) and the flood chronology. With regard to the former, the number of clean animals, the explanation is simply that it is a precise figure given immediately before the flood (7:1–2) instead of the general figure given before the ark was built (6:20). Provision had to be made to ensure that there would be sufficient livestock after the flood.[32]

The matter of chronology is more complex, and it involves the structure of the whole narrative. Many scholars have pointed out the difficulty of reconstructing a chronology of the flood from the figures given and have concluded that the confusion is the result of R^P having conflated the two different chronologies of J and P without resolving the chronological inconsistencies.[33] But recent research has demonstrated the whole narrative to be far more coherent than was once recognized.

Wenham has shown the whole flood story (6:10–9:19) to be chiastic in structure (fig. 1.3). The mere presence of a chiasmus is not proof that there can be no sources behind it. Indeed, as shall be argued subsequently, the genealogical material in particular appears to be from another source.[34] Yet there comes a point at which a given source hypothesis is simply no longer reasonable. It stretches the imagination

---

31. *Sentence*, 40.

32. The need for clean animals to offer as sacrifices is also significant. Cf. Wenham, *Genesis 1–15*, 176–77.

33. But commitment to the Documentary Hypothesis has caused some scholars to embrace interpretations that border on the ludicrous. Westermann, *Genesis 1–11*, 397, for example, claims that P believed the waters rose for 150 days (7:24) and then abated for 150 days (8:3). But it is obvious that the two verses speak of a single 150-day period.

34. See chap. 4.

Figure 1.3

The Structure of the Flood Story
(6:10–9:19)*

A	Noah (6:10a)
B	Shem, Ham, and Japheth (10b)
C	Ark to be built (14–16)
D	Flood announced (17)
E	Covenant with Noah (18–20)
F	Food in the ark (21)
G	Command to enter the ark (7:1–3)
H	7 days waiting for flood (4–5)
I	7 days waiting for flood (7–10)
J	Entry to ark (11–15)
K	Yahweh shuts Noah in (16)
L	40 days flood (17a)
M	Waters increase (17b–18)
N	Mountains covered (19–20)
O	150 days water prevail ([21]–24)
P	GOD REMEMBERS NOAH (8:1)
O'	150 days waters abate (3)
N'	Mountain tops visible (4–5)
M'	Waters abate (5)
L'	40 days (end of) (6a)
K'	Noah opens window of ark (6b)
J'	Raven and dove leave ark (7–9)
I'	7 days waiting for waters to subside (10–11)
H'	7 days waiting for waters to subside (12–13)
G'	Command to leave ark (15–17 [22])
F'	Food outside ark (9:1–4)
E'	Covenant with all flesh (8–10)
D'	No flood in the future (11–17)
C'	Ark (18a)
B'	Shem, Ham, and Japheth (18b)
A'	Noah (19)

*Gordon J. Wenham, The "Coherence of the Flood Narrative," *VT* 28 (1978): 338. This chiastic structure is confirmed in Bernhard W. Anderson, "From Analysis to Synthesis: The Interpretation of Genesis 1–11," *JBL* 97 (1978): 23–39. Anderson sees a chiastic structure to Gen. 6:9–9:19 which, though developed in less detail than Wenham's analysis, also has God's remembrance of Noah as its center.

to suppose that the structure of the flood story is the result of a patchwork of two complete, contradictory documents.

The chiastic structure not only renders the documentary approach unlikely, but also helps to resolve the issue of the chronology of the narrative. In particular, Gordon J. Wenham points out, the chronological data have been reported somewhat artificially in order to maintain the narrative structure. Thus the seven-day waiting period is reported twice (7:4–10) in order to balance the fourteen days of waiting in 8:10–13.[35]

Even so, the present chronology in the text is not the confusion it is sometimes implied to be. On the basis of his calculations, Wenham concludes that the only significant problem is fitting both the forty days of 7:12 and the 150 days of 7:24 into the five months between 7:11 and 8:4. This can be resolved if it is assumed that the forty days are part of the 150, and not a separate period of time.[36]

This alone should be sufficient to indicate the fruitlessness of the documentary position here, but evidence for the coherence of the flood narrative is more significant yet. When compared form-critically to the other major ancient Near Eastern flood accounts (especially the account in Gilgamesh, but also the Atrahasis, Ras Shamra, and Sumerian versions), the Genesis narrative is found to have a remarkably high number of formal parallels to those versions. Wenham has isolated seventeen features the Genesis and Gilgamesh accounts have in common, and these usually occur in the same sequence. There are, to be sure, significant theological differences between Genesis and the other versions, but formally they are of the same category. Wenham points out that of the seventeen common formal elements, J has only twelve and P has only ten. Wenham comments that "it is strange that two accounts of the flood so different as J and P, circulating in ancient Israel, should have been combined to give our present story which has many more resemblances to the Gilgamesh version than the postulated sources."[37]

35. Wenham, "Coherence," 339.
36. Wenham, *Genesis 1–15*, 180. In "Coherence" (343–45), Wenham also mentions a problem in coming to a common figure if all the data regarding the dates of the events of the flood are totaled and compared. He notes that the writer apparently "was not concerned to tell how Noah spent all the time on the ark," and thus concludes that it is "unfair to accuse him of inconsistency" (344). See his presentation for details.
37. "Coherence," 347. Full analysis of the formal characteristics is found in "Coherence," 345–47, and *Genesis 1–15*, 159–69.

Against Wenham and other scholars, J. A. Emerton attempts to resuscitate the traditional source division of the flood narrative.[38] For our purposes, there are three significant points in the case he makes.

First, Emerton argues against Wenham's chiastic reading of the text on the grounds that there are imperfections in the chiasmus. He notes, for example, that 7:11 is parallel to 8:2 and that 8:21 echoes 6:5, but that neither is part of the chiasmus. But Emerton's objections are based on a stilted understanding of how a chiasmus functions. It is not a mathematical equation; there is no reason a section of a chiasmus cannot parallel a portion of the text not in the chiastic structure. Regarding 7:11 and 8:2, which record the beginning and end of the rain, it is not reasonable to expect these to be coordinated in a chiasmus. The chiasmus goes from the beginning to the end of the flood, but the rains obviously began at the beginning of the flood but ended well before the end of the flood. In addition, the fundamental validity of the chiastic structure of the narrative is confirmed by two independent studies by Bernhard W. Anderson and Yehuda T. Radday.[39] Both scholars see chiastic structure in the flood narrative and both analyses, though neither is identical to Wenham's, have God's remembrance of Noah as the center.

Second, Emerton has no real answer for Wenham's formal comparison of Genesis to Gilgamesh and other ancient flood narratives. He can only hypothesize to account for the lack of formal elements in the J and P narratives. He contends that we do not know how much of J the redactor failed to preserve and that P may have suppressed some material as theologically offensive. He argues, for example, that the closing of the ark door "may have been regarded by P as unnecessary, or even as anthropomorphic."[40] It is curious that R[P] did not share this concern and suppress this detail from J. At any rate, between Wenham and Emerton, it is clear which scholar is working with ancient texts and which is working with his imagination.

Third, Emerton continues to urge that the chronology of the narrative is impossible. He writes, "According to vii 4, 12, it rained for forty

38. "The Unity of the Flood Narrative in Genesis. Part I," *VT* 37 (1987): 401–20, and "Part II," *VT* 38 (1988): 1–22.

39. See Anderson, "From Analysis to Synthesis: The Interpretation of Genesis 1–11," *JBL* 97 (1978): 23–39; see also Radday, "Chiasmus in Hebrew Biblical Narrative," in *Chiasmus in Antiquity*, ed. John W. Welch (Gerstenberg Verlag, 1981), 99–100. Note also that Andersen, *Sentence*, 124–25, describes chiastic structuring in Gen. 7:6–17. The structure of the whole narrative is thus highly complex and is probably more intricate than any single analysis has yet uncovered. Nevertheless, these independent studies confirm that chiasmus is a dominant organizing motif in the narrative.

40. "Unity, Part II," 15.

days . . . , whereas vii 24 and viii 3 speak of a hundred and fifty days."[41] And, "There is thus a strong case for the view that the hundred and fifty days are the period between the beginning of the flood and viii 2 when the rain stopped. There is a discrepancy between the hundred and fifty days of rain and the forty days of rain."[42] In fact, the text nowhere implies that the rain lasted 150 days. Genesis 7:24 and 8:3 refer to the time from the beginning of the flood until the water had abated enough for the ark to ground (8:3–4). Otherwise, one narrator is a complete fool, since he believed that the water abated enough for the ark to ground on the very day the rain ceased after a 150-day deluge! Emerton attempts to justify his interpretation with an ingressive translation of 8:3, that the water *began* to abate at the end of the 150 days.[43] He asks, "Are we to suppose that a hundred and ten days elapsed between viii 2 and the beginning of the process of decreasing in viii 3?"[44] The answer, of course, is no. But Emerton has only saddled the text with a translation contrary to context and then criticized it for not making sense.

The Genesis account is thus structurally unified and formally of a type of literature (flood narrative) that is far older than the alleged R^P . It employs ancient narrative technique, as evidenced in its profound concern for narrative structure, but even so cannot be said to be chronologically confused. The "contradictions" are more imaginary than real. It is difficult to see why the documentary approach should be considered to have any validity here.

The Criterion of Style

The notion that J and P have radically different styles is a result of artificially dividing the text. The "arid" style of the genealogies of P is simply a by-product of the fact that they are genealogies—it has nothing to do with their being in P. Whybray points out that the genealogies ascribed to J "have precisely the same 'arid' character as those attributed to P."[45] He also observes that there is no real uniformity of style within a single document source.[46]

41. "Unity, Part I," 402–3.
42. Ibid., 405.
43. Contrast Speiser, *Genesis,* 49.
44. "Unity, Part I," 403–4.
45. *Pentateuch,* 60.
46. Ibid., 59. Whybray cites Westermann, *Genesis,* trans. John J. Scullion (Minneapolis: Augsburg, 1974), 766–77, who notes that there are considerable differences among the styles of Gen. 12:10–20 (J), Gen. 24 (J), and the J portions of Gen. 37–50.

One rarely sees in modern works on the Documentary Hypothesis the kind of elaborate lists of "characteristic vocabulary" of the documents that were common in the older critical works.[47] The criterion is itself quite artificial; as Whybray notes, we know nothing of the common speech of the people of ancient Israel, and we cannot be sure that the words cited as synonymous pairs are in fact synonymous. One may have been chosen over the other for the sake of a special nuance in a given circumstance, or indeed for the sake of variety.[48] Regarding the case of הוליד / ילד, see the discussion by Cassuto.[49]

A recent development in this area is in computer-aided analysis of the text. Because this is a new field, models for analysis are still in development. Nevertheless, among the more sophisticated and linguistically sensitive works in this field is the analysis of Genesis done by Radday and Haim Shore. Their work, *Genesis: An Authorship Study*, is an exhaustive linguistic analysis which takes into account as many variables and factors as possible, and they are particularly interested in checking their results against the Documentary Hypothesis. They conclude, "All these reservations notwithstanding, and with all due respect to the illustrious Documentarians past and present, there is *massive evidence* that the pre-Biblical triplicity [i.e., of J, E, and P] of Genesis, which their line of thought postulates to have been worked over by a late and gifted editor into a trinity, is actually a unity."[50]

The Theological Unity of Each Document

Of all the arguments for the Documentary Hypothesis, this is the least significant[51] because it is based on the assumption that the hypothesis is true rather than being an independent argument for the theory. Opponents of the theory have often observed that many of the source narratives are incomplete[52] and that in any case it is not difficult to separate a single biblical narrative into two artificially complete "documents."[53] This makes theological analysis all the more tenuous.

47. See Rolf Rendtorff, *The Problem of the Process of Transmission in the Pentateuch*, trans. John J. Scullion, JSOTSS 89 (Sheffield: JSOT Press, 1990), 146–50.

48. Whybray, *Pentateuch*, 56–57.

49. *Documentary Hypothesis*, 43ff.

50. Yehuda T. Radday and Haim Shore, *Genesis: An Authorship Study* (Rome: Pontifical Biblical Institute, 1985), 190, italics added.

51. Cf. Segal, *Pentateuch*, 19–20.

52. See the discussion of Gen. 27 in Cassuto, *Documentary Hypothesis*, 85ff.

53. Cf. the parodies of the documentary methodology in William Henry Green, *The Higher Criticism of the Pentateuch* (1895; reprint, Grand Rapids: Baker, 1978), 119–25. Green "dissects" the parables of the prodigal son and the good Samaritan.

One has the sense that, even among scholars trained in the Documentary Hypothesis, an increasing number have difficulty taking analyses like those by Walter Brueggemann and Hans Walter Wolff[54] seriously as presentations of the theological background of Genesis. Even scholars with both feet firmly planted in the critical tradition make little use of the classic documentary criteria in tradition-historical analyses of theological strata. Thomas L. Thompson notes that, under continued scholarly scrutiny, the Elohist has disappeared from view entirely and the Yahwist is fast fading from existence, even as P grows beyond all reasonable bounds. The hypothesis has no value as a guide for continued research.[55] Whybray, too, in outlining especially the recent contributions by Rolf Rendtorff[56] and H. H. Schmid, demonstrates how the consensus for a "theology of the Yahwist" among critical scholars is collapsing.[57]

The Hypothesis Proven in Some Specific Texts

The preceding arguments are the classic arguments given in defense of the Documentary Hypothesis. I suspect, however, that many scholars continue to be converted to the hypothesis not because of the force of those arguments, the weaknesses of which are well known, but because of one or two specific test cases. Westermann's discussion of the evidence tends to confirm this.

At the end of the first volume of his commentary on Genesis, Westermann reviews the classic arguments for the Documentary Hypothesis. He deals with language and style, the divine names, contradictions, doublets, and theological viewpoint. Although (in contrast to the objections of scholars like Cassuto) he generally supports the arguments, in every case he carefully qualifies the value of these criteria. He frequently notes that a given criterion cannot be used "mechanically," or must be used "with particular caution." The use of "caution" is of course not an admission that the arguments are exploded, but it does suggest that confidence in the criteria has eroded considerably.[58]

---

54. Brueggemann and Wolff, *Vitality*.

55. Thompson, *Origin Tradition*, 49. He calls the hypothesis "a creed empty of substance."

56. Rendtorff, *Problem*, 119–36.

57. *Pentateuch*, 93–108. He especially summarizes arguments developed in Rendtorff, *Pentateuch*, and H. H. Schmid, *Der sogenannte Jahwist* (Zurich: Theologischer Verlag, 1976).

58. Westermann, *Genesis 1–11*, 576–84. Contrast the more optimistic assessment of the criteria in Eissfeldt, *Old Testament*, 182–88.

At several points, however, Westermann leans on specific texts as justification for continued adherence to the hypothesis. He insists that Genesis 4:26 and Exodus 6:3 continue to have full force in regard to the question of the divine names,[59] that the flood narrative must be a composite of two sources,[60] and that Genesis 1–2 is a classic example of a doublet.[61]

The first two arguments here have already been discussed; the last will be taken up in chapter 10. I want to make a single point here. It is possible that Genesis 1:1–2:3 and Genesis 2:4ff. do in fact spring from separate sources, but that these sources have nothing to do with the four documents of the Documentary Hypothesis. I suggest that although they represent different sources, the application of the wrong criteria to Genesis 1–2 has sent scholars off on a wild goose chase. In short, there is no text in Genesis which is best explained by the Documentary Hypothesis.

The Hypothesis Verified by the History of the Priesthood

It appears that many scholars continue to support the hypothesis because of questions regarding the history of Israel. In particular, the hypothesis seems to offer the best explanation of why the term *Levite* is used inconsistently in the Old Testament. This matter is discussed in chapter 11. At this point, suffice it to say that the traditional solution offered in conjunction with the Documentary Hypothesis is historically anomalous. A far better solution can be obtained by reading the Pentateuch as a work that was substantially produced, as the text affirms, during the period of the exodus.

Conclusion

The Documentary Hypothesis must be abandoned. Regardless of the theological presuppositions with which one approaches the text, and regardless of whether one wishes to affirm the tradition of Mosaic authorship or move in new directions, one must recognize the hypothesis to be methodologically unsound.

59. *Genesis 1–11*, 579. This is a curious position in light of his comments on 4:26 (339–40).

60. Ibid., 582.

61. Ibid., 582–83. To be precise, he considers 1:26–30 to be the parallel of 2:4b–24, but he still adheres to the classic source division.

In the last century, Homeric scholars thought they had discovered sources behind the *Iliad* and the *Odyssey*. The concept is comparable to the Documentary Hypothesis of the Pentateuch.[62] Walter Leaf and M. A. Bayfield (1898) thought they saw several works, including the "Wrath of Achilles" and the "Aristeia of Diomedes" as "strata" behind the *Iliad*.[63] Other scholars, such as Adolf Kirchhoff (1859) and P. D. C. Hennings (1903) similarly divided the *Odyssey*.[64] Such hypotheses are now antiquarian scholarly curiosities.[65] One can only hope that the same fate awaits their sister theory, the Documentary Hypothesis.

62. The seminal work was F. A. Wolf, *Prolegomena to Homer* (1795; trans. Anthony Grafton, with an introduction by James E. G. Zetzel [Princeton: Princeton University Press, 1985]). Wolf had been influenced by J. G. Eichhorn's *Einleitung ins Alte Testament*. See Zetzel's introduction, 18–26.

63. *The Iliad of Homer*, 2 vols. (1898; reprint, London: Macmillan, 1968), 2:xv–xxiii. Linguistic evidence is cited as the primary ground for source division on p. xxi.

64. See W. B. Stanford, *The Odyssey of Homer*, 2d ed., 2 vols. (New York: St. Martin's, 1959), 1:xxx–xxxi.

65. A vigorous attack on source division in Homer is John A. Scott, *The Unity of Homer* (New York: Biblo and Tannen, 1965). It is doubtful that any single theory of origin dominates modern Homeric studies, although many support the Parry-Lord hypothesis as developed in Albert B. Lord, *The Singer of Tales* (Cambridge: Harvard University Press, 1960). On the other hand, Andre Michalopoulos, *Homer* (New York: Twayne, 1966), 34, writes: "Today the consensus of the vast majority of Homeric scholars is that the epics were written by one man." For a good survey of the history of Homeric scholarship, see Howard Clarke, *Homer's Readers* (London and Toronto: Associated University Presses, 1981). It is not my purpose here to support any particular view of Homer but merely to point out that in Homeric studies origin theories using nineteenth-century criteria are now abandoned.

2

Form-Criticism
and Tradition-Criticism

Twentieth-century critical investigations of Genesis have relied heavily on the tools of form-criticism and tradition history. Form-criticism is the standard translation of the German terms *Formgeschichte* and *Gattungsgeschichte*. As the name implies, form-criticism is the attempt to classify units of the biblical text according to the pattern or form to which they adhere. Categories under which a text is classified include structure, genre, setting (often referred to by the German term *Sitz im Leben*), and intention. The method has been most rigorously applied to Genesis, the Psalms, and the synoptic Gospels.

A simple example is Psalm 1. Its structure is built around the two ways of the wise and the wicked, its genre is determined by the fact that it is not a prayer or a hymn but a lesson, the setting is probably the temple, and its intention is to provide a simple, easy-to-remember spiritual lesson on the importance of devotion to God. It could be classed as a "wisdom psalm."[1]

Tradition history (*Traditionsgeschichte* or *überlieferungsgeschichte*) is the attempt to trace the history of a given text from its earliest, oral stage through to its commitment to writing, and finally to its redaction into the present text of the Bible. Primary emphasis is on the shape and use of a story in its oral stage. Tradition historians often urge that in

1. See Artur Weiser, *The Psalms*, trans. Herbert Hartwell, OTL (Philadelphia: Westminster, 1962), 102–3.

the oral stage a story functions with a radically different purpose from that for which it is used in the biblical text. The relationship of form-criticism to tradition history is problematic because of the lack of agreement among practitioners on this question. For some, tradition history is dependent upon and an outgrowth of form-criticism; for others, form-criticism and tradition history are virtually one and the same.[2] Indeed, the two can be said to have been born simultaneously.

Nevertheless, although the tools of form-criticism do have valid use in Old Testament studies, tradition history, as a method, is virtually useless. At the end of this chapter, some suggestions are made for the legitimate use of form-criticism.

The Rise of Form-Criticism and Tradition History

Hermann Gunkel

Form-criticism is associated with Hermann Gunkel (1862–1932). The roots of his method go back at least as far as the research of the brothers Grimm into folktale composition and transmission. Nevertheless, it was Gunkel, working at the turn of the century, who brought the methods and conclusions of the then-current folklore research into Pentateuchal studies.

Gunkel was interested in going behind the written texts of the Old Testament to find the preliterary stages of the growth of the tradition. Fundamental to his method is the distinction between "legend" and "history." Legend, he contended, is part of an oral tradition, concerns the life of a family, and tends to be poetic. History, on the other hand, is based in written texts, concerns a political environment, and is prosaic.[3]

In his commentary on Genesis (1901), Gunkel divided the book into two portions: chapters 1–11, which are mythical in nature, and chapters 12–50, which contain the legends of the patriarchs. Genesis was thus for him a folk book, that is, a collection of legends. Patricia G. Kirkpatrick notes that in 1909 Axel Olrik published his views on the principles

---

2. Cf. Richard N. Soulen, *Handbook of Biblical Criticism,* 2d ed. (Atlanta: John Knox, 1981), s.v. "Tradition Criticism" for a summary of some major views.

3. Patricia G. Kirkpatrick, *The Old Testament and Folklore Study,* JSOTSS 62 (Sheffield: JSOT Press, 1988), 24. For Gunkel's own discussion of this point, see Hermann Gunkel, *The Folktale in the Old Testament,* trans. Michael D. Rutter (Sheffield: Almond, 1987), 21–27.

that govern oral literature, and that Gunkel, when he published the third edition of his commentary the following year, was able to claim the added authority of Olrik's research into folklore.[4]

Gunkel went on to postulate the original setting, or *Sitz im Leben*, of the legends behind Genesis: the campfire scene and the popular festivals where professional storytellers presented their stories. He also followed the arguments of Hugo Gressmann, who claimed that the patriarchal narratives did not spring from Canaanite myths but were instead from old Hebrew folktales about the lives of individual shepherds. In 1917, Gunkel published *Das Märchen im Alten Testament (The Folktale in the Old Testament)*, in which he sought to demonstrate the presence of folktale motifs throughout the Old Testament by comparison with folktales from around the world.[5] He concluded that folktales were very much a part of the Old Testament landscape, and that these came into existence through a long process of oral development "just the same in Israel as everywhere else."[6]

Gunkel thus contended that behind the written documents of the Pentateuch was an oral prehistory that covered several centuries. He further contended that through critical techniques it was possible to recover from the written text the process through which the oral stories had journeyed.[7]

Axel Olrik

Further studies continued the new approach to the Old Testament. Olrik (1864–1917) was a Danish folklorist who published his observations on the characteristics of oral narrative. These observations, sometimes called Olrik's laws, were never set down in a fixed order, but R. N. Whybray has set forth a classification of the laws in three categories.

Whybray notes that the three major areas of concern in Olrik's laws are general structural characteristics, internal structural characteristics, and characterization. The first category would include "the law of perspicuity or clear arrangement," which means that oral narrative has clear structure and uses only details that directly serve its purpose.

---

4. Kirkpatrick, *Old Testament*, 25.
5. For this summary, I am dependent primarily on Kirkpatrick, *Old Testament*, 24–26.
6. Gunkel, *Folktale*, 173.
7. See R. N. Whybray, *The Making of the Pentateuch* (Sheffield: JSOT Press, 1987), 138, and Kirkpatrick, *Old Testament*, 33.

Another law in this category is "the law of [epic] unity of plot," which means that the plot moves toward a single conclusion. The second category includes "the law of repetition," which means that oral narrative uses repetition for emphasis, and the "law of three," which means that oral tales tend to use the number three for characters, objects, and events. The third category includes "the law of concentration on the central character," which states that an oral narrative revolves around a single character, and the "law of two to a scene," which states that oral works restrict any one episode to only two characters.[8]

Olrik's "laws" not only bolstered Gunkel's case but also have provided justification for continued optimism among Old Testament scholars who believed they had the means to separate narrative that was originally oral from that which was originally literary.

Andre Jolles

Jolles (1874–1946), himself not an Old Testament scholar, published *Einfache Formen* (*Simple Forms*) in 1929, a work in which he tried to identify the types of short forms of narrative found in simple societies. For Old Testament studies, however, his most important contribution was his use of the term *Sage* (legend or saga). He looked back to Norse family sagas, especially those from Iceland (ca. A.D. 1300), for his archetypical examples of the *Sage*. He believed these family sagas came from a time when the family was the basic social unit, and that they arose orally rather than as written texts. Most significantly, Jolles claimed that examples of the family saga of this type could be found in the patriarchal narratives of Genesis. His ideas have had enormous influence on biblical scholars, especially Gerhard von Rad, Martin Noth, and Claus Westermann.[9]

The Assumptions behind Form-Criticism and the Traditio-Historical Model

Many of the assumptions of the early pioneers of form-criticism and folklore study, assumptions that were taken up by subsequent genera-

8. Whybray, *Pentateuch,* 146–47. Whybray lists twenty of Olrik's "laws," but he notes that Olrik's own presentation is "unclear and inconsistent" (145). For another presentation of Olrik's laws, see Thomas L. Thompson, *The Origin Tradition of Ancient Israel,* JSOTSS 55 (Sheffield: JSOT Press, 1987), 44.

9. Cf. Whybray, *Pentateuch,* 152–55, and Kirkpatrick, *Old Testament,* 81–83.

tions of scholars, cannot be maintained. Gunkel's belief that simple narrations come from primitive, preliterate societies is particularly open to question, as Kirkpatrick notes: "The proposition that the primitive mind had a limited concentration span and would therefore have only understood legends of short duration is itself a simplistic notion and one which can no longer be upheld. Indeed it is questionable whether Gunkel ever had other than 'Rousseauesque' reasons for maintaining such an argument."[10]

John Van Seters, who accepts Olrik's laws as valid,[11] also notes that one cannot hold to the equation that simple forms are the earliest and complex forms are the most recent.[12] He notes that "Gunkel's fundamental mistake . . . has led subsequent scholars astray."[13] Van Seters also challenges Gunkel's evolutionary model and his attempt "to relate his literary history to sociopolitical levels of development in ancient Israel."[14] Whybray, too, notes that "Gunkel's assumption of a lineal progression of culture marked by a series of stages in the development of *Sage* into more 'artistic' composition (*Kunstwerk*) is an over-simple view which takes no account of the complexities of actual pre-literate, or indeed, literate, societies."[15]

Gunkel's notions of the original setting of the Genesis legends are also questionable. The romantic picture of professional storytellers narrating their legends to early Israelites gathered around the campfire is a product of modern imagination.[16] Any tradition history that springs from this model must be considered doubtful. Also, the position of Gunkel and his followers that the idiom *until this day* reflects an etiological purpose has been challenged in a significant article by Brevard S. Childs. Childs concludes that the formula "seldom has an etiological function of justifying an existing phenomenon, but in the great majority of cases is a formula of personal testimony added to,

10. *Old Testament,* 28–29.
11. *Abraham in History and Tradition* (New Haven: Yale University Press, 1975), 158–61.
12. *In Search of History* (New Haven: Yale University Press, 1983), 37–38. While I do not subscribe to the full methodology of Van Seters's book (see chap. 3), it is valid to note that other ancient works which were clearly the product of a single author (Van Seters's example is Herodotus) plainly contradict the rules for the growth of a tradition alleged for Israelite literature
13. Ibid., 38 n. 84.
14. Ibid., 212.
15. *Pentateuch,* 151.
16. Ibid., 173–74.

and confirming, a received tradition."[17] As such, the formula is of no value in determining an oral precursor to a written text.[18]

For the purposes of this discussion, Olrik's "laws" are open to question on two grounds. First, it is not clear that they are all valid as markers of oral composition; and second, it is not clear that, even where they may have validity, they apply to the Old Testament. One of the laws, that oral literature tends to use repetition, is exploited by Gunkel and his followers. However, the folklorist Ruth Finnegan observes that the concept of repetition is too wide to be valuable for separating oral from written compositions and that even written literature can employ repetition and formulae.[19] One might add to this that a truly formulaic literary style, as seen in the epithets of Homeric literature, is not characteristic of Genesis.

The fact that written literature can contain the characteristics of Olrik's laws is especially significant. Whybray comments that "some of the 'laws'—for example, those of clear arrangement, progression, openings, closings, concentration on a central character—may be found in almost any kind of narrative literature, including modern novels."[20] He adds that "there is no reason why the conventions and techniques of oral composition should not have been carried over and used in purely written compositions."[21] This would only make the process of separating originally oral works from originally written works all the more difficult.[22]

Even if the laws are to some extent valid in folklore study, they do not necessarily apply to Genesis. Van Seters, although accepting the validity of the laws, concludes that in Genesis "oral forms and motifs are confined to a rather small part of the tradition, certainly much less than Gunkel originally proposed."[23] His limitation to the application of Olrik's laws to Genesis is supported by Whybray.[24]

---

17. Brevard S. Childs, "A Study of the Formula, 'Until This Day,'" *JBL* 82 (1963): 279–92. The quote is from p. 292. For a more detailed examination of the data Childs investigates, see Burke O. Long, *The Problem of Etiological Narrative in the Old Testament,* BZAW 108 (Berlin: Verlag Alfred Töpelmann, 1968). Long's results (108) "parallel" those of Childs.

18. Cf. Van Seters, *Search,* 49–50.

19. Ruth Finnegan, *Oral Poetry* (London: Cambridge University Press, 1977), 130; cited in Kirkpatrick, *Old Testament,* 55. Whybray also draws extensively on Finnegan's research into oral literature and folklore. See *Pentateuch,* 160–67.

20. *Pentateuch,* 150.

21. Ibid.

22. See also Thompson, *Origin Tradition,* 44–45.

23. *Abraham,* 309–10.

24. Whybray, *Pentateuch,* 151.

Oral Tradition in the Old Testament
and the Ancient Near East

Bruce K. Waltke points out the difficulties in the study of oral tradition in the Old Testament.[25] He observes that the two presuppositions behind the oral traditio-historical approach are that most of the Old Testament had a long oral prehistory before being committed to writing and that, in the process of oral transmission, the stories were altered to suit changing circumstances. Neither the biblical texts nor the ancient Near Eastern parallels support those assumptions.

From Ebla, a millennium earlier than Moses, come writings of every kind, including administrative documents, lists, epic tales, hymns, and incantations. Mesopotamian writings illustrate the care with which texts were transcribed. Law codes (such as Hammurabi's) include warnings that the written statutes are not to be defaced or altered in any way. Sumerian proverbs that date to around 1500 B.C. (in Akkadian collections) are found in neo-Babylonian collections of around 600 B.C. with no significant alteration. Even hymns were written down rather than left to human memory. In addition, there are no grounds for supposing that stories went through long processes of oral transmission. "The great Akkadian creation epic *Enuma elish* was probably composed during the time of Hammurabi (c. 1700 B.C.), and its earliest extant copy, clearly not the original, is dated only one hundred years later."[26] Although redaction of written sources took place (as in the case of the epic of Gilgamesh), "there is no evidence of a flexible oral tradition."[27]

The situation is similar for Hittite, Egyptian, and Ugaritic cultures. In the Old Testament, frequent appeal is made to written sources (Josh. 10:13; 2 Sam. 1:18), and laws, prophetic messages, and even songs were transcribed at the time of their composition (Exod. 24:7; Deut. 31:9, 19, 30; Isa. 8:16; Jer. 36). Variations in Old Testament synoptic material cannot be described as variations in oral traditions. Whybray comments that the Proto-Semitic inscriptions at Sinai (from the mid-

25. "Oral Tradition," in *A Tribute to Gleason Archer*, ed. Walter C. Kaiser, Jr., and Ronald F. Youngblood (Chicago: Moody, 1986), 17–34.

26. Ibid., 20.

27. Ibid., 23.

28. On this point, Waltke, "Oral Tradition," 27 n. 35, cites Helmer Ringgren, "Oral and Written Transmission in the Old Testament," *ST* 3 (1950–51): 34–59. See also the discussion in Whybray, *Pentateuch,* 180–81. Whybray also notes that some of the "errors" that Ringgren deals with appear to be oral or aural in nature, but that these have nothing to do with oral composition.

dle of the second millennium) at least imply that there is no reason that Old Testament stories could not have been written down at an early date.[29]

Waltke also notes that it is hard to see how evidence from Old Icelandic sagas, from a people so far removed from Israel in time, space, and cultural conventions, can outweigh all the contrary evidence from the Bible itself and the ancient Near East.[30]

The Question of Sitz im Leben

Some scholars are now calling into question whether one can determine the original intention and setting of oral narrative.[31] The very possibility of a quest for a Sitz im Leben has been challenged by Thomas L. Thompson. He argues that we do not have the data necessary to reconstruct an "interpretive context external to the actual texts of ancient tradition" and that in any case such a reconstruction is unnecessary since the "text does speak to us."[32]

There is much here with which we can sympathize. Many of the proposed historical settings for texts amount to nothing more than presumptuous guesswork. Furthermore, the situation is far more doubtful if one is claiming to have found the oral tradition behind the text and the setting for it. Thompson's words are a wise caution and a frank admission of how little we really know of the social and historical backgrounds of our texts. And certainly the biblical text as we have it does speak to us!

On the other hand, complete skepticism is not the proper response. Some texts do imply that they were written to function in a specific setting. To give but a simple example, a number of psalms obviously have the temple worship as their setting. The narratives of Genesis, to be sure, are more difficult in this regard than the Psalms. It is best to approach the problem with caution while remaining open to the possibility that the texts may give us clues regarding their original setting.

---

29. Pentateuch, 140–41.

30. Waltke, "Oral Tradition," 29, cites G. Widengren, "Oral Tradition and Written Literature Among the Hebrews in Light of Arabic Evidence, with Special Regard to Prose Narratives," AcOr 23 (1959): 225, to this effect. Widengren is astonished that the cultural gap between Israel and Iceland has had "no discouraging effect" on Old Testament scholars.

31. Cf. Whybray, Pentateuch, 217.

32. Thompson, Origin Tradition, 196–97.

Again, we can only work with the texts we have and not with an alleged oral tradition antecedent to the texts.

Form-Critical Methods since Hermann Gunkel

Albrecht Alt

Using form-critical methodology, Albrecht Alt (1883–1956) argues that the separate seminomadic tribes that eventually became Israel carried the cults of their founders (i.e., of Abraham, of Isaac, and of Jacob—according to Alt, all were originally unrelated to one another) with them in their wanderings. Once in the land of Canaan, they attached the names of their patriarchal cult founders to shrines already established in the land and identified the tribal god with the *El numina* of the local sanctuaries. With interaction among followers of the various deities (the god of Abraham at Mamre, the god of Isaac at Beersheba, etc.), they were merged into the one God of the Fathers, and the patriarchs were incorporated into a single genealogy.[33]

Van Seters and Kirkpatrick have criticized both Alt's method and his proposal. Van Seters discounts Alt's use of historical analogy (Alt uses the religion of the Nabateans as an analogue) and states, "He has lost any objective control over his method so he can always make it fit. One can begin with virtually any idea as a historical analogy, reconstruct the original 'lost' traditions, and then account for how they were reworked by later writers."[34] Van Seters also notes that Alt can point to no Genesis cult legend "with which he can associate the two phases of his historical reconstruction."[35] Kirkpatrick observes that Alt could be quite inconsistent in following his own criteria, particularly in his insistence that the God of the Fathers is from a preliterary tradition. Such a position is completely at odds with his own method.[36]

One might add that there are in fact no objective grounds for the isolation of the *El* deities from their literary contexts as separate oral traditions, to say nothing of substantiating the highly complex, multilayered history of tradition Alt has proposed. The hypothetical and subjective nature of

33. For an English translation of Alt's essay see Albrecht Alt, "The God of the Fathers," in *Essays on Old Testament History and Religion,* trans. and ed. R. A. Wilson (Oxford, 1966), 3–77. For summaries of Alt's position, see Kirkpatrick, *Old Testament,* 34–35, and Van Seters, *Abraham,* 139–41.

34. *Abraham,* 141.

35. Ibid.

36. Kirkpatrick, *Old Testament,* 36.

Alt's discussion is obvious.[37] Indeed, even those who follow the form-critical methodology are by no means led to Alt's conclusions.[38]

Martin Noth and Gerhard von Rad

For most of the twentieth century, tradition history has been dominated by two men, Gerhard von Rad (1901–1971) and Martin Noth (1902–1968). Their synthesis, as summarized by Douglas A. Knight, includes the following elements: The Pentateuch as we have it is the final result of a long process of passing down the traditional beliefs of the Israelite people from generation to generation. This transmission was often oral, and each generation modified the tradition to suit its own needs. The traditions passed down independently of one another, but five themes (stressed by Noth) were thought to be central. These were the guidance out of Egypt, the guidance to the arable land, the promises to the patriarchs, the guidance in the wilderness, and the revelation at Sinai. Noth holds that the central cult of the amphictyony was the place where the themes were merged.[39] Von Rad regarded a few simple "creeds" (especially Deut. 26:5b–9) as central to the faith of premonarchic Israel, but he gives the Yahwist credit for merging the themes into a linear narrative. Both scholars were more interested in the prehistory of the text, the tradition, than in the theological interests of the redactor who brought the final form of the Pentateuch into being. This method was thought to be theologically useful; von Rad in particular used it to extract the early Israelites' interpretation of history

37. Cf. Alt, "God of the Fathers," 20–24. Alt argues that the *Elim* are "merely relics" (21). While it is true that the *Elim* point to older, localized, or tribal names under which God was worshiped, this of itself does not establish their status as oral legends over against any other theory of composition. Note also Alt's casual (and unjustified) dismissal of Gen. 46:1 as irrelevant to his discussion (22 n. 59). This verse is in fact relevant: it attaches Jacob to the shrine and the God of Isaac (it begs the question to set the verse aside as redactional).

38. See Hugh C. White, "The Divine Oath in Genesis," *JBL* 92 (1973): 165–79. White concludes his formal analysis with an assertion that "the divine appearance thus does not reflect the influence of the epiphany religion of settled Canaanite peoples; the divine epiphany at sacred places was a necessary part of the oath ceremony of nomadic tribes" (178).

39. The term *amphictyony* was originally applied to the sacral leagues of the first millennium B.C. in Greece and Italy, such as the League of Delphi and the Etruscan League of Voltumna. On the analogy of these associations to the organization of the twelve tribes of Israel at Shechem, Noth and Alt applied the term *amphictyony* to premonarchic Israel. The use of the term, however, is not appropriate. See R. K. Harrison, *Introduction to the Old Testament* (Grand Rapids: Eerdmans, 1969), 332–34.

from the text and use it to develop the theological model of *Heilsgeschichte* (salvation history).[40]

In recent years their analyses of the Pentateuch have undergone what Knight describes as a "dissolution." Knight points out twelve areas in which critical scholars have examined von Rad's and Noth's solutions and found them wanting. Studies have shown, for example, that it is not possible to determine with certainty the presence of orally transmitted narrative in a written text, that the "creeds" are not necessarily independent of other themes, and that the "amphictyony" has some major shortcomings as a historical model for ancient Israel. The legitimacy of separating scientific history from theological interpretation has been challenged, and the whole idea of *Heilsgeschichte* as an interpretive program has been found to lend itself excessively to facile and reductionist interpretation.[41]

Whybray has been even more pointed in his criticism of Noth's methodology. He notes that Noth supposes he can distinguish earlier from later material in the text on the basis of style (which often means Noth's own subjective reading of the text). Noth also uses the dubious criterion that short and concise narratives are the earliest. In addition, he takes the possibility that a story may change its protagonist and turns this into a universal assumption upon which his whole critical history depends.[42]

At times, Noth's arguments are almost bizarre. Whybray observes that, for Noth, the presence of the foremen and elders of the people in Exodus 3:16, 18; 4:29; and 5:6–19 was enough evidence to exclude Moses altogether from the theme of "guidance out of Egypt." On the other hand, tremendous significance is attached to "grave traditions," although he is inconsistent even here.[43] Worst of all, Whybray observes, "much of Noth's detailed reconstruction of the Pentateuchal traditions was obtained by *piling one speculation upon another*," as in the case of his treatment of the narratives of Abraham and Lot.[44]

40. Douglas A. Knight, "The Pentateuch," in *The Hebrew Bible and Its Modern Interpreters,* ed. Douglas A. Knight (Chico, Calif.: Scholar's Press, 1985), 265–68. See p. 266 for Knight's justification for treating the two men's work as a synthesis. For von Rad's presentation of his theory, see "The Form-Critical Problem of the Hexateuch," in *The Problem of the Hexateuch and Other Essays,* trans. E. W. Trueman Dicken (London: SCM, 1966), 1–78. For Noth's presentation, see Martin Noth, *A History of Pentateuchal Traditions,* trans. Bernhard W. Anderson (Englewood Cliffs, N.J.: Prentice-Hall, 1972).

41. Knight, "The Pentateuch," 268–72.

42. Whybray, *Pentateuch,* 187–88.

43. Ibid., 188–90.

44. Ibid., 194. See Whybray's discussion on 194–96 for a detailed analysis of Noth's treatment of the Lot narratives.

The Scandinavian Scholars

Whybray's analysis of the writings of the Scandinavian scholars Ivan Engnell, E. Nielsen, and R. A. Carlson is especially instructive. This school is well known for its advocacy of an oral traditio-historical approach to the Pentateuch as opposed to a literary approach and in particular for its opposition to the Documentary Hypothesis. Other scholars, while using the form-critical methodology and interacting with traditio-historical critics, continued to rely upon the Documentary Hypothesis.[45] Yet the Scandinavians cannot be counted as supporters of even the methods employed by scholars such as Noth. Whybray concludes that although they agreed with Noth and others that a complex oral tradition is behind the present biblical material, the skepticism of the Scandinavians regarding the possibility of recovering that tradition was so profound as to nullify Noth's entire program.[46]

John Van Seters

It was earlier noted that Van Seters challenges Gunkel's wholesale application of Olrik's laws to Genesis. Nevertheless, Van Seters has developed criteria for analyzing texts that to some degree resuscitate Olrik.[47] These criteria include the notion that the simplest form of a story is the earliest,[48] that a second account may both summarize and add new details, that a story may assume knowledge of an earlier version of the same story (the "blind motif"), and that verbal similarity indicates literary dependence (unless the similarities are in common expressions). Also, citing Albert B. Lord's *Singer of Tales*, he attempts to show how oral composition variants differ from written literature. Oral works do not combine genres, do not summarize, and lack the "blind motif."[49]

Following these criteria, Van Seters attempts to establish that Genesis 12:10–20 arose as a primitive folktale, a piece of oral literature. He further contends that Genesis 20 is a literary account dependent on

45. Cf. J. A. Emerton, "The Origin of the Promises to the Patriarchs in the Older Sources of the Book of Genesis," *VT* 32 (1982): 14–32, and Z. Weisman, "National Consciousness in the Patriarchal Promises," *JSOT* 31 (1985): 55–73.

46. *Pentateuch*, 202.

47. See Thompson, *Origin Tradition*, 46.

48. However, Van Seters himself seems to have come to reject the notion that simpler = earlier (see Van Seters, *Search*, 38).

49. Van Seters, *Abraham*, 162–63. For his application of Olrik's laws to a text, see p. 169.

12:10–20 (because of "blind motifs") and that Genesis 26 is a literary conflation of the previous two accounts.[50] Van Seters's arguments have been effectively demolished by Thompson and Kirkpatrick. Thompson has shown that Genesis 12:10–20 does not fit Van Seters's own criteria for oral literature[51] and that his methods place unreasonable constraints on the range of possibilities for both oral and written literature.[52] Kirkpatrick has demonstrated that Van Seters operates from an inadequate understanding of oral composition. Regarding Lord's *Singer of Tales,* she points out that one cannot regard the methods of Yugoslavian bards as normative for ancient Israelite storytellers. She particularly challenges his assertion that oral composition variants do not summarize and questions "the possibility of identifying an oral folktale behind a written text."[53] I must add that I find Van Seters's citation of Lord especially strange. Lord's work does not establish Van Seters's criteria, but Lord does say that an "*oral* text will yield a predominance of clearly demonstrable formulas, with the bulk of the remainder 'formulaic.'"[54] Yet Genesis 12:10–20 is clearly not formulaic!

To summarize, one may say that no scholar has demonstrated convincingly an ability to distinguish and separate an oral tradition within the text of the Old Testament.

Other Inadequacies of Contemporary Form-Critical Procedures

Recent form-critical analyses have, if anything, further demonstrated the bankruptcy of the method as currently practiced. Instead of being a tool for the investigation of a text, it is now a quick and easy way to attach labels of every conceivable kind to the texts. We now read of so-called annals, chronicles, biographies, histories, lists, fables, novellas, myths, adoption reports, dream reports, death reports, marriage reports, family sagas, and heroic sagas, to name but a few.[55] The point

---

50. Ibid., 167–83.
51. Thompson, *Origin Tradition,* 53.
52. Ibid., 54–55. The blind motif is simply a function of the repetition of scenes.
53. *Old Testament,* 62–64. The quote is from p. 63.
54. Albert B. Lord, *The Singer of Tales* (Cambridge: Harvard University Press, 1960), 130.
55. This list is a sampling from George W. Coats, *Genesis: With an Introduction to Narrative Literature,* FOTL (Grand Rapids: Eerdmans, 1984), 317–20.

here is not to lampoon the proliferation of forms but to question whether much of this may be rightly called form-criticism at all.

Some of the alleged forms are merely labels attached to texts according to content. George W. Coats, for example, calls Genesis 23 a "death report."[56] But the text has no formal pattern or structure that may be called a "death report" pattern. The only apparent reason for calling it a "death report" is that verses 1–2 mention that Sarah died and verse 19 records her burial. But this is not a formal pattern; it is only a matter of story content. By this standard, every time the Bible mentions that someone died, such a reference could be called a "death report."[57] The same may be said of designating Genesis 36:2–3 as a "marriage report."[58]

Other alleged forms are anachronistic. The term *novella* is often used to describe the Joseph narrative. Novella is a Renaissance genre;[59] no extrabiblical examples appear from the ancient Near East. As used to describe biblical texts, the term has no clear formal definition or structure. Coats's definition of novella states that it is a story that develops a tension and then resolves it, is this-worldly, may have subplots, and is not set within oral tradition.[60] Since it is difficult to see how one may separate material which is set within an oral tradition from that which is not,[61] this definition could be applied to virtually any passage in Genesis. The texts Coats categorizes as novellas (Gen. 13–14; 18–19; 15:1–21; 24:1–67; 38:1–30; 37:1–47:27)[62] have nothing in common from a form-critical perspective. The more extended definition of novella offered by Humphreys[63] is no more helpful; particularly doubtful is his assertion that a biblical text designated a novella is written primarily to entertain.[64] Of course, some will object that some texts are more novella-like than others, but when one looks for objective crite-

56. Ibid., 164.

57. See chap. 7 for further discussion of the formal pattern of Gen. 23.

58. Coats, *Genesis*, 246–47.

59. W. Lee Humphreys, "Novella," in *Saga, Legend, Tale, Novella, Fable*, ed. George W. Coats, JSOTSS 35 (Sheffield: JSOT Press, 1985), 82. Humphreys notes that the novella is a genre of the fourteenth-century Italian Renaissance and that Boccacio's *Decameron* is the most typical. He observes that it is a modern genre and simply a short novel. But, against Humphreys, it is difficult to imagine any formal parallel between Gen. 37–50 and the *Decameron*.

60. *Genesis*, 8, 319.

61. See Thompson, *Origin Tradition*, 47.

62. *Genesis*, 319.

63. "Novella," 86–96.

64. Ibid., 94. On the genre of the Joseph narrative, see my discussion in chap. 9.

ria, the only apparent distinction is that some texts are *longer* than others! This distinction, as a formal criterion, is explicit in von Rad.[65]

Other alleged forms simply have inappropriate names. The saga is an Icelandic narrative of a type not found in the Old Testament. Jolles brought the term to Old Testament studies. He believed that the Icelandic sagas began as oral traditions at the time of Iceland's settlement, and that the patriarchal stories of Genesis were of the same type.[66] His suggestions influenced a number of Old Testament scholars, especially Claus Westermann and Klaus Koch.[67]

As used in English, especially in Old Testament studies, the term *saga* is hopelessly ambiguous.[68] In addition, the Icelandic sagas, although often used as analogues for the Genesis narratives in traditio-historical studies, are extremely violent and tragic stories that revolve around heroic figures and as such are utterly unlike their alleged Old Testament counterparts.[69] Finally, modern folklorists are by no means certain that an oral, preliterary stage is behind the Icelandic sagas, as most Old Testament scholars assume.[70] Van Seters, who criticizes Westermann's use of Jolles's conclusions, writes: "What is most damaging to Westermann's view is that he did not attempt to actually describe a particular example of an Icelandic saga and then compare it with the stories in Genesis. If he had, the inappropriateness of the comparison would have been self-evident."[71]

Conclusion

The form-critical theories of Gunkel and his followers are founded on doubtful folktale theories and on false analogies between the literature of other cultures and the Old Testament. The tradition histories that grew out of those theories can be challenged at every point and are

65. Von Rad, *Genesis*, 248.

66. *Einfache Formen* (1930, 1958 [2d ed.]), 62–90, cited in Van Seters, *Search*, 222 n. 44.

67. Van Seters, *Search*, 222–23. See also Kirkpatrick, *Old Testament*, 84, and Claus Westermann, *Genesis 12–36*, trans. John J. Scullion (Minneapolis: Augsburg/Fortress, 1985), 51. Note that although Westermann accepted Jolles's ideas, he preferred not to use the term *Sage* in his analysis, as he considered it too ambiguous.

68. Cf. Van Seters, *Abraham*, 131–38, Kirkpatrick, *Old Testament*, 81–83, and Whybray, *Pentateuch*, 143–44.

69. Whybray, *Pentateuch*, 157.

70. Kirkpatrick, *Old Testament*, 83.

71. Van Seters, *Search*, 223–24.

based upon inconsistent or arbitrary methods. Many of the assured results of the past two generations of Old Testament study must be and are being set aside.

Nevertheless, this does not mean that form-criticism as a tool is to be abandoned. Instead, it must be used properly. The following five guidelines are suggested for the use of form-criticism:

1. Granted the nature of the Old Testament as a written text of limited size, form-criticism should be used only for the analysis of the patterns of written material. There are no grounds for claiming it to be a means for uncovering the oral stage of a text.
2. Although the content of a text has obvious bearing on its classification, texts should be categorized primarily according to form, not content. Incidental details of content are not grounds for formal classification.
3. Classifications that are anachronistic or otherwise doubtful (e.g., "novella," "saga") should be avoided.
4. A text's classification should, if possible, have clear ancient parallels. Otherwise, the classification should be a distinctly biblical genre. In other words, the only legitimate grounds for claiming that a text is of a genre not found elsewhere in the ancient world is that it is of a type found only in the Bible.[72]
5. Hypotheses about the original setting and intention of a text should be based only on the material of the text itself and not on a hypothetical reconstruction of the prehistory of the text.

If these guidelines are observed, meaningful results may be obtained concerning the texts of Genesis.

---

72. It is clear from the form-criticism of the Psalter that there are forms in biblical literature that are not attested elsewhere. Other genres, such as apocalyptic, are found only in the Bible or in works that imitate the biblical genre.

3

Mosaic Authorship and Historical Reliability

The author of the Book of Genesis remains anonymous. In fact, the entire Pentateuch was written anonymously, although large portions of the legal material are attributed directly to Moses (Exod. 24:4; 30:11, 17; 33:1, 5; 39:1, 5, 29; Lev. 1:1; 4:1; 6:1; Num. 4:1; Deut. 1:1, 5; 5:1; 31:22, 30; 33:1). From this evidence, it is not irrational to conclude that Moses is the person primarily responsible for the writing of the Pentateuch, which is indeed the common assumption of postexilic Judaism (1 Chron. 15:15; 22:13; 2 Chron. 23:18; 24:6; 25:4; 30:16; 35:12; Ezra 3:2; 7:6; Neh. 1:7; 8:1; 13:1; Sir. 24:22; also Philo, Josephus, the Mishna and Talmud). Jesus and his followers shared this view (Matt. 8:4; Luke 16:31; 24:27, 44; John 1:17; Acts 3:22), although the New Testament does not endorse some extreme views, such as the theory of Philo and Josephus that Moses proleptically described his own death.[1]

In the previous chapters I have argued that the Documentary Hypothesis is unsatisfactory as a guide to source analysis and that tradition history and form-criticism, as currently practiced, have had questionable results as well. This is also the conclusion to be found in *The Making of the Pentateuch* by R. N. Whybray.

1. Cf. R. K. Harrison, *Introduction to the Old Testament* (Grand Rapids: Eerdmans, 1969), 497.

R. N. Whybray's Proposal

Having abandoned the two major thrusts of current critical methodology, Whybray proposes a new, much simpler solution. He takes as his starting point an issue alluded to already, that in postexilic Judaism one hears specific assertions that Moses is the author of the Law. He also notes that literary studies have gone far to demonstrate that the Pentateuch is an integrated, unified work. He thus takes the step of concluding that the Pentateuch has a single author and that it was composed no earlier than the sixth century B.C.[2]

Whybray's proposal is built upon criticism of Gerhard von Rad's "theology of the Yahwist" offered by Rolf Rendtorff. He especially supports Rendtorff's point that Exodus 1–14 seems to know nothing of Genesis because it does not cite any of the promises made to the patriarchs. Thus, for example, Exodus 1:7 should have mentioned the promise given to Abraham that he would have many descendants.[3] Whybray also builds upon the work of John Van Seters, who, believing Herodotus and the Deuteronomistic historian to be roughly contemporary, compares the two and claims to find many points of similarity. For Whybray, the comparison indicates the Pentateuch may be the work of a single author working more or less with the same approach as Herodotus: to forge a national identity for his readers by composing a national history from a rather loose collection of sources and especially from his own imaginative reconstructions.[4]

A major factor for Whybray is the lack of explicit references to the Pentateuch in preexilic writings. He argues that the few references to the patriarchs that are found in the preexilic texts can be attributed to the Deuteronomistic editor. Otherwise, only Hosea 12:2–4, 12–13 allude to the patriarchs, but Hosea appears not to have derived his information from Genesis.[5] Whybray is thus able to conclude that the author of the Pentateuch is a late figure.[6] He appears to favor an exilic date for the work.[7]

2. *The Making of the Pentateuch* (Sheffield: JSOT Press, 1987), 221–42. Whybray of course does not deny the use of sources to his author.

3. Ibid., 100–102.

4. Ibid., 225–30.

5. Ibid., 48–49.

6. Ibid., 103, 235.

7. Ibid., 229–30. Whybray cites with approval the opinions of Van Seters, H. H. Schmid, and Rendtorff that the Pentateuch ought to be associated with the exile.

Preliminary Assessment

Whybray's hypothesis is for several reasons problematic. Although one may concede that the preexilic literature is not filled with citations of the Pentateuch, the situation is not what Whybray implies it to be, and the interpretation he places on this phenomenon is altogether unsatisfactory.

Arguments from silence are notoriously slippery, and the argument by Rendtorff that Exodus knows nothing of Genesis is especially suspect. It is true that Exodus does not cite chapter and verse from Genesis, as a later exegete would, but is it reasonable to expect such citations from a biblical writer? The implicit references to the promises speak far more powerfully to the attentive reader. Such is the mark of a truly great writer and a truly great book! The reader, having read the text of Genesis, can hardly fail to miss the point of God's sending Moses back to Egypt under the authority of the God of Abraham, Isaac, and Jacob (Exod. 3:15). Similarly, Exodus 1:5–8, besides its explicit reference to the Joseph narrative, certainly does allude to the promises of many offspring given to the patriarchs, and it is all the more profound for its subtlety. It is noteworthy that Whybray excises Exodus 1:6, 8, on the grounds that they "provide cross-references" and are from a "final redactor."[8] The removal of references to Genesis is special pleading on Whybray's part, but at any rate, one wonders how it is that the "final redactor" missed what Rendtorff and Whybray regard to be an obvious place to refer to the patriarchal promises in Exodus 1:7.

In addition, the situation in the exilic and postexilic material is not as dramatically different as Whybray implies. In the four books of Haggai, Malachi, Zechariah, and Daniel, there is but one reference to Moses (Mal. 4:4), and no reference to Abraham or to Isaac. References to Jacob in Malachi (1:2; 2:12; 3:6) are of the same sort one often finds in all the prophets—a reference to the nation rather than the individual. Allusions to episodes in Genesis are no more common in much of the postexilic material than in the rest of the Old Testament.[9] But it would be absurd to say that this is evidence that Genesis postdates these works.

Also, Whybray slants the data in his favor by asserting that almost all the references to Moses and the patriarchal history are Deut-

---

8. Ibid., 102.
9. The only exceptions are the genealogical chapters of 1 Chron. and a few Psalms.

eronomistic or otherwise late. References to the covenant promises to Abraham are found in Exodus 33:1; Leviticus 26:42; Numbers 32:11; and 2 Kings 13:23. Joshua 24:2–10 summarizes almost the entire Pentateuch. Aside from the many references in Joshua, Moses and the Law are mentioned in Judges 3:4; 1 Samuel 12:6–8; 1 Kings 2:3; 8:9, 53, 56; 2 Kings 14:6; 18:6, 12; 21:8. Micah 6:4 mentions the leadership of Moses, Aaron, and Miriam in the exodus, and 2 Kings 18:4 alludes to the episode of the bronze serpent. It is questionable whether one can excise all of this as late or Deuteronomistic material, especially since material is described as Deuteronomistic because it mentions Moses and the Law. As an argument for the late date of the Pentateuch, this is circular reasoning.

Hosea and the Pentateuch

Whybray's reference to Hosea is particularly interesting. Umberto Cassuto pointed out that Hosea alludes to the Pentateuch in six different categories: patriarchal narratives of Genesis, the exodus story, the Decalogue, narratives relating to the life of Moses, Deuteronomy 11:13–21, and Deuteronomy 33:1–43.[10]

Under the first category Cassuto observes that Hosea 11:8–9 alludes to the destruction of the cities of the plain and that the verb *destroy* (v. 9) is perhaps a catchword that points to Genesis 19:13, 14, and 29.[11] Cassuto also demonstrates that Hosea 12:4–5 and 13 (English = 3–4 and 12) are best understood as allusions to Genesis rather than to other traditions.[12] The verb pair *he struggled* (12:4 [3]) and *he prevailed* (12:5 [4]) is a direct allusion to Genesis 32:29 (English = 28), where the same verbs are employed. The verb *to struggle* (*sarah*) in these verses is attested nowhere else in the Bible, which implies that Hosea is in effect citing Genesis.

Under the second category Cassuto sees allusions to the exodus in Hosea 2:2 (English = 1:11), 5:6; 11:1; and 13:15. For specific verbal parallels, compare in the Hebrew text Hosea 2:2[13] to Exodus 1:10,

10. "The Prophet Hosea and the Books of the Pentateuch," reprinted in Umberto Cassuto, *Biblical and Oriental Studies,* trans. Israel Abrahams, 2 vols. (Jerusalem: Magnes, 1973), 1:79–100.

11. Ibid., 81–82.

12. Ibid., 82–87.

13. On Hos. 2:2 [1:11] and its relationship to Exod. 1:10, see especially C. F. Keil, *Hosea,* trans. James Martin (reprint; Grand Rapids: Eerdmans, 1954), 47.

Hosea 5:6 to Exodus 10:9, Hosea 11:1 to Exodus 4:22, and Hosea 13:15 to Exodus 14:21–29.[14] Under the third category Cassuto finds allusions to the Decalogue in Hosea 4:2; 12:10 [9]; and 13:4. Once again, there are clear parallels in the vocabulary of the Hebrew text. Compare Hosea 4:2 to Exodus 20:13–15 and Hosea 12:10 and 13:4 to Exodus 20:2. Cassuto also notes that the very theme of Hosea, the adultery of Gomer as the equivalent to the idolatry of the Israelites, is the theme of two facing commandments, the second and the seventh.[15]

In the fourth category Cassuto compares Hosea 13:2 to the incident of the golden calf. For further evidence, compare especially the Hebrew of that verse to Exodus 32:4 and Deuteronomy 9:12, 16.

In the fifth category Cassuto points out that the Hebrew texts of Hosea 2:10, 14, 16, 23 and 3:1 allude respectively to Deuteronomy 11:14, 17, 16, 17 again, and 13.[16] In the last category verbal parallels in the Hebrew between Hosea and Deuteronomy 32 are numerous: Hosea 1:9 = Deuteronomy 32:21; Hosea 5:14 = Deuteronomy 32:39; Hosea 8:14 = Deuteronomy 32:15, 18, and 22; Hosea 9:10 = Deuteronomy 32:10; Hosea 13:5–8 = Deuteronomy 32:10, 15, 24.[17]

The parallels to Deuteronomy 32 are especially meaningful since all citations in Deuteronomy are from a single chapter, but those in Hosea are scattered throughout the book. Cassuto rightly observes that it is more plausible that Hosea made use of ideas found in the poem of Deuteronomy 32 than that the author of the poem, which is a harmonious unity, "studded his entire poem, from beginning to end, with expressions and ideas culled from different prophecies of Hosea, without even echoing the central idea of Hosea, the concept that God's love for Israel was like that of a groom for his bride."[18] Cassuto concludes from his whole study that "there is nothing in the entire Book of Hosea to compel us to suppose that the Pentateuchal material existed in his day in a form different from that before us today." He goes on to claim that much of the Pentateuch "already existed in its present form in Hosea's time and was known to broad circles of people."[19]

14. Cassuto, "The Prophet Hosea," 87–89.
15. Ibid., 89–92.
16. Ibid., 93–95.
17. Ibid., 95–99.
18. Ibid., 100.
19. Ibid.

Deuteronomy and the Josianic Reformation

If 2 Kings 22 is taken as it stands, instead of read through the lenses of a reconstructed history, it too helps to clarify the situation. The text states that workmen who were remodeling the Jerusalem temple found a copy of the Law that had lain neglected for some time. This rediscovered copy thus became a major incentive for the reformation that followed (see 2 Kings 23). Following the work of W. M. L. de Wette (1805), however, many scholars have considered it axiomatic that in fact Deuteronomy was written at the time of the Josianic reformation.[20] Deuteronomy thus dates to about 621 B.C., as does the "Deuteronomic" theology, which dominates much of Joshua to 2 Kings.

Yet the position that Deuteronomy was written at so late a date is far from established. Scholarly challenges to the standard reconstruction began as early as 1911, when J. B. Griffiths pointed out that only three of twenty-five laws said to be distinctive to Deuteronomy have any bearing on the Josianic period.[21] Since then, challenges to linking Deuteronomy's composition to the Josianic period have come from many different directions.[22]

The most significant development in the study of this question was the discovery that Deuteronomy is formally a covenant treaty that structurally parallels the second-millennial treaties between Egypt and the Hittites. The specific details are well-known and need not be repeated here, but the conclusion, that Deuteronomy is a second-millennium work, remains a viable position despite its rejection by many scholars.[23] Arguments to the contrary, which try to relate Deutero-

20. To be precise, many scholars would contend that the origin of Deuteronomy came when the basic form of the book first appeared around 750 B.C. in the northern kingdom. Then, a Deuteronomic redaction of the original core took place later in Judah in conjunction with the Josianic reformation. A later redaction then occurred after the exile. For surveys of recent thought on Deuteronomy, see J. Alberto Soggin, *Introduction to the Old Testament*, OTL (Philadelphia: Westminster, 1976), 114–26, Werner H. Schmidt, *Introduction to the Old Testament*, trans. Matthew J. O'Connell (London: SCM, 1984), 120–9, and J. A. Thompson, *Deuteronomy*, TOTC (London: Inter-Varsity, 1974), 47–68.

21. J. B. Griffiths, *The Problem of Deuteronomy* (1911), cited in Harrison, *Introduction*, 43.

22. See Harrison, *Introduction*, 43–46.

23. This thesis was developed by Meredith Kline in *The Structure of Biblical Authority* (Grand Rapids: Eerdmans, 1972). Kline built upon the work of G. E. Mendenhall, "Ancient Orient and Biblical Law," *BA* 17 (1954): 26–46 and "Covenant Forms in Israelite Tradition, *BA* 17 (1954): 50–76. For a good survey of both the relevant material and the scholarly literature, see K. A. Kitchen, *The Ancient Orient and the Old Testament* (Chicago: Inter-Varsity, 1966), 90–102.

nomy to first-millennium Assyrian treaties, are not persuasive.[24] In the current environment, it is not difficult to maintain the position that the bulk of Deuteronomy is Mosaic in origin.[25]

The implications of this for the present study are twofold. First, if Deuteronomy is substantially Mosaic in origin, there is no reason to date the "Deuteronomistic" comments in the Former Prophets to the seventh century. References to the "law of Moses" (e.g., 1 Kings 2:3) need not be considered late additions. Second, this allows the account in 2 Kings 22 to be understood to mean exactly what it says. The Law was for some time quite literally gathering dust in the period of the divided kingdom. The reasons for this neglect are unknown, but it helps explain how it is that there are relatively few explicit references to the Law in much of the literature from this period.

The Greek Historians and the Pentateuch

Van Seters's *In Search of History* is an attempt to locate the beginning of Israelite written history in the wider context of the ancient world. An ambitious survey of historiographic documents from the Greeks, Mesopotamians, Hittites, Egyptians, and Levanters, this analysis has much to commend it and should stimulate other scholars to do related research. It is also a work upon which Whybray leans for his theory of Pentateuchal origin. Important aspects of Van Seters's analysis are troublesome, however, and his thesis is less than fully persuasive.

The programmatic notion of Van Seters is that true history writing (as distinguished from mere historiography) is a specific genre that seeks to discover the causes of the present circumstances in which a nation finds itself. It is thus national in character and is a literary contribution to the corporate identity of the people.[26] He develops this definition from the writings of Dutch historian Johan Huizinga (espe-

---

24. The arguments of R. Frankena, "The Vassal Treaties of Esarhaddon and the Dating of Deuteronomy," *OTS* 14 (1965): 122–54, and M. Weinfeld, *Deuteronomy and the Deuteronomic School* (Oxford: Clarendon, 1972), 59–157, both of whom hold to a seventh-century date for Deuteronomy, are treated in Peter C. Craigie, *The Book of Deuteronomy*, NICOT (Grand Rapids: Eerdmans, 1976), 24–29. Note that Craigie does not rest his entire case on the presence or absence of the "historical prologue" (contrast Thompson, *Deuteronomy*, 51–52). See also Kitchen, *Ancient Orient*, 95–96.

25. For a good survey of the case for this position, see Harrison, *Introduction*, 637–53.

26. John Van Seters, *In Search of History* (New Haven: Yale University Press, 1983), 1–6.

cially from a remark by Huizinga that history is "the intellectual form in which a civilization renders account to itself of its past.").[27] Van Seters uses his definition as a sieve for separating true history writing from mere "historiography."

Van Seters argues that the first true historians were Herodotus and the Deuteronomistic historian and distinguishes their writings from the chronicles, annals, and king lists of other ancient Near Eastern civilizations. These other forms of historiography to some degree contributed to the development of true history writing (the "chronicle," a genre he attributes to the neo-Babylonians, is thought to have been significantly influential), but they fall short of actually being within that genre. Thus he is able to contend that the study of Herodotus especially sheds light on the Deuteronomistic History, since the two are in effect parallel developments. The linking of Herodotus to the Deuteronomistic History allows Van Seters to assert that the works have two fundamental similarities: both had a very paratactic style (individual narrative units are set alongside one another with little concern for transition) and both freely created many of their stories.

Specific problems related to these assertions are to be noted. First, the definition of *history* presented by Van Seters, as Lawson Younger has demonstrated, is a serious misrepresentation of what Huizinga actually said. History is a much broader concept than Van Seters allows. Younger has thus shown, by way of example, that Van Seters's reasons for excluding Hittite historiography from genuine history writing are artificial.[28] The Hittite material is troublesome for Van Seters since it appears to display a relatively high sophistication in history writing a good deal earlier than his thesis will allow. This opens the door to speculation about whether Hittite influence may have encouraged the early development of Israelite history writing.[29] Van Seters's grounds for excluding certain Mesopotamian texts from the genre of history are also suspect.[30] This further challenges the notion that true history writing is a mid-first-millennial development and begs the question of whether the extensive use of analogy between the Deuteronomistic History and Herodotus is legitimate.

27. Johan Huizinga, "A Definition of the Concept of History," in *Philosophy and History: Essays Presented to Ernst Cassirer* 9 (cited in Van Seters, *Search*, 1).

28. Review of *In Search of History*, by John Van Seters, *JSOT* 40 (1988): 110–14.

29. This connection is explicitly made in H. Cancik, *Grundzüge der hethitischen und alttestamentlichen Geschichtsschreibung*, 3ff. (cited in Van Seters, *Search*, 103, n. 19). Van Seters has pointed out some problems in Cancik's methodology, but it does not appear to me that he has effectively removed the problems the Hittite material poses.

30. See Van Seters, *Search*, 67–68, concerning the so-called letters to the god, and 83–84, concerning the Synchronistic History. See also Younger, review of *Search*, 116.

Van Seters bolsters his case for linking the two by dating the beginning of Israelite history writing to the sixth century B.C.[31] (i.e., near the time of Herodotus) and by postulating that the Phoenicians served as a cultural bridge to Greece.[32] Younger observes that the former position is circular reasoning and the latter is a leap of faith.[33]

Indeed, as one who has done a fair bit of study in the Greek texts of Herodotus, I do not find Van Seters's arguments for a close comparison to the Deuteronomistic History convincing. He demonstrates a few similarities of narrative technique in the two works, but this is far from establishing that they "ought to be studied together."[34] A more detailed comparison makes such an assertion all the more dubious.[35]

Herodotus was above all a pioneer of historical investigation. He was something of a world traveler in his day; he probably visited the Euphrates valley, Susa, Egypt, Scythia, Macedonia, Tyre, Cyrene, and Sicily.[36] His interest in travel and geography even extended to descriptions of boats and navigable rivers. On the basis of these travels, he was able to incorporate local legends into his history as well as describe things he had personally seen. He made use of poetic sources, especially Homer, but Hecataeus was the only prose resource we can be sure he knew (although it is clear that other prose accounts of local legends were available).[37] He also named a few eyewitnesses to the events he described, including Archias the Spartan (3.55) and Thersander of Orchomenus (6.16). He often referred to the monuments of the places he visited, including the Pyramids (2.101), the temple of Bel at Babylon (1.181), the inscriptions of Darius (4.87), and an enormous number of trophies and monuments from Greece. He made use of temple records of oracular responses, especially from Delphi (e.g., 1.65).[38] He also utilized official Persian documents, as indicated in the Persian army list of book 7. Herodotus knew

31. *Search*, 8.
32. Ibid., 53–54.
33. Younger, review of *Search*, 114–15.
34. *Search*, 39.
35. For good introductions to Herodotus, see W. W. How and J. Wells, eds., *A Commentary on Herodotus* (London: Oxford University Press, 1912), 1:1–50, and the more recent and detailed work by J. A. S. Evans, *Herodotus* (Boston: Twayne, 1982).
36. For a survey of his travels, see R. P. Lister, *The Travels of Herodotus* (London: Gordon and Cremonesi, 1979).
37. Dionysius of Halicarnassus, *Thucydides* 5, gives a list of such writers. See Evans, *Herodotus*, 142–45, for discussion.
38. John Hart, *Herodotus and Greek History* (London: Croom Helm, 1982), 183–86, argues that the Delphic oracles recorded in Herodotus should be regarded as genuine unless there are compelling reasons for thinking otherwise. In other words, they should not be dismissed as fictional.

only Greek, however, and was dependent on others for the interpretations of these materials and non-Greek inscriptions.[39]

Herodotus was concerned about the accuracy of the evidence he received. This is not to say he was in all points a mature historian; flaws in his methodology have been long recognized.[40] Still, he pointed out independent confirmation of a story in 2.147 and even noted where the evidence was contradictory and thus the actual facts of a case uncertain (e.g., 4.154). He distinguished between myth and human history and frequently was quite skeptical or ironic in his handling of myths.[41]

It is true that one scholar, Detlev Fehling, essentially denies the role of investigator to Herodotus and claims that he invented most of his sources and, having "worked everything he knew" into his history, fabricated many details and even entire stories in order to fill out the narrative.[42] Working from Fehling's thesis, Van Seters makes similar claims for the Deuteronomistic historian, and Whybray extends them to the author of the Pentateuch.[43] And yet, as Van Seters well knows, Fehling's views have by no means swept the field in Herodotus studies.[44] Henry R. Immerwahr, by contrast, stresses the selectivity of Herodotus in his use of sources.[45] Scholars writing after Fehling continue to reckon with Herodotus as an investigator whose references to sources must be taken seriously.[46] One writer, Stewart Flory, treats Herodotus's use of fact and fiction in a way far more sensitive and perceptive on the concept of truth in the *Histories* than Fehling's blunt assertions that Herodotus was a liar.[47]

---

39. He may have also known Carian, a language of southwest Asia Minor (1. 171–72).

40. For a good survey of his strengths and weaknesses as a historian, see K. H. Waters, *Herodotus the Historian* (London: Croom Helm, 1985), 152–64.

41. Binyamin Shimron, *Politics and Belief in Herodotus, Historia* 58 (Stuttgart: Franz Steiner, 1989), 17–25.

42. *Die Quellenangaben bei Herodot* (1971); English translation, *Herodotus and His 'Sources'*, trans. J. G. Howie (Leeds: Francis Cairns, 1989). The quote is from p. 248 (English).

43. *Search*, 43–51, and *Pentateuch* 225–29, 238–39.

44. Cf. Van Seters, *Search*, 47.

45. *Form and Thought in Herodotus* (Cleveland: Case Western Reserve University, 1966), 33.

46. Evans, *Herodotus*, 142–53, concludes that Herodotus must be regarded as an oral historian. Also, unlike Fehling, *Herodotus*, 240–45, Evans accepts the historicity of Herodotus's travels (6–12). Similarly, Waters, *Herodotus the Historian*, 76–92, deals with Herodotus as an oral historian and considers it "almost certain" that Herodotus met with high-ranking Persians, 77. See also Shimron, *Politics and Belief*, 12.

47. Stewart Flory, *The Archaic Smile of Herodotus* (Detroit: Wayne State University, 1987), 49–79.

Even if Herodotus has done a good deal of fabricating, this does not prove that the biblical material can be similarly indicted. Fehling argues that Herodotus uses many devices characteristic of "lying-literature." These include both assurances of credibility as well as assertions by an author of his own doubts about the stories (something like, "I doubt that this is true but this is what I am told"), and also "evidence" in the form of inscriptions, descriptions of votive offerings, and other literary devices meant to lure the reader into credulity.[48] But these characteristics of "lying-literature" are not found in the Deuteronomistic History! The only characteristics it contains that might be used by some as evidence of its fictional nature are the use of typical numbers and the formula *to this very day*. These traits are hardly grounds for maintaining that entire narratives are late fabrications.

Herodotus treated both Greeks and non-Greeks with remarkable impartiality. Unlike many of his countrymen, who had only contempt for the "barbarians," Herodotus praised not only the Babylonians (2.109), Phoenicians (5.58), and Egyptians (2.43), peoples to whom he believed the Greeks were culturally indebted, but also the Persians, whom he described as fair, honest, and loyal (e.g., 1.136–39; 3.128). This even-handedness was a great asset to Herodotus as historical investigator; it enabled him to examine fairly and enthusiastically cultures not his own. Two curious facts about his history, however, are that he rarely used lists of archons, priests, or kings for dating purposes (although he certainly knew of such) and that he had no chronological framework, an oversight that led to inconsistencies and distortions in the narrative.[49]

The Joshua–Kings narrative is significantly different from Herodotus's writings. This is above all because the biblical narrative is consciously a work of canonical Scripture and not a work of historical investigations. Indeed, by the criteria Van Seters applies to other Near Eastern historiographical texts,[50] and if Herodotus is to be the benchmark, the Deuteronomistic historian was not a historian at all.[51] This is not to say that the incidents he described are not historically accurate, but to note that he was not an investigator of history and culture.

48. Fehling, *Herodotus*, 120–41.
49. See How and Wells, *Commentary*, 438–42, and Immerwahr, *Form and Thought*, 25–34.
50. Van Seters, *Search*, 320, does attempt to show that the Deuteronomistic History fits under his definition of history by claiming that the Deuteronomist is "articulating the people's identity." This assertion, in my view, is utterly groundless.
51. In referring to the Deuteronomistic historian, I am not subscribing to any particular theory of the origin of Joshua–Kings. I am only using common terminology for the sake of discussion.

Unlike Herodotus, the Deuteronomistic historian was not a world traveler or a student of culture. He did not speak of local traditions or describe incidents or objects that he personally observed. He did not refer to Israelite inscriptional evidence, to say nothing of foreign monuments or official documents. No individuals were cited as witnesses or informants, and no pieces of evidence were weighed for their reliability. He did not give personal opinions based on probability or strength of evidence. Impartiality with foreigners was not an issue because he had no interest in foreigners except as they interacted with Israel and Judah. Otherwise, they were simply peoples outside the covenants—the nations. Rather than investigate the past, the Deuteronomistic historian used the past to make his theological points. The sources he cited ("the chronicles of the kings of Israel," etc.) were regarded to be authoritative documents to which the reader might refer.

On the other hand, the biblical account does follow the patterns set by Near Eastern historians. Altogether unlike Herodotus, Joshua–Kings is dominated by the names of judges, prophets, and kings set within a chronological framework. Also, while it is true that both Herodotus and the Joshua–Kings material use vivid narrative technique, two of the most dramatic accounts of the biblical text, the court history and the Elisha stories, are excluded by Van Seters from the Deuteronomistic History as later additions.[52]

We might also note that Van Seters's Deuteronomistic History is really not paratactic in the way Herodotus is. This is because Herodotus follows a highly anecdotal method of narration. While it is true that the biblical history is to some degree episodic, it adheres closely to its theme and does not at all compare to Herodotus for the use of far-flung and at times apparently incongruous asides. While Herodotus does have an overall purpose in his use of anecdotes, his purpose and his method are not at all comparable to biblical history.[53]

Most significantly, the Deuteronomistic historian was dominated by a theological program. At the heart of this is the Davidic covenant (2 Sam. 7) and the conviction that both Israel and Judah were destroyed for their refusal to honor the terms of the covenant with Yahweh.[54]

---

52. *Search*, 277–91, 306.

53. Cf. Immerwahr, *Form and Thought*, 46–78. Van Seters, *Source*, 31–40, cites Immerwahr extensively, but even in Van Seters's discussion the only significant point is that biblical scholars have been too hasty to claim evidence of source division and redactional influence. Otherwise, Herodotus and the Bible are clearly not the same. See also Flory, *Archaic Smile*, for an illuminating commentary on Herodotus's anecdotal style. Here again, however, I can see no parallel to the Deuteronomistic History.

54. Van Seters, *Search*, 271–77, argues that this text is thematically central to the Deuteronomistic History.

Herodotus, too, operated in a religious context, as indicated by his references to the oracles and to human acts of hubris. In Herodotus, however, this is merely a religious viewpoint that affects (and sometimes obscures) his historical investigations. His work is fundamentally a political history and not a theological program,[55] such as we find in the Deuteronomistic History. It is not without reason that the Jews referred to the biblical corpus as the Former Prophets. If this distinction holds for the Deuteronomistic History, moreover, how much more so for the Pentateuch! One can only wonder if Whybray is really prepared to say that Herodotus and the Pentateuch are in the same genre and "ought to be studied together."

The late date Van Seters assigns to the beginning of Israelite history writing is problematic on other grounds as well. In addition to the alleged parallels to Herodotus, he argues that the evolution of history writing in Israel followed the example of the neo-Babylonian chroniclers and that the "book of the deeds of Solomon" and the "book of the chronicles of the kings of Israel/Judah" are Israelite examples of such chronicles. Thus, these works must be considerably later than the events they describe. In fact, they must postdate the neo-Babylonian material, although they may have drawn on earlier inscriptions and annals for their material.[56]

Van Seters's efforts to establish this reconstruction can only be described as fanciful. He is attempting to make a genre analysis of books that no longer exist and that none of us has ever seen! Nevertheless, in keeping with his thesis, Van Seters argues that the "book of the deeds of Solomon" is "a collection of the records of Solomon's reign, especially inscriptions, that were extant in the time of the compiler" and that the collection probably included a commemoration for the building of the temple. Thus the work is chiefly made up of "references to building activity, inventories, and lists."[57]

The biblical author, however, who presumably had the book before him, stated that it contained "all which [Solomon] accomplished, and his wisdom" (1 Kings 11:41). This connotes a much more extensive work than what Van Seters implies. The meaning of "and his wisdom" is unknown, but it may describe information that was the basis for the summation in 1 Kings 4:29–34. Indeed, here as in all other such references in Kings,[58] it appears that the author, having extracted what

55. See especially Shimron, *Politics and Belief*, 26–47.
56. Van Seters, *Search*, 292–302, 357.
57. Ibid., 301–2.
58. E.g., 1 Kings 14:29; 15:23; and 15:31.

information he deemed essential for his theological (not historical!) purposes, was referring the curious or skeptical reader to a prior, much more detailed history of Solomon's reign. The form, date of composition, and content of this material is unknown to us, but Van Seters's analysis is inconsistent with the implications of the text.

To return to Whybray and the Book of Genesis, it is difficult to see how the Greek historians have any real bearing on the question of the date of the Pentateuch unless one wishes to contend for the very doubtful position that the latter was influenced by the former. Although formal parallels between Greek literature and the Bible can be instructive, the ancient Near Eastern milieu of Genesis and the Hellenic environment of Herodotus are in truth worlds apart with respect to their literary histories. Even where two works are obviously of the same genre, and there is clear literary dependence, it does not follow that the respective writers had similar motives or wrote out of similar circumstances, to say nothing of their being contemporaries. An obvious example is provided by a comparison of Homer's epics to Vergil's *Aeneid*. The fact that true history writing did not begin in Greece until the fifth century has no bearing on how or when the Pentateuch was composed. Van Seters can provide no reliable support for Whybray's thesis.

The Inadequacy of Whybray's Hypothesis

The most significant point of all is that Whybray's principal argument, the lack of reference to the Pentateuch in preexilic writings, is not adequately explained by his theory and cannot be used to support it. An argument from silence (that preexilic works do not mention incidents from the lives of the patriarchs), can be reasonably used only to try to prove that the preexilic Israelites never heard of the patriarchs or at least knew none of the stories concerning the patriarchs. It cannot be used to suggest that a given book about the patriarchs had not yet been written. The reason for this is simple. If the preexilic Israelites believed they were the offspring of the patriarchs, and if they knew some stories about the patriarchs, and if they further believed that God gave promises to the patriarchs related to their habitation of the land of Canaan, then the presence or absence of Genesis as a complete, written text is a moot point. In either case, the comparatively few references to Abraham in the preexilic prophets cannot be taken to mean the people did not know who Abraham was. Thus, some other explanation must be sought for the infrequent reference to the Genesis material.

Whybray must concede that his hypothesis does not imply that the author of the Pentateuch had no sources. It did not spring out full-grown like Athena from the brow of Zeus. Indeed, discussing the antiquity of the possible sources of the Pentateuch, Whybray rightly remarks that "no dates subsequent to the events described can be ruled out *a priori*."[59] To be sure, Whybray prefers to think of much of Genesis as a fictional reworking of ancient folktales,[60] but even in Genesis he cannot escape sources altogether.

Yet the fact of sources is troublesome if not fatal for Whybray's approach. Only two possibilities exist; either the preexilic Israelites generally believed that they were the descendants of Abraham, Isaac, and Jacob and had some common traditions about them, or they did not. If they had no such traditions, then one must explain how it was that the exilic community suddenly and completely accepted the novel history of the patriarchs (not to mention the exodus and the laws) as both true and canonical. Indeed, so persuasive was this newly written Pentateuch that the Deuteronomist even went back and inserted references to Moses and the patriarchs into the Deuteronomistic History![61] It is equally implausible to suppose that a few kernels of tradition were expanded and fictionalized into the present Pentateuch. If the Israelites during the period of the monarchy did know and accept the patriarchal traditions, then the nonmention of the patriarchs in a given piece of preexilic literature is a nonissue with respect to the date of Genesis as a book. And the concession that the author of Genesis used sources is a concession that the preexilic Israelites knew these traditions. At any rate, it is unthinkable that the Israelites could have existed until the exile as a nation without any common origin tradition.

The issue, therefore, is not whether the preexilic Israelites knew about the patriarchs. They assuredly did. The question is why reflection on the patriarchal history is rare in the rest of the Old Testament (including the postexilic material). The answer can only be that the patriarchal stories were no longer living traditions in the community. To put it another way, the stories of Genesis have no *Sitz im Leben* in Israel's history after the exodus. Genesis was not written for, nor does

---

59. *Pentateuch*, 236.

60. Ibid., 239–40.

61. According to Van Seters, *Source*, 323, the Deuteronomistic History is prior to the Pentateuchal sources.

it address, the questions being asked in the period of the judges or the monarchy, or the exilic or postexilic communities. The sources of Genesis spoke to a community that existed long before national Israel, and the written text of Genesis had a function quite apart from the historical and theological problems encountered in the monarchy, the divided kingdom, or the exilic situation.

Genesis is thus best taken as a work with a premonarchic setting. The questions of what relationship exists between Genesis and the rest of the Pentateuch and of whether the Babylonian exile provides a reasonable setting for Genesis are taken up in chapter 12.

The Historicity of the Text

Conservative attempts to sustain the credibility of the Genesis material are often brushed aside as naive. In recent years, however, evangelical scholars have dealt with thorny historical problems with a high degree of academic precision and sensitivity.

The Tower of Babel

Dale S. DeWitt has examined the issue of the historical background of the episode of the tower of Babel.[62] He observes that scholars have generally either regarded the story as pure myth[63] or as an example of literary dependence on the *Enuma elish*.[64] But he builds a strong case for setting the story of the tower in the context of Sumerian history. He observes that "land of Shinar" (v. 2) is properly Sumer, and that the language of the text can be read in a local rather than a universal sense.[65]

He further notes that there are many parallels between Genesis 11:1–9 and what is known of Sumerian civilization. First, a Sumerian text from late in the Third Dynasty of Ur states that the Sumerians

---

62. "The Historical Background of Genesis 11:1–9: Babel or Ur," *JETS* 22 (1979): 15–26.

63. "Myth" in the sense of being outside the realm of history. Thus, Robert Davidson, *Genesis 1–11* (Cambridge: Cambridge University Press, 1973), 6, 10–11, cited in DeWitt, "Babel or Ur," 15.

64. Thus, E. A. Speiser, *Genesis*, AB (New York: Doubleday, 1964), 75–76.

65. He treats the reference to Babel in v. 9 as an editorial comment meant either as a satire on paganism or as a means of linking Ur to the subsequent city of Babylon (17–18).

once had been a people of one language but that Enki had confounded their speech.[66] The historical background of this is the invasion of Sumeria by Semitic and other peoples, who both introduced new languages and brought about the fall of Sumerian civilization. DeWitt comments that in both the Sumerian text and Genesis the multiplication of languages is attributed to the actions of deity. Nevertheless, he continues, this breakup had historical causes, specifically invasions by Amorites and Elamites. He notes that elsewhere in the Bible historical actions are attributed to divine causality.[67]

Also, DeWitt states that the ideology surrounding the Sumerian ziggurat accords well with what Genesis 11:4 states of the builders' purpose. They believed the ziggurat established a link between heaven and earth ("a tower that reaches to heaven") and was the greatest visible sign of their own glory and power ("make a name for ourselves"). Furthermore, the use of oven-fired bricks in the making of ziggurats is confirmed at least as early as the Third Dynasty of Ur, as is the use of bitumen mortar (Genesis 11:3 records the use of "tar" instead of mortar).[68]

Finally, DeWitt observes that the fall of the Third Dynasty of Ur resulted in a scattering of the Sumerian peoples ("And the Lord scattered them all over the earth" [v. 8]).[69] The collapse of Sumerian civilization is thus emblematic of divine condemnation of all human hubris.

The Historical Circumstances of the Patriarchal Period

K. A. Kitchen has pointed out that the patriarchal narratives are well-suited to the Palestinian situation in the early second millennium B.C. He gives several reasons for this judgment.

"Power-alliances between Mesopotamian states (Gn. 14) are typical for c. 2000–1750 BC."[70] He writes that this does not seem

---

66. See S. N. Kramer, "The Babel of Tongues: A Sumerian Version," *JAOS* 88 (1968): 108–11, cited in DeWitt, "Babel or Ur," 19.

67. DeWitt, "Babel or Ur," 20.

68. Ibid., 15, 20–24.

69. Ibid., 24–25. DeWitt is somewhat perplexed about relating the biblical account to the date of the fall of the Third Dynasty of Ur (pp. 25–26), but in my view needlessly so. As this work will demonstrate, the story of the tower of Babel and the genealogical material that follows it are from different sources, and it is not necessary to suppose that the tower episode chronologically antedates the lifetimes of the individuals in the genealogy.

70. Kitchen, *Ancient Orient*, 47.

to be the case before or after this period, but cites an eighteenth-century B.C. Mari letter that mentions alliances of ten, fifteen, and twenty kings and notes that "[a]t least five other Mesopotamian coalitions are known" from this period.[71] Kitchen also observes that the names of the four eastern kings of Genesis 14 fit this period.[72]

Kitchen further claims that the personal names of the patriarchs have parallels in Egyptian and Mesopotamian documents, and all are within the period of the nineteenth to seventeenth century B.C. Abraham, he states, is comparable to Aburahana from the Posener execration texts, and Zebulon is similar to Zabilanu from Egyptian and Old Babylonian sources.[73] Thomas L. Thompson questions the validity of the parallel to Abraham from the execration texts and argues that, although the name *Abraham* is West Semitic, it cannot be isolated to any chronological period. He states that names similar to Abraham "are found from the time of the Mari texts down through the Neo-Assyrian period."[74] His conclusion seems overstated, however, since his single neo-Assyrian example is questionable, yet he excludes earlier names that are at least as plausible. Although it is true that we cannot contend that the name *Abraham* demands a second-millennial date, it is equally true that the name by no means excludes it.[75]

Kitchen's reasoning continues: "Seasonal occupation of the Negeb region on the south-west borders of Palestine is archaeologically attested for the twenty-first to nineteenth centuries BC (Middle Bronze Age I)—but *not* for a thousand years earlier or for eight hundred years afterwards."[76] Patriarchal sojourning is indicated in Genesis 20:1 and 24:62. Here, Kitchen is primarily dependent on the

71. Ibid., 45.
72. Ibid., 43–44.
73. Ibid., 48.
74. *The Historicity of the Patriarchal Narratives*, BZAW 133 (Berlin: de Gruyter, 1974), 22–36. The quote is from p. 35.
75. For further discussion, see D. J. Wiseman, "Abraham Reassessed," in *Essays on the Patriarchal Narratives*, ed. A. R. Millard and D. J. Wiseman (Winona Lake, Ind.: Eisenbrauns, 1983), 141–60, especially 158–60.
76. *Ancient Orient*, 49. Cf. Yohanan Aharoni, *The Archaeology of the Land of Israel*, trans. Anson F. Rainey (Philadelphia: Westminster, 1982), 85–86, for his description of the Negeb in what he calls "Middle Canaanite I." Carl Armerding argues that after Middle Bronze Age I, the "first real expansion" in the Negeb came in the united Israelite monarchy, *The New International Dictionary of Biblical Archaeology*, ed. E. M. Blaiklock and R. K. Harrison (Grand Rapids: Zondervan, 1983), s.v. "Negev."

work of Nelson Glueck. Van Seters challenges Glueck at this point and, following Kathleen Kenyon, argues that Middle Bronze Age I culture was essentially seminomadic and that the settled communities of the sort Genesis describes are "inappropriate to this period."[77] Thompson, however, has demonstrated the weakness of Kenyon's arguments on this point.[78] The position that Middle Bronze Age I archaeology is compatible with the patriarchal migrations remains secure.

Kitchen continues: "Freedom and wide scope of travel is particularly evident in the Old Babylonian period."[79] He notes that caravans traversed the area from Hazor to Elam and from Babylon to Asia Minor, and cites the Mari archives as a primary source of evidence. He also notes that seminomads "sometimes took to crop-cultivation and more settled life."[80]

The Old Assyrian tablets from Cappadocia (nineteenth century B.C.) afford the best parallels to the multiple appellations of the deity found in Genesis. These include the "God of Abraham," the "Fear of Isaac," and the "Mighty One of Jacob." But these are not, as Albrecht Alt suggested, separate deities. To cite Kitchen: "[A]s so often in the Ancient Near East, they are but multiple epithets of a single God."[81]

Social customs and laws known to exist in the second millennium B.C. have parallels in Genesis. For example, "the price of twenty shekels of silver paid for Joseph in Genesis 37:28 is the correct average price for a slave in about the eighteenth century BC; earlier than this, slaves were cheaper (average, ten to fifteen shekels), and later they became steadily dearer."[82] In addition, Kitchen supports the position that Genesis 23 is best illustrated by the Hittite property laws and should not be regarded as a neo-Babylonian dialogue contract.[83] He rightly notes that Genesis 23 is a report of a purchase and not an actual contract.[84] Finally, he supports the view that the biblical portrait of cus-

---

77. *Abraham*, 105–7.

78. *Historicity*, 165–71. Thompson is not speaking with an apologetic intent where Genesis is concerned.

79. *Ancient Orient*, 50.

80. Ibid.

81. Ibid., 50–51.

82. Ibid., 52–53.

83. Contra Gene M. Tucker, "The Legal Background of Genesis 23," *JBL* 85 (1966): 77–84.

84. *Ancient Orient*, 154–56. See also M. J. Selman, "Comparative Customs and the Patriarchal Age," in *Essays on the Patriarchal Narratives*, ed. A. R. Millard and D. J. Wiseman (Winona Lake, Ind.: Eisenbrauns, 1983), 91–139, p. 124.

toms governing the options available for a childless couple are best illustrated by the Ur and especially Nuzi material (see pp. 73–79).[85]

Recent Challenges to the Historicity of the Patriarchal Narratives

Two recent works, both mentioned already, have argued that the patriarchal narratives cannot be read as historical in any sense. These are Thompson's *Historicity of the Patriarchal Narratives* and Van Seters's *Abraham in History and Tradition*. Because of the significance of these works and the erudition with which they are argued, at least a few words of response are in order.

Some Needed Corrections

To begin with, it is clear that these criticisms of the patriarchal narratives have supplied much-needed corrections to Genesis studies. Thompson in particular has exploded a number of alleged parallels to Genesis and historical reconstructions of the patriarchal age. I question, however, whether the best of these reassessments really impinge upon the historicity of the patriarchal narratives so much as upon certain scholarly reconstructions which may themselves be incompatible with the details of the text of Genesis. A few examples will illustrate this.

The Benjamites

The transliteration of the name of a tribal group at Mari to *Bin-ia-mi-na-a* led a number of scholars to believe that this tribe could be identified with biblical Benjamin. Thus, it was postulated that the tribe separated from its parent group and came southward from Syria to Canaan. Thompson, however, has demonstrated that the name in question must be translated not as Benjamin but as either "the tribe of *Iamina*" or "the southern tribe." He further notes the term probably does not refer to a single tribe at all but to portions of several tribes in two specific geographical areas of Mesopotamia. The group mentioned in the Mari tablets has no relation whatsoever to the Israelite tribe of Benjamin.[86]

85. Ibid., 153–54.
86. Thompson, *Historicity*, 58–66.

If the Mari group could have been identified with biblical Benjamin, however, it would have only shown that the Bible had seriously garbled the history of the origin of Benjamin. Thompson's work here in no way challenges the historicity of the Bible! He has only overthrown a scholarly opinion, which was in fact contradictory to Genesis.

Abraham the Caravaneer?

Building on critiques made by other scholars, Thompson has also put to rest the theory of C. G. Gordon and William F. Albright that the patriarchs were merchant caravaneers who roamed about trading with the local population. The theory was justified by an interpretation of the Hebrew texts of Genesis 34:10 and 42:34 to mean that the patriarchs were free "to trade" in the land instead of the correct rendition that they were allowed "to move about freely." Albright, moreover, attempted to sustain this thesis with an impossibly low date for Early Bronze IV/Middle Bronze I and by connecting Abraham to "Hapiru caravans." Regarding the latter, Thompson has noted that the Hapiru are described in the texts more as pirates than as traders.[87]

Once again, however, the Bible never implies that Abraham was a caravaneer. The conservative scholar Kitchen, in fact, long ago rejected the caravaneer theory.[88]

An Amorite Migration into Palestine?

Another theory associated especially with the Albright school asserts that the Early Bronze IV/Middle Bronze I era saw a migration of West Semites ("Amorites" or "Aramaeans") first northward from Ur to Haran and then southward into Palestine. The debate involves interpretation of pertinent terminology, the identification and history of the West Semitic peoples, and the implications of texts from diverse areas, especially the Mari texts and Egyptian execration texts. The depth and breadth of Thompson's research into these questions is truly to be admired. His overall conclusion is that the theory of a major West Semitic migration northwards from Ur to Haran and then southwards to Canaan is implausible. Thompson further argues that the Egyptian texts do not support the picture of newly arrived West

87. Ibid., 171–86.
88. *Ancient Orient*, 49 n. 71.

Semites coming down from Palestine during this period and that the archaeology of Middle Bronze I Palestine does not indicate that the region was overrun by seminomads.[89] One reviewer, to be sure, observes that Thompson has overstated his case, especially where the Egyptian evidence is concerned.[90] Still, it is clear that a theory of an Amorite migration has been significantly damaged.

Once again, however, we are brought back to a singular point: the Bible never says that Abraham was part of a mass movement of people. To the contrary, this study will attempt to demonstrate that a major theme of the patriarchal narratives is the alienation and isolation of the patriarchs in a world of strangers. Apart from his wife, his estranged nephew Lot, and a few followers, Abraham had no kindred or fellow travelers. Jacob was so concerned about his isolation among the indigenous people that he complained bitterly (and with some fear) that his sons made his name "a stench among the people living in this land" (Gen. 34:30). Simply put, the patriarchs were alone. While some scholars may have derived a certain amount of satisfaction from the idea that the patriarchal migrations were confirmed by archaeological research, close examination shows this "confirmation" to be itself problematic for the biblical narratives. Because it was patriarchal the migration is presented as an isolated family movement; in fact, historical confirmation of this claim is neither necessary nor possible.

The Sojourning of the Patriarchs

Van Seters argues that ancient Near Eastern studies indicate three characteristics of a nomadic people: transhumance (seasonal migration of nomads with their families and flocks to flourishing pastures), hostility to the native populations, and migration. He argues that the patriarchs cannot be said to meet any of these criteria.[91]

In response, we note that the text never implies that the patriarchs were migrants in the sense described by Van Seters. They are represented as landless immigrants.[92] While they may have engaged in some transhumance, they were not outlaws or part of a major migration. As

---

89. *Historicity,* 52–187, 316–21.

90. Aelred Cody, review of *The Historicity of the Patriarchal Narratives,* by Thomas L. Thompson, *Bib* 57.2 (1976): 263.

91. *Abraham,* 13–38.

92. See also Wiseman, "Abraham Reassessed," 141–58. The fact that Abraham was an immigrant does not preclude his having earned the respect and influence among the local population which Genesis ascribes to him.

Van Seters himself notes, Abraham is described as a resident alien, "a term not entirely appropriate as a general designation for nomad."[93] Also, J. J. M. Roberts comments that "Van Seters's radical contrast between sedentary and nomadic life (p. 9) ignores the fact that second-millennium nomadism of the Mari region was characterized by a combination of sedentary and nomadic features." Roberts also observes that the Mari "nomads" themselves were eager to obtain land.[94] The biblical presentation is entirely consonant with such a picture.

The Wife-Sister Narrations and Nuzi

In another analysis, which displays admirable thoroughness, Thompson shows how E. A. Speiser's zeal to relate the Genesis "wife-sister" motif (12:13; 20:2; 26:7) to the Nuzi material effectively causes him to lose his sense of perspective on both. Speiser contends that in the Hurrian upper class at Nuzi, a man not only married a woman but also adopted her as his sister. He believes this occurred because Hurrian culture was fratriarchal, and that the wife-sister position of the woman gave her greater protection and higher social (even religious) status while at the same time enhancing the husband's authority. If this is true, one can conclude that the West Semites at Harran (a center of Hurrian society) adopted this custom; Genesis implies as much for the patriarchs although, according to Speiser, it badly garbles the details. Rather than a simple matter of legal status, the Bible presents the wife-sister motif as a matter of duplicity and cowardice on Abraham's part. Thus, the Genesis "wife-sister" stories have a historical kernel, Speiser concludes, but the stories themselves are not historical.[95]

Thompson shows that almost every aspect of this theory collapses under scrutiny. First and foremost, the notion that Hurrian husbands adopted their wives as sisters is based on a misinterpretation of the texts. The man who adopts a woman as sister does not marry her but has the right to give her in marriage (and thus receive a portion of the bride price). Second, Hurrian society was not fratriarchal but patriar-

---

93. Ibid., 16.

94. Review of *Abraham in History and Tradition*, by John Van Seters, *JBL* 96 (1977): 109. Roberts's evidence is contrary to Van Seters, *Abraham*, 16, who calls the theme of land inheritance "utterly foreign to the nomadic way of life."

95. See *Genesis*, 91–94, for Speiser's own summary of his views on the subject. For a full account of his position, see E. A. Speiser, "The Wife-Sister Motif in the Patriarchal Narratives," in *Biblical and Other Studies*, ed. Alexander Altann (Cambridge: Harvard University Press, 1963), 15–28.

chal. Third, the adoption of a woman as sister did not convey special status upon her. Finally, Speiser's method involves a serious methodological problem. To maintain that a parallel exists between his interpretation of Hurrian customs and the patriarchal stories, he must acknowledge that no real parallel exists for the present stories in Genesis but postulate that the original details have been seriously confused. In short, his parallel is based on an imaginary background for Genesis![96]

Once again, however, Thompson's work on the Nuzi material has only put to rest an alleged parallel which in fact implies that the Genesis version of events was nonhistorical. Thompson, of course, does not accept Genesis as historical. He argues that Genesis 12:10–20 develops the theme of "despoiling the Egyptians." He further observes that the motif of brothers and sisters marrying one another is common for gods and titans, and also that in Eighteenth-Dynasty-Egyptian material *sister* is a term of endearment for one's beloved.[97]

On the other hand, although Genesis 12:10–20 may be read as perhaps proleptic of the exodus, this in no way explains the "wife-sister" motif there or in the parallel stories (20:1–18; 26:1–11), which do not occur in Egypt. Sibling marriages among the gods and the use of *sister* as a term of endearment are both meaningless parallels. The patriarchs are not godlike in the tales—in Isaac's case, the wife-sister motif is a plain and simple lie and thus is in no way parallel to the myths! Similarly, Abraham does not call his wife "sister" in a context of endearment, as in the Egyptian love poetry.[98] Whatever one wishes to make of these stories, neither the parallels offered by Speiser nor those by Thompson are significant.

Other Alleged Parallels from Nuzi and Elsewhere

A number of scholars have attempted to point out cultural parallels between the second-millennial Nuzi texts and the Genesis stories.

96. See Thompson, *Historicity,* 234–45, for details, including a full analysis of relevant Nuzi texts. For a more recent look at the Nuzi marriage contracts, see Jonathan Paradise, "Marriage Contracts of Free Persons at Nuzi," *JCS* 39 (1987): 1–36. Paradise is not directly concerned with the issues Thompson raises, but his discussion does not cast doubt on Thompson's work.

97. *Historicity,* 246–48.

98. The use of the terms *brother* and *sister* for one's lover is found especially in the Egyptian love poetry of the Papyrus Chester Beatty I and the Papyrus Harris 500.

Van Seters and Thompson reject this approach and attempt to demonstrate that other, later parallels are more persuasive. While they have in many cases corrected some previous excesses, I believe that the Nuzi texts do provide light on much of Genesis, as the following examples illustrate.

The Surrogate Mother

A number of ancient texts, especially the Nuzi text HSS 5:67, have been cited as parallels to the Genesis accounts of a wife giving her slave to her husband as a surrogate mother. Van Seters rejects the parallel and argues that an Egyptian text from the late twelfth century and especially a seventh-century text from Nimrud are better parallels and establish a first-millennial environment for the Genesis stories.[99] Thompson, however, who has done a much more careful analysis of all relevant texts, remarks that the Egyptian text does not necessarily concern a concubine and that the Nimrud text "is in fact not remarkably close to our Genesis stories."[100]

Thompson himself lists seven objections to seeing the biblical texts and HSS 5:67 as parallels,[101] but his objections are much more appropriate for the Rachel and Leah narrative (Gen. 30) than for the Hagar narrative (Gen. 16; 21:1–21). There is no doubt that the story of Jacob's wives and concubines is distinct and not to be related to HSS 5:67; the former deals with a man who has two wives and two concubines,[102] whereas the latter restricts a man to a single wife with the provision that he may take a concubine to bear children in case the wife should be infertile. The Rachel and Leah story thus describes the problems inherent in a polygamous situation (a fact that does not require but does not exclude an early-second-millennial environment).

The Hagar episode, on the other hand, is closer to HSS 5:67 than Thompson allows. In both cases, the man is monogamous and takes a concubine only because the wife is infertile. In both cases, the wife chooses the concubine. Also, both texts make clear that in case the wife should after all bear a son, the wife's son would be heir. A signif-

---

99. Van Seters first made his case in "The Problem of Childlessness in Near Eastern Law and the Patriarchs of Israel," *JBL* 87 (1968): 401–8. See also *Abraham,* 70.

100. *Historicity,* 254–55, 266–67. The quote is from p. 267.

101. Ibid., 256–58.

102. The only significant similarity is Rachel's use of Bilhah to have children during her own period of infertility.

icant difference is that the Nuzi text forbids the expulsion of the concubine's children, an event that does occur in the biblical story.
Thompson considers this to be decisive and argues that Abraham's
unnatural expulsion of his son to the desert is a variation on the literary theme of the cruelly abandoned child.[103] In fact, Abraham's hesitation and concern about dismissing Hagar and Ishmael (Gen. 21:11)
answer Thompson at both points. Abraham is both anxious for
Ishmael's safety and may also be aware that sending him away violates
common legal standards; only a word from God persuades him to
grant Sarah's request. Also, the malicious behavior of Hagar (16:4) and
Ishmael (21:9) indicates that Sarah is not a wicked stepmother.[104]

This is not to suggest that HSS 5:67 and the Hagar stories are in all
points alike. The former is a Hurrian prenuptial agreement whereas the
latter is an Israelite narrative. Nor can the parallel be used to establish a
precise dating for the patriarchal period since Abraham was not Hurrian.
Nevertheless, the Nuzi material does provide a remarkable illustration
for the Genesis account. Other second-millennial texts, such as those
from Alalakh, and especially the Code of Hammurabi, also provide
interesting parallels to the episodes involving Hagar. On Thompson's
own analysis, moreover, the latest alleged parallels (those from Egypt
and Nimrud as well as neo-Babylonian and later Greco-Egyptian texts)
are the weakest.[105] One may conclude that the story of Ishmael's birth
and expulsion best fits in a second-millennial environment.

Stealing the Gods

Rachel's theft of her father's gods (Gen. 31:19) in the context of
Jacob's struggle with Laban has occasioned a great deal of debate.
Some scholars have argued from Nuzi parallels that Laban had no sons
at the time he contracted to allow Jacob to marry his daughter. He
therefore adopted Jacob in accordance with a practice well docu-
mented from Nuzi. Jacob thus should have had a right to a portion of
the property even though Laban subsequently had sons, but Laban
systematically maneuvered to exclude him. This is seen to be at the
base of the conflict between the two men.

103. *Historicity*, 258.
104. This also answers Thompson's suggestion (257) that Sarah need not have been
concerned to send Hagar and Ishmael away if Nuzi-like customs were in effect, since
Isaac's position as heir was secure. Genesis indicates that her worries were not strictly
legal but that she saw a danger to Isaac in the malice of Ishmael.
105. *Historicity*, 260–68.

Both Thompson and Van Seters reject the notion that an adoption of Jacob is implied in the texts.[106] Their arguments are substantial, and the point is to be conceded. The decisive factor is Thompson's observation that in a marriage that involved the adoption of the son-in-law, no bride-price was paid.[107] Jacob, on the other hand, paid the very substantial price of seven years of labor per wife! Also, of course, Genesis never says that Laban adopted Jacob but, to the contrary, states that the families of Jacob and of Laban were financially separated (31:1).

The question of whether any parallels are to be found at Nuzi, however, does not end here, for Nuzi also describes both marriages in which a bride-price was paid and the terms of employment for hired shepherds. Martha A. Morrison has demonstrated a close correspondence between the customs reflected in the Nuzi and Old Babylonian texts and the Jacob-Laban narrative.[108]

Morrison begins by describing the general terms of contracts between hired shepherds and the herd owners, and she notes parallels between these and the Genesis texts. The shepherds of Nuzi and the Old Babylonian world tended the sheep in return for a share of the profits minus any losses incurred through negligence. The shepherds were free men, however, and in case of a dispute, they could go to court and contend that a sheep had died not through their negligence but by an act of God (the legal term in the Hammurabi Code is "the touch of a god") or because of wild animals. But in actual practice, the owners won almost all disputed cases.

At shearing time in the spring, accounts would be settled and herd assignments for the following year would be made. Morrison describes how the annual shepherding cycle was tied to the agricultural cycle such that the two complemented one another. In particular, shepherds tended their flocks near the cultivated fields during the time of plowing and planting so that they might help with the work. They removed their flocks far away during the growing season for the safety of the young plants and returned at harvest.

In Genesis, similarly, Jacob is a free man who works under the term of a stipulated contract (30:31–36), but he too felt the bitterness of having to bear financial damage of sheep that had been lost through no negligence of his own (31:39). At the episode of Reuben's mandrakes,

---

106. It must be observed that this is a relative and not an absolute assessment of the date. The difficulties of the comparative method in general and of the study of HSS 5.67 in particular are noted in Selman, "Comparative Customs," 127, 130–34.

107. *Historicity,* 269–80, and *Abraham,* 78–81.

108. Thompson, *Historicity,* 274.

Jacob is keeping his flocks near enough to home that he can return at night. This is said to have been "during the wheat harvest" (30:14), just as in the agricultural cycle already described. During the first month of Jacob's residence with Laban, moreover, he apparently worked with no contract and no specified wages. At the end of that month, however, he and Laban entered an agreement for him to work for the hand of Rachel (29:14b–20). This may well have been at shearing time, when new contracts would be drawn up. Seven years later, the contract is fulfilled. Note that all the people were together and thus able to attend Laban's feast, as would be the case at shearing time (29:21–22).

It is also interesting that Jacob's third period of service, six years, is close to the turnover time of six-and-a-half years for the Nuzi flocks— the time frame within which the sheep of the original flock would have died. During this time, most of Laban's flock could have died and been replaced by the variegated animals that all went to Jacob. Thus, Laban's sons complained that Jacob had taken everything (31:1).[109]

This returns us to the conflict between Jacob and Laban and to Rachel's theft of the gods. Morrison explains that in Nuzi a dowry was generally given to a bride as part of a marriage contract. She observes, however, that Rachel and Leah complain that their father gave them no dowry but instead simply sold them off. Laban himself used the money (i.e., Jacob's service) that was paid for them (a bride-price was often returned to the bride as a dowry). Laban had never performed his paternal duties and in his daughters' eyes had never completed the marriage contract. For them, the wealth Jacob had accumulated over the previous six years had in effect become their dowry (31:14–16).[110]

Still the question remains: Why did Rachel steal the gods? Household gods were generally passed down to the principal heir. They represented the property and fertility of the family, and their loss was a family disaster. To be without them was to be disenfranchised as a family, so to speak. Contrary to some interpreters, however, Rachel does not take the gods to insure that Jacob would become Laban's heir. Jacob had never been in the line to inherit (and in light of their migration to Canaan, inheritance would never be a possibility anyway).

Instead, her theft arises from the strong emotional attachment a family had for its gods and from the legitimation of the family the gods would provide. This was important to Rachel in light of Laban's failure to give a dowry;

---

109. "The Jacob and Laban Narrative in Light of Near Eastern Sources," *BA* 46. 3 (1983): 155–64.
110. Ibid., 156–60.

it was as though she and Leah had become nonpersons, and the possession of the gods would remedy this. Another Nuzi text, HSS 14:8, although its interpretation is difficult, plainly attests to such cultural tendencies.[111]

Although Morrison does not conclude that the Genesis material *must* be placed in the second millennium, her evidence plainly shows it not to be anachronistic, and her work is in effect a challenge to Van Seters, who argues that the best parallels to this material are from neo-Babylonian and Achaemenid "dialogue documents."[112] Thompson, on the other hand, cites incidental parallels from much later sources.[113] The important point, however, is the *consistency* with which the entire narrative fits in the early-second-millennial environment in Morrison's interpretation over against the sketchy and isolated parallels claimed by Thompson and Van Seters.[114]

In conclusion, one may say that some Nuzi materials illustrate and in some cases assist in explaining the Genesis narratives. Also, they help to establish that the narratives belong in a second-millennial environment and should not be regarded as the creations of mid-first-millennium authors. This is not to say that the parallels are in all points precise, and the reader must bear in mind the cultural (and temporal) distance between Nuzi and the patriarchs. Claims that the Genesis stories have been verified by Nuzi are extravagant. Even so, the Nuzi material enhances and in no way diminishes the credibility of the biblical account.

Anachronisms and Other Indications of a Late Date for Genesis

Although anachronisms do not deprive a text of all historical trust-worthiness,[115] they have naturally been a focal point of studies aimed at determining the historicity and origin of the narratives in Genesis. Van Seters has especially tried to demonstrate that the only legitimate parallels to the Abraham stories occur in the middle- to late-first millennium (and thus the texts themselves are from that period). To do

111. Ibid., 160–61.
112. Ibid., 161–64. Morrison describes two alternative interpretations of the Nuzi text and shows how both are compatible with her reading of the Genesis material (162).
113. *Abraham*, 97–98.
114. *Historicity*, 278–80, citing Josephus and Arabic tales.
115. A. R. Millard, "Methods of Studying the Patriarchal Narratives as Ancient Texts," in *Essays on the Patriarchal Narratives*, ed. A. R. Millard and D. J. Wiseman (Winona Lake, Ind.: Eisenbraun's, 1983), 35–51. See especially 46–48.

this, however, he at times overstates his case severely. For example, he rejects any connection between Ur of the Chaldeans (Gen. 11:31) and the Third Dynasty of Ur.[116] Van Seters instead contends that the period of Nabonidus best fits the Genesis material.[117] Yet the evidence he cites is circumstantial, and Roberts, quoting Van Seters, aptly comments that "the migration from Ur to Harran is hardly 'a specific historical allusion to Nabonidus'" (p. 38).[118] Other examples may be given as well.

Genesis 14

Van Seters attempts to demonstrate the nonhistorical character of Genesis 14 from several considerations. He asserts that the names of the kings of Sodom and Gomorrah, Bera and Birsha, respectively mean "in evil" and "in injustice" and thus are simple pejoratives of no historical value. He further argues that a punitive expedition of kings from Mesopotamia to Palestine is more consistent with the first millennium than the second.[119] Also, he argues that verses 1–11 are formally comparable to a neo-Assyrian or neo-Babylonian campaign report. The formal elements of the report are the reason for the campaign (usually the subjugation of a rebellious client state); the preparation for the campaign; the route taken and the battles fought; and the results of the campaign (an account of cities destroyed or booty taken). He contends that the latest form of this type of narrative is the "chronicle form," which uses the third person.[120]

Gordon J. Wenham, on the other hand, recognizes that the names Bera and Birsha are "striking," but he gives alternative etymologies and concludes that the names probably rest on older traditions. He also shows that the names of the kings of Admah and Zeboim (respectively, Shinab and Shemeber) have a more authentic ring.[121] At any rate, the transformation of an individual's name to a pejorative is not

---

116. The most significant problem here is actually that Ur is said to be "of the Chaldeans." Gordon J. Wenham, *Genesis 1–15*, WBC (Waco: Word, 1987), 272, notes that this is "probably a gloss on the old tradition." See also W. S. LaSor's comments in *ISBE* (rev. ed.), s.v. "Ur."

117. *Abraham*, 23–26.

118. Roberts, review of *Abraham*, 112.

119. *Abraham*, 112–20.

120. Ibid., 299–300. The texts he has in mind are the Assyrian victory inscriptions (*ANET*, 275–301) and the Babylonian Chronicles (*ANET*, 301–5).

121. *Genesis 1–15*, 309.

an indication that the person in question is not historical, although it may indicate scribal tampering. An example would be the transformation of the name of Saul's grandson, Meribbaal ("Baal is [my] advocate") to Mephibosheth ("utterance of shame").[122]

While it is true that the first millennium attests punitive campaigns from Mesopotamia to Palestine, the particular system of alliances described in Genesis 14 has been compared by Kitchen to the particular political situation that prevailed in the early second millennium. With regard to Van Seters's formal analysis, it is noteworthy that this type of campaign report is known far earlier than he indicates. The Annals of Karnak give a detailed account of the victory of Thutmose III (ca. 1490–1436 B.C.) at the battle of Megiddo, and it includes all four formal elements described by Van Seters in the same sequence. It is also in third person (like the Bible, unlike the neo-Assyrian texts) and, although it supplies chronological information, it is in narrative rather than chronicle style (like the Bible, unlike the neo-Babylonian texts).[123] The mid-second-millennial parallel is thus stronger than any of the first-millennial formal parallels, and it would seem that the form of Genesis 14 does not have the chronological significance Van Seters supposes.

Thompson's treatment of Genesis 14 is somewhat strange. He compares it to a Serbo-Croatian poetic account of the beginning of the First Balkan War (1912). The account was recorded and interpreted by Milman Parry, and is part of the Parry-Lord school of Homeric studies. As a parallel to Genesis 14, however, this account is utterly worthless unless one is prepared to demonstrate that Genesis 14 comes from oral poets who followed exactly the same composition techniques as Yugoslavian bards. And Thompson does not even attempt to do so.[124]

Wenham has given an excellent summation of evidence for the historicity of Genesis 14. He states that the names of the eastern kings, the route of the invasion, the unusual Hebrew term for "trained men" (v. 14, a word attested only in a nineteenth-century Egyptian text and a fifteenth-century Taanak letter), and the details given about Melchizedek are all compatible with a second-millennial date. He also refutes

122. Cf. 1 Chron. 8:34 to 2 Sam. 9:6–12.
123. See *ANET*, 234–38. On the form of the account, note the following: rebellion [year 22, month 4 of second season, day 25]; preparation and planning [year 23, month 1 of third season, days 5 to 16]; battle [year 23, month 1 of third season, day 19]; and plunder [year 23, month 1 of third season, day 23].
124. *Historicity*, 188–89. See pp. 190–95 for other miscellaneous objections to Gen. 14 as historical.

the charge of inconsistency, that we have Abraham the mighty warrior in Genesis 14 and Abraham the isolated weakling elsewhere.[125] While the historicity of Genesis 14 may not be "proven," it is by no means as doubtful as Thompson and Van Seters make it out to be.

Genesis 17 and the Rite of Circumcision

Van Seters considers Genesis 17 to be a unified work of P. He argues that in the Abraham material, P is only a supplement to J, and that the author of P had J as a source for his own work. In addition, he contends that the "cultic institution of circumcision" in Genesis 17 "represents P's own contribution to the tradition corpus."[126]

My only question here is whether such a late date for an origin tradition for circumcision is reasonable. From the biblical data, it is an inescapable conclusion that circumcision was well-established by David's time and thus antedates him. Would the Israelites wait so long, until P, to give an account of how the rite originated? It is important to note that, on Van Seters's analysis, the idea that P made use of an ancient tradition is virtually excluded. But the position that the account of the origin of circumcision is so late as to be a creation of P is not credible.

Arabs in Genesis?

Van Seters notes that neo-Assyrian, neo-Babylonian, and Persian sources describe contact with and subjugation of Arabs, but that Arabs do not occur in historical sources prior to the mid-eighth century. And yet, he argues, Abraham "is presented as the father of the Arabs," and this further establishes a mid-first-millennial date for Genesis.[127] In fact, however, Genesis makes no such claim for Abraham. Whatever connections later interpreters have sought to make between Ishmael and the Arabs, Genesis does not mention Arabs and consistently refers to "Ishmaelites" instead. As Roberts remarks, this is somewhat odd if Genesis is as late as Van Seters contends.[128]

---

125. *Genesis 1–15*, 318–20. Van Seters, *Abraham*, 115, argues that the pictures of Abraham are inconsistent.

126. See *Abraham*, 279–93. The quote is from pp. 281–82.

127. Ibid., 35–37. The quote is from p. 36.

128. Review of *Abraham*, 112.

The Camel in Genesis

John J. Davis has drawn together available evidence on the use of the camel in the ancient Near East.[129] A number of scholars, including Albright[130] and more recently Van Seters,[131] have considered the references to camels in Genesis to be anachronistic on the grounds that the camel was not domesticated in the patriarchal age.

A negative assessment based on an apparent lack of evidence is dangerous. Prior to 1950, animal bones were discarded by archaeologists as having no significance, and it is in any case difficult to know from the bones of an animal whether it was domesticated. In addition, the camel is not commonly used around urban centers, and camel remains are thus not likely to be found at those sites.[132]

Even so, evidence for the domestication of the camel prior to the patriarchal age is considerable. Some authorities in fact consider it to have been domesticated from the fourth millennium B.C. Painted or figurine camels have been found from predynastic Egypt, and a braided cord of camel hair, which dates to the Third or Fourth Dynasty of Egypt, was found in the northern Faiyum scarp. A Sumerian lexical text from Ugarit lists the camel as a domestic animal, and another Sumerian text, from Nippur, refers to camel's milk. In Palestine, camel bones have been found in Middle Bronze Age layers at Gezer, Megiddo, and Taanach.[133] Davis concludes that the camel was known in the ancient Near East prior to the third millennium and domesticated prior to the second.[134]

The Possibility of Mosaic Authorship

Most theological conservatives continue to maintain Mosaic authorship of the Pentateuch, but this viewpoint has been effectively ignored. Two reasons can be given for this situation. Some extreme conservatives would simply attribute it to a lack of faith on the part of their opponents. This attitude does not foster interaction. Much the same

129. "The Camel in Biblical Narratives," in *A Tribute to Gleason Archer*, ed. Walter C. Kaiser, Jr., and Ronald F. Youngblood (Chicago: Moody, 1986), 141–52.

130. *From Stone Age to Christianity*, 2d ed. (New York: Doubleday, Anchor Books, 1957), 165.

131. *Abraham*, 17.

132. Davis, "Camel," 144.

133. Ibid., 145.

134. Ibid., 146.

may be true of the other side as well. Scholars who have embraced theories such as the Documentary Hypothesis may not be as open to criticism from outside their ranks as they should be.

A second important factor must also be considered. Mosaic authorship, by itself, does not answer the fundamental question: What are the sources of Genesis? Moses was not alive during any part of the history of the Genesis narrative, and theological conservatives generally have not tried to explain where he obtained his material.[135] Considering that even the latest portions of the Genesis narrative are asserted to have taken place some four hundred years before Moses, this is a significant complication.

Still, it is possible to speak of the Mosaic authorship of the Pentateuch. This does not mean that Moses wrote every word of the present text; indeed, as will be argued, the idea of a post-Mosaic redaction is essential to an intelligible analysis of the data. Nevertheless, in the face of biblical evidence that Moses was highly educated (reared in Pharaoh's household) and the father of the new nation, one cannot doubt that he was a figure of sufficient stature to have written the law. Unless we are prepared to say that the people of Israel hopelessly confused and misunderstood their own history, the attempt of Martin Noth to demote Moses to a position of minor significance in the history of Israel must be recognized as a piece of unwarranted hyperskepticism.[136]

In addition, a considerable amount of internal evidence for the Egyptian provenance of the Pentateuch, together with the Pentateuch's accurate portrayal of second-millennium legal and social customs and its tendency to use some archaic Hebrew forms, suggests that its origin antedates the Israelite monarchies.[137] In fact, certain forms in standard biblical Hebrew are borrowed from second-millennium Egyptian.[138]

135. See Gleason L. Archer, Jr., *A Survey of Old Testament Introduction* (Chicago: Moody, 1973). Archer devotes an enormous amount of space to attacking various critical theories and gives considerable space to asserting that Moses could have written the Pentateuch (109-18), but he says nothing about *how* he could have written it. The question of sources, in particular, is left unexamined. The same pattern is followed in other conservative writings. Cf. Harold G. Stigers, *A Commentary on Genesis* (Grand Rapids: Zondervan, 1975), 7–32.

136. See Martin Noth, *The History of Israel* (London: SCM, 1958), 135–37.

137. Archer, *Survey*, 109–18, is helpful here. See also Harrison, *Introduction*, 537–41.

138. See Jesse L. Boyd III, "An Example of the Influence of Egyptian on the Development of the Hebrew Language During the Second Millennium B.C.," in *A Tribute to Gleason Archer*, ed. Walter C. Kaiser, Jr., and Ronald F. Youngblood (Chicago: Moody, 1986), 191–95.

One may infer that these forms were adopted during the sojourn and were made a permanent part of standard Hebrew by their inclusion in the Pentateuch.

Nevertheless, with respect to Genesis, the question of sources remains. Although I affirm that Genesis is part of the prophetic word of Scripture, this cannot mean that the histories and genealogies contained in it came to Moses or anyone else by direct revelation. Only a limited amount of the text should be assumed to be visionary in origin. This is in accord with what is seen in the other Old Testament historical books, which explicitly used sources (see Num. 21:14; Josh. 10:13; 2 Sam. 1:18; 1 Kings 11:41; 14:29; 15:7, 23, 31; 2 Chron. 16:11; 20:34; Ezra 4:11). No analogy exists in the Bible, on the other hand, for historical narrative having its source in direct revelation.

It should not be assumed, however, that Moses only collected and strung together a list of documents. He certainly modified, edited, and carefully arranged the materials in his use. He probably operated in a way analogous to Luke's collection of materials for his Gospel (Luke 1:1–4). Although he used sources, he arranged and edited the material in such a way that he produced a new and original document, not a collection of sources mechanically added to one another.

Recognition of the editorial process has two implications. First, any attempt to isolate documents behind Genesis must remain hypothetical. Dogmatism is impossible here! The text, as it now exists, is in its present form because of the work of Moses and post-Mosaic redactors. One cannot assume that any passage in its present form is a word-for-word representation of the original source. Second, finding the sources of Genesis is not the same as identifying the structure of Genesis, which is a result of the redaction process. The question of sources and the question of structure must not be confused.

The Post-Mosaic Redaction

The assertion that Moses is the principal author of the present text of Genesis need not mean that it came from his hand exactly as we have it now.[139] To the contrary, one may confidently assume that the work has undergone post-Mosaic redaction. The main reason such a redaction would have taken place was not to substantially change the

139. Cf. Segal, *Pentateuch*, 34–35.

book in any way but rather to make it intelligible to a later generation of readers.

Genesis is written in standard Hebrew, archaic forms notwithstanding. Although one may well argue that the Pentateuch played a major role in the development of standard Hebrew, there is no reason to think that there could not have been any revisions to keep up with semantic developments in the Hebrew language. In addition, the location of geographical settings by names that were common in a later period is an indication of redaction. The most well-known example is the reference to Dan as a place name in Genesis 14:14, an obvious anachronism. But it proves no more than that the text has undergone some revision. The same may be said of the reference to Israelite kings in Genesis 36:31.[140]

Summary and Conclusion

This chapter has attempted to demonstrate that it is possible to speak meaningfully of Genesis as a work that goes back to Moses himself. One may grant that the work has had some later revision, but these changes need not have been so substantial as to invalidate the concept of Mosaic authorship. In addition, the position that Genesis is historical and reliable rather than fictional or confused has been defended.[141]

All of this is preliminary to the study at hand. No attempt has been made to prove conclusively that Genesis is true or that Moses wrote it; indeed, it is no more possible to "prove" that Abraham actually lived, apart from a dramatic archaeological find, than it is to "prove" that there was once a document J or that the Pentateuch is the work of a single author from the exilic period. Nevertheless, if one may rightly assert that the Mosaic authorship of Genesis and the veracity of the book are intelligent options, then one may proceed to attempt to develop a hypothesis regarding the sources of

140. There are a number of editorial revisions and comments in Deuteronomy as well. See Deut. 2:10–12; 3:11, 13b; 34:1–12.

141. John Goldingay has correctly written that "historical factuality is a necessary though not a sufficient basis for faith. It is not possible to have the advantages of history without the risks." See "The Patriarchs in Scripture and History," in *Essays on the Patriarchal Narratives,* ed. A. R. Millard and D. J. Wiseman (Winona Lake, Ind.: Eisenbrauns, 1983), 1–34; the quote is from p. 34.

Genesis and their original intentions and settings. Mosaic authorship thus becomes a paradigm within which one may operate.

A dramatic development in the philosophy of science came in the publication of *The Structure of Scientific Revolutions,* by Thomas S. Kuhn. In that book, Kuhn argues that scientific discoveries are not built up piece by piece through the gradual accumulation of facts, as many people have long assumed, but by a scientific revolution in which one paradigm is overthrown by a new paradigm. Once a paradigm is dominant, all theories and interpretations of phenomena will be so structured as to fit into the paradigm. Much attention will be drawn to "facts" that fit easily into the paradigm, and elaborate explanations will attempt to account for observations which do not fit. Crisis ensues when anomalies are so obvious and troublesome that the old paradigm is seen to be inadequate. This situation will continue until a new paradigm overthrows the old.[142]

In the study of Genesis, the old paradigms of the Documentary Hypothesis and tradition criticism are clearly in a crisis state. Hopelessly complex theories that attempt to account for all the problems are reminiscent of the complexities of Ptolemaic astronomy. Other theories (such as Whybray's and Thompson's)[143] are now being offered. But the simplest explanation of all, that the Book of Genesis means what it says and that its origins go back to a much earlier date than the rest of the Old Testament, has been given only cursory consideration because it is "precritical." The chapters that follow will attempt to demonstrate that the oldest paradigm is in fact the best paradigm of all. The paradigm will be offered as an alternative to the current critical "consensus" (if one may still use that term), a consensus that is becoming obsolete. And "what is obsolete and aged will soon disappear" (Heb. 8:13).

142. Thomas S. Kuhn, *The Structure of Scientific Revolutions,* 2d ed. (Chicago: University of Chicago Press, 1970).

143. Thompson, *Origin Tradition,* 61–131. See app. B of this work for a discussion of Thompson's theory.

PART

The Structure and Sources of Genesis

4

The Toledoth *and Narrative Sources of Genesis*

With any approach to the reconstruction of the history of the text of Genesis, several stages of development must be taken into account. A four-stage development of the text is here proposed: the initial recollection and transmission; the reduction of these stories to writing and the pre-Mosaic redaction of the unstructured oral sources into complex literary units; the Mosaic redaction; and the post-Mosaic redaction(s).

During the period of the initial recollection, the patriarchs recounted the stories of their life histories to their children. Also during this period, the patriarchs would have passed on to the next generations whatever written materials they possessed. In the second stage, the various stories would have been redacted into complex narrative structures and preserved in written form. It is impossible to know whether the stories were collected into complex narrative structures during the oral stage or after a preliminary transcription of the simple recollections. The complex literary structures are narrative works that were probably derived from several recollection sources. These complex narrative units can be isolated from the present text of Genesis on a form-critical basis. The third stage, the Mosaic redaction, gave the book its present form and most of its present content. This stage may be properly called Urgenesis. The fourth stage, the post-Mosaic redaction(s), gave the work its present shape.

The initial recollection of the stories may well have been oral, but it is important to note that no prolonged oral tradition-history is implied in this model. A relatively brief period of oral recollection (less than one hundred years) is reasonable.[1] Unless one is prepared to argue that all the stories of Genesis were written down in the generation in which they occurred (or that the stories began as written documents), which is highly unlikely, oral sources are inescapable.[2] Nevertheless, we have no tools for meaningful research into the oral stage of the history of the sources; the concept is no more than a hypothetical probability.

At some stage this oral material was transcribed, and unless the transcription went directly from the oral sources to the present text of Genesis, intermediate steps were required. Furthermore, it is reasonable to suppose that at or soon after the first transcriptions of the oral sources, the material was structured into discrete units in ancient Near Eastern patterns. Of course, some of the oral material could have been formed into larger and more formal narrative structures prior to transcription, but one need not assume this to have been the case. The assumption that an oral stage must lie behind the forms is fallacious (see chap. 2).

At some stage, however, these pre-Genesis sources must have been fashioned into a work that had the general structure of the present Book of Genesis, a work here called Urgenesis. It is possible that the Book of Genesis, exactly as it now exists, sprang directly from the sources, but this is not likely unless Genesis is a very late work. Changes in Hebrew vocabulary, grammar, and morphology, the changing of place names, and the addition of new data (e.g., 36:31–42) indicate that Genesis was redacted subsequent to the initial framing of the book.[3] Although the four-stage development of the text postulated here may not in all points conform exactly to the actual historical process, it is a reasonable and workable hypothesis.

Even if this four-stage development hypothesis is valid, however, a major question is whether anything can be determined about the nature and extent of the individual sources. Here, the questions concern the types, structures, and purposes of the sources (i.e., form-crit-

---

1. According to Patricia G. Kirkpatrick, *The Old Testament and Folklore Study,* JSOTSS 62 (Sheffield: JSOT Press, 1988), 113–14, 150 years is the maximum length of time for which an oral history may be transmitted accurately.

2. See R. N. Whybray, *The Making of the Pentateuch* (Sheffield: JSOT Press, 1987), 236.

3. See chap. 3.

ical matters) as well as how they came into Moses' possession. Also, how have the sources been woven into a coherent whole? Source and structure are separate but related matters. And finally, is the present structure of Genesis primarily due to the Mosaic redaction, or has the text been so thoroughly re-edited in the post-Mosaic period that the original Mosaic structure is lost? In this chapter, we will attempt a preliminary assessment of the nature of the sources and then deal with the other questions in subsequent chapters.

The *Toledoth* Sources

The Meaning of Toledoth

In attempting to piece together the sources and prehistory of Genesis, a term of major significance and much discussion is *toledoth*. The word *toledoth* is often translated "generations" or "account," and is familiar to the Bible reader in the formula, "these are the generations of . . . ." It occurs in the Bible thirty-nine times, including twelve times in Numbers 1, which enumerates the populations of each of the tribes,[4] and once in Numbers 3:1. The word *toledoth* occurs nine times in 1 Chronicles[5] where the descendants of various individuals and members of eponymous clans are given. Ruth 4:18ff., under the term *toledoth*, lists the lineage of Perez down to David. In Exodus 6:16 and 6:19, *toledoth* is used in reference to the descendants of Levi, while in Exodus 28:10 it relates to the twelve sons of Jacob.

All other occurrences (thirteen) are in Genesis.[6] In every case outside of Genesis, *toledoth* refers to the lineal descendants of an individual or to members of an eponymous clan. This is in accord with its root, *yld,* "to give birth." Of particular interest is the phrase "according to their *toledoth*."[7] In this case, "their *toledoth*" does not mean "their descendants" but "their family genealogy," since the clan members whose *toledoth* it is are themselves the individual members of the *toledoth* records. Used in this way, therefore, *toledoth* is a technical term for a method of keeping family and clan records. In Numbers 1, similarly, "their *toledoth*" means "their genealogical registration."[8] On this

---

4. Num. 1:20, 22, 24, 26, 28, 30, 32, 34, 36, 38, 40, 42.
5. 1 Chron. 1:29; 5:7; 7:2, 4, 9; 8:28; 9:9, 34; 26:31.
6. Gen. 2:4; 5:1; 6:9; 10:1, 32; 11:10, 27; 25:12, 13, 19, 36:1, 9; 37:2.
7. E.g., Gen. 10:32; 25:13; Exod. 6:16; 1 Chron. 5:7; 7:9.
8. Thus NASB.

basis, the understanding that the *toledoth* is a manner of keeping records is well established. Another significant point is that the *toledoth* pattern generally does not include the birth of the eponymous clan head himself (a probably insignificant exception occurs in Genesis 25:19, in which after "the *toledoth* of Isaac," we are told that Isaac was the son of Abraham).[9]

In Genesis, however, *toledoth* is used in some unusual ways. The first example, Genesis 2:4, is notable for giving the *toledoth* of the heavens and the earth. Also, although the *toledoth* texts of certain individuals are often confined to descriptions of their descendants, sometimes the *toledoth* of a person appears to introduce historical events that go far afield from giving simple genealogical records (Genesis 6:9 and 37:2 are especially problematic). The *toledoth* of a patriarch frequently includes a few significant details concerning the circumstances of his life relevant to his fathering of children (e.g., how old he was when the eldest was born, where he and the clan lived and moved, how old he was when he died; see Genesis 5:1ff.; 11:27ff.; 25:19ff.). Numerous scholars have sought the key to the usage of *toledoth* in Genesis, but no consensus has been reached.[10]

The Wiseman-Harrison Theory

A good deal of attention has been given to the question of whether the thirteen occurrences of *toledoth* mark off the tablet sources of Genesis. The latter position was set forth by P. J. Wiseman in *Ancient Records and the Structure of Genesis*[11] and has been vigorously defended by R. K. Harrison.[12] Wiseman and Harrison assert that the *toledoth* lines mark off eleven original tablets behind Genesis (eleven tablets rather than thirteen; the occurrences of *toledoth* in 10:32 and 25:13 are repetitive and do not mark off separate tablets). The theory is supported by the ancient tablets from Mesopotamia. There, tablets often began or ended with catchlines as titles or colophons. These

9. See *Theological Wordbook of the Old Testament*, ed. R. Laird Harris, Gleason L. Archer, Jr., and Bruce K. Waltke, 2 vols. (Chicago: Moody, 1980), 1:380.

10. For a good survey of views see M. H. Woudstra, "The *toledoth* of the Book of Genesis and their Redemptive-Historical Significance," *CalThJ* 5 (1970): 184–89. Woudstra's own position is not sufficiently well developed to be persuasive.

11. Reprinted as P. J. Wiseman, *Clues to Creation in Genesis*, ed. D. J. Wiseman (London: Marshall, Morgan and Scott, 1977), 3–105.

12. R. K. Harrison, *Introduction to the Old Testament* (Grand Rapids: Eerdmans, 1969), 543–53.

would serve to indicate the proper sequence for a series of tablets (since they obviously could not be bound together). Therefore, in contrast to the Documentary Hypothesis, this theory is supported by ancient Near Eastern literary practice and does not have a "scissors-and-paste" view of how the ancients handled their documents.

A great difficulty with the Wiseman and Harrison position, however, is that it considers each *toledoth* statement to come at the end of each segment of text (i.e., that each *toledoth* represents an original colophon). This curiously coincides with the Graf-Wellhausen position that 2:4a belongs with 1:1–2:3 and not with 2:4ff. A complete tabular analysis of the Wiseman-Harrison position is seen in figure 4.1. The stories of Joseph are thought to have been a later supplement to the tablet sources.[13]

Figure 4.1
The Wiseman-Harrison Theory of the *Toledoth* Sources

Tablet	Extent	Content
1	1:1–2:4	origins of cosmos
2	2:5–5:2	origins of humanity
3	5:3–6:9a	histories of Noah
4	6:9b–10:1	histories of sons of Noah
5	10:2–11:10a	histories of Shem
6	11:10b–11:27a	histories of Terah
7	11:27b–25:12	histories of Ishmael
8	25:13–25:19a	histories of Isaac
9	25:19b–36:1	histories of Esau
10	36:2–36:9	histories of Esau
13	36:10–37:2	histories of Jacob

R. K. Harrison, *Introduction to the Old Testament* (Grand Rapids: Eerdmans, 1969), 548.

On close examination, this view of the *toledoth* statements is untenable. Genesis 25:12 is the *toledoth* of Ishmael. With the Harrison model, this verse refers to Genesis 11:27b–25:12, the life history of Abraham. Aside from the fact that it is astonishing that Ishmael was

13. Ibid., 551–53.

in possession of tablets describing all of Abraham's life (including the period after Ishmael's expulsion) or that for some other reason that record was called the "*toledoth* of Ishmael," 25:12 is actually followed by a short section, verses 13–18, which describes the names and journeys of the Ishmaelite clans. Common sense would indicate that this small section is the *toledoth* of Ishmael, 25:12–18. But the theory states that this Ishmaelite section is in fact the *toledoth* of Isaac (25:19)![14]

A similar situation occurs in Genesis 36:1, the *toledoth* of Esau, which according to the theory refers to 25:19–36:1, the stories of Isaac and Jacob. Here again, this is in spite of the fact that Genesis 36 lists the descendants of Esau and the Edomite kings. These difficulties are fatal to the Wiseman and Harrison presentation. With the exceptions at 10:32 and 25:13, as well as a possible exception at 36:9,[15] the general rule is that the *toledoth* lines introduce rather than conclude sections.[16]

An Alternative Approach

A possible solution, however, is that the *toledoth* lines are in fact source titles, not colophons, and that they are introductory, as they appear to be. In that case, we may assert that indeed the *toledoth* lines do refer to ancient sources that existed prior to the complete text of Genesis. In the *toledoth* sources, therefore, we have an obvious set of pre-Mosaic documents.

But what are the contents of these *toledoth* sources? If the *toledoth* lines represent tablets that contained all the narrative material from one

14. Wiseman, *Clues*, 44, obscures this difficulty by asserting that Gen. 11:27–25:19 together constitute the *toledoth* of Ishmael and Isaac, but this violates his own standards of how the *toledoth* lines function in the text.

15. Gen. 36:9 may be a repetition of 36:1 (the *toledoth* of Esau), which verses together would form an *inclusio*. See n. 16 for an alternate possibility.

16. An attempt to modify and resurrect the Wiseman-Harrison theory is in Dale S. DeWitt, "The Generations of Genesis," *EvQ* 48 (1976):196–211. DeWitt asserts that the *toledoth* lines refer not just to the preceding narratives but also to the following genealogies. He therefore proposes that each tablet had a title, narrative, and colophon *toledoth* line on the front and a genealogy and summary colophon on the back. His proposal fails for several reasons: he is unable to give an example from the ancient Near East for the tablet format he proposes; with his view, the "colophon" lines sometimes come in at peculiar places, and some of his hypothetical tablets do not follow his formal structure at all (6:1–9:18 is especially problematic); DeWitt must arbitrarily assign portions of the text to various tablets in order to maintain his theory (he artificially divides 12:1–25:11 into the "Ishmael" [12–16] and "Isaac" [17:1–25:11] tablets; his assertion that 2:7a is a tablet title is equally peculiar). In fact, there is simply no compelling reason to adopt this modification of the colophon theory.

toledoth line to the next, these tablets must have been of highly irregular length. The *toledoth* of Ishmael introduces a section of a mere seven verses (vv. 12–18), whereas that of Terah (11:27) introduces a section of more than thirteen chapters. Obviously the story of Abraham (contained in chapters 12 to 24) is of more significance to Israel than that of the Ishmaelite tribes. Nevertheless, the highly varied content of the Abraham chapters and the length of the narrative make it unlikely that it was ever one single tablet. The best solution to this problem is to understand that the *toledoth* lines introduced sources, but that those sources did not necessarily contain all the material from one *toledoth* catchline to the subsequent use of the word *toledoth*. In other words, a considerable amount of Genesis is from non-*toledoth* (narrative) sources.

Indeed, we shall argue that the *toledoth* sources of Genesis are exclusively genealogical in nature, although they may contain such details as clan movements or the ages of the patriarchs at death. Certainly the *toledoth* source of Terah (11:27) did not contain all of the stories of Abraham (as far as 25:11), the *toledoth* source of Isaac did not contain all of the Jacob narrative (25:19–35:29), and the *toledoth* source of Jacob did not contain all the Joseph narrative (37:2–50:26).

We therefore should assert that Genesis probably contains a number of sources, each indicated by a *toledoth* title, but that these sources have been supplemented by other revelations and pieces of tradition. We are now left with two broad classifications: *toledoth* sources and narrative (non-*toledoth*) sources.

The Extent of the Toledoth Sources

The question of the number, type, and length of the narrative sources will be considered again, but first it is necessary to separate the *toledoth* sources from the narrative sources. To do this, the probable length of the *toledoth* sources must now be considered.

In a few cases, the sources do extend all the way to the next *toledoth*, as in 25:12–18. The *toledoth* of the sons of Noah goes to and includes the second reference to the *toledoth* of the sons of Noah (10:32). In this instance, Genesis 10:32, the *toledoth* is a colophon, but this is not a real exception to the rule that *toledoth* lines are generally title lines. The *toledoth* line here is obviously retrospective to 10:1, and the two form an *inclusio*. The *toledoth* of Shem (11:10) extends to 11:26, where it is followed by the *toledoth* of Terah in 11:27. The *toledoth* of Esau (36:1) extends through the chapter, to 36:43, a terminus set by the next *tole-doth* line, 37:1–2a (the *toledoth* line in 36:9 may or may not introduce a separate source; see p. 99). In some cases, therefore, the terminus of a *toledoth* source is set by a subsequent *toledoth* line.

In other cases, the terminus of a *toledoth* source is not set by the next *toledoth* line. The *toledoth* of Adam (5:1) certainly extends to 5:32, but does not include 6:1–8, a section that is part of the flood narrative. The *toledoth* tablet of Terah (11:27) probably extends only as far as 11:32, Genesis 12:1ff. being part of a separate narrative source on Abraham.

In all of these examples, it is best to adopt a minimalist position on the length of the *toledoth* sources: only material strictly relating to genealogical history is of the *toledoth* type and represents a *toledoth* source. This includes the names of descendants of an individual as well as notations about his age at the birth of his first-born and at the time of his death, and other information strictly relevant to the matter of the rise of succeeding generations (e.g., family migrations between the birth of one generation and the next), with occasional bits of incidental information. This approach accords not only with the most natural and apparent meaning of the term *toledoth* in most of the Genesis occurrences but also with the usage of the word in texts outside of Genesis.

Four *toledoth* texts in Genesis are especially problematic, however: that of the heaven and the earth (2:4), that of Noah (6:9a), that of Isaac (25:19), and that of Jacob (37:2).

The *toledoth* of the heavens and the earth (2:4) is unique. Here alone, inanimate objects are said to have *toledoth*. Contrary to the Documentary Hypothesis, 2:4a does not belong with 1:1–2:3. First, *toledoth* normally introduces a section in Genesis, and no compelling reason exists for seeing this as an exception. Second, the *toledoth* of a person or clan generally does not include the story of the birth of the person or eponymous clan head himself. Instead, the *toledoth* of an individual is the list of those who came from him. It is anomalous that the story of the creation of heaven and earth should be called the *tole-doth* of heaven and earth. One would expect that the *toledoth* of heaven and earth would concern what followed or arose from the creation of heaven and earth. Third, 2:4a, if appended to 1:1ff., is anti-climactic to the point of being meaningless.[17] The *toledoth* line, therefore, belongs with what follows.

---

17. Claus Westermann adheres to the Documentary Hypothesis, but it is curious that in his massive commentary on the text of this chapter, *Genesis 1–11*, trans. John J. Scullion (Minneapolis: Augsburg/Fortress, 1984), 74–173, he says almost nothing about 2:4a (see p. 81). The verse simply does not belong with what precedes.

But Genesis 2:4 introduces narration rather than genealogy (2:4–4:26). Can this be considered a *toledoth* source? If so, it is certainly unlike all the others. It is far more like the stories that we have described elsewhere as narrative sources.

As a resolution to this dilemma, one might best postulate that 2:4ff. is from a narrative source that, in the redaction, was for literary purposes given the heading, "These are the *toledoth* of," in deliberate imitation of the *toledoth* sources. The reason for such a bold move is not hard to imagine. The whole of Genesis is structured around the genealogical history of Israel, the people of God, as they emerge from all the other nations. No better way of beginning this story could be found than to follow the creation narrative itself with a statement that all of this history, indeed all human history, flows out of the creation of earth itself. Adam was made of clay and, in that sense, was born of the soil. The story of the fall is itself the *toledoth* of heaven and earth. Genesis 2:4ff., therefore, is a narrative source that begins with a *toledoth* line; it is not a true *toledoth* source.

The *toledoth* of Noah (6:9) could extend to 9:29, which records the age of Noah at his death. It is most unlikely that all the flood narrative, 6:11–9:27, is part of that source. But 9:18–19 and 28–29 are of the *toledoth* source type: they give the names of Noah's sons, the number of years of Noah's life after the flood, and his age at death. This suggests that original *toledoth* source material has been split, as necessary, by narrative material. The original *toledoth* of Noah probably included notice of the names of his sons (6:10; 9:18–19), his age at the beginning (7:6) and end of the flood (9:28), and his age at death (9:29).

The *toledoth* of Isaac (25:19) is divided in our text by the narrative of Jacob. The *toledoth* source at least included 25:19–20, as well as a notice of the birth of Esau and Jacob, and 35:22c–29. The *toledoth* source may have included the material in 25:21–26, the story of the births of Esau and Jacob. Alternatively, 25:21–26b may be part of an original narrative source; in this case, the original Isaac *toledoth* source would have contained a shorter notice of the birth of the twins, which was deleted in the Urgenesis redaction as redundant. Genesis 25:26c should be taken as part of the *toledoth* source, since it gives the characteristic notice of the age of Isaac at the birth of Esau and Jacob.

The problem with the *toledoth* of Jacob is that the story of Joseph abruptly begins (37:2b) immediately after the *toledoth* line. Insomuch as the Joseph narratives are in no way confined to Jacob's genealogical history, it does not seem possible that this story could be the *toledoth* source of Jacob. On the other hand, a clear example of a normal *toledoth* source appears in 46:8–27. This passage contains a list of Jacob's descendants and a note about the family migration to Egypt (vv. 26–27), both of which are fairly common in *toledoth* sources. The solution must be that this is another example of a redaction—the *toledoth* title line was separated from its contents, 46:8–27, and the Joseph narrative was inserted between the two. The interruption was necessary to explain how the sons of Israel, including the two sons of Joseph, came to be in Egypt and had their national beginnings there. In other words, in the present redaction, the Joseph narrative explains 46:26–27 within the *toledoth* of Jacob. Notably, the list of Jacob's offspring is introduced in 46:8 without the familiar *toledoth* line, which had been separated from the rest of the source and left in 37:2a in the redaction of the *toledoth* and narrative material.[18]

The number and extent of the *toledoth* sources are set forth in figure 4.2.

The Narrative Sources

One can obviously assert that everything that is not a *toledoth* source is a narrative source. This is true, but more precision than that is desirable. How can we distinguish among the narrative sources?

As a starting point, we should observe that much of the material of Genesis is divided into discrete stories that are analogous to the pericopae of the Synoptics. Stories that are self-contained units—in other words, units that can be lifted from their contexts without destroying the flow of the larger narrative of Genesis—were probably originally independent tradition units. We will proceed on the assumption that this approach is methodologically sound.[19] Note, however, that we are here speaking of complete stories, not minor details and episodes within stories.

Two simple examples of narrative sources would be (a) the tower of Babel (Gen. 11:1–8); (b) the slaughter of the town of Hamor and Shechem (Gen. 34). These are only two preliminary examples, however; most of the narrative structure of Genesis is quite complex. A complete analysis of the narrative sources of Genesis is not possible until other factors have been considered.

18. Gen. 37:1 is probably redactional.
19. This does not mean that the discrete source units were necessarily handed down by separate communities, or that those who told one set of stories were unaware of the existence of the other stories. It is the sources, not the tradents (those who preserve the traditions of a community and insure they are transmitted to the next generation) of the sources, that are isolated in this manner.

Figure 4.2

The *Toledoth* Sources

Text	Description
5:1–32	Of Adam; includes information on the years of each patriarch
6:9a, 10; 7:6; 9:18–19; 28–29	Of Noah; interrupted by flood narrative
10:1–32	Of Noah's sons; contains incidental details on Nimrod and Babylon
11:10–26	Of Shem; contains information on the years of the patriarchs
11:27–32	Of Terah; describes a family migration
25:12–18	Of Ishmael; describes a family migration
25:19–20; 35:22b–29	Of Isaac; interrupted by the Jacob narrative
36:1–43	Of Esau; describes a family migration and lists Edomite tribal chiefs; may have originated between two separate sources, as indicated at v. 9
37:1–2a; 46:8–27	Of Jacob; interrupted by the Joseph narrative; describes a family migration

Still, recognition of the importance of separating discrete narrative units in the text is helpful in three ways. First, it assists in separating the sources from one another. The story of Shechem related in Genesis 34, for example, is clearly a distinct tale with its own history.

Second, adherence to this rule will keep the critic from falling into the hypercriticism exhibited in the documentary school, whereby the text is fragmented into myriad sources. The story of Melchizedek, for example, is part of the wider context of Genesis 14 and need not be regarded as an originally independent narrative that was artificially inserted into the story of the rescue of Lot. Indeed, as will be shown on formal grounds (p. 139), the Melchizedek story is essential to Genesis 14. In the ancient Near Eastern world, as K. A. Kitchen has demonstrated, a single text could contain a variety of literary styles and types of material.[20]

20. *Ancient Orient and Old Testament* (Chicago: Inter-Varsity, 1966), 125–26.

Separating the sources in the way outlined here also is helpful in a third way, because it allows for meaningful form-critical research in the Genesis narratives. Significant insights into the text are available when it is approached in this way.

The Earliest Transmission of the Source Material

It is now necessary to determine how the sources were assembled and transmitted in their earliest stages. At the beginning of this chapter, a four-stage development of the Genesis text was outlined, and it is the first, the stage at which the patriarchs passed on their own personal histories as well as whatever records they may have possessed, we must consider here.

The Toledoth Sources

As genealogical records, the *toledoth* sources of Genesis are essentially the same type of genealogical sources as found in Numbers, Ezra, Nehemiah, 1 Chronicles, Matthew, and Luke. The Bible, therefore, attests to the keeping of such records from time immemorial, and it is probable that each family and clan kept its own set of genealogical records. These records were probably kept in written form from very early times and updated with the rise of each new generation.[21] It is unnecessary to postulate lengthy oral prehistories for the *toledoth* sources.[22]

The fact that they were written does not mean that the present text of Genesis contains any *toledoth* source in toto. To the contrary, the *toledoth* sources were probably used selectively and in accordance with the purposes of the redactor.[23] First of all, the genealogies are plainly

21. The question of the origin of some of the very early genealogies has given rise to a good deal of speculation. Scholars once argued that the Sumerian King List stood behind the genealogies of Gen. 5 and 11, but that position has been abandoned. See Gerhard F. Hasel, "The Genealogies of Gen 5 and 11 and their Alleged Babylonian Background," *AUSS* 16 (1978): 361–74.

22. See Kitchen, *Ancient Orient*, 135–38. On the other hand, one cannot exclude the possibility that the genealogies existed in oral form for a period of time. Cf. Robert R. Wilson, "The Old Testament Genealogies in Recent Research," *JBL* 94 (1975): 178–86.

23. A deliberate and selective use of genealogical material for redactional purposes is evident in Genesis, but this does not mean that the genealogies are "contrived ties," as asserted by Terry J. Prewitt, "Kinship Structures and the Genesis Genealogies," *JNES* 40 (1981): 87–98.

not continuous, but contain some major gaps.[24] Second, the present text displays a symmetry that appears to have been deliberate (e.g., ten generations before the flood and ten generations after it). All of this probably indicates redactional activity. Other evidence exists as well. Sometimes, for example, the genealogies name but one offspring of a patriarch (Gen. 5:4; 11:10–26; Ruth 4:18ff.). The original records behind these may have been considerably more extensive, since many genealogies do name siblings (e.g., Gen. 36). In particular, if Genesis 11:10–26 (the line of Shem down to Terah, with information on the ages of various patriarchs) is compared to Genesis 10:21–31 (the offspring of Shem in the table of nations), it is apparent that the two texts may go back to a single original, which was used in two different ways in the two passages. The original source may have included at least as much as, if not more than, the two passages contain together. Although, for the sake of convenience, it is preferable to refer to texts such as Genesis 11:10–26 as *toledoth* sources, it is necessary to realize that what we actually have are witnesses to the *toledoth* sources, not the *toledoth* sources themselves.

The Narrative Sources

The question of the origin and nature of the narrative sources is more complicated. First of all, it is difficult to imagine, for example, how the Jacob narrative could have begun as a written source. The only way this is possible, in fact, would be if Jacob himself had written a first-hand account of his adventures. Written autobiography was not unknown in the ancient Near Eastern world; extant Egyptian literature includes "The Autobiography of Weni" (Sixth Dynasty),[25] "The Autobiography of Harkhuf" (Sixth Dynasty),[26] the famous "Tale of Sinuhe" (Twelfth Dynasty)[27] and "The Journey of Wen-Amon to Phoenicia" (Twenty-first Dynasty).[28] Numerous first-person accounts from ancient Near Eastern kings are extant, and those often give details of the life of the king.[29] This material at least indicates that written accounts of the life of the patriarchs existed very early.

24. Kitchen, *Ancient Orient*, 36–39.
25. See Miriam Lichtheim, *Ancient Egyptian Literature*, 3 vols. (Berkeley: University of California Press, 1973), 1:18–23.
26. Ibid., 1:23–27.
27. Ibid., 1:222–35.
28. *ANET*, 25–29.
29. Cf. "The Story of Idrimi, King of Alalakh," *ANET*, 557.

On the other hand, nothing in the present texts is first-person. It is unlikely that original autobiographies were transformed into third-person narratives at a redactional stage. Similarly, there is no reason to suppose that Abraham or Isaac wrote his own life story in the third person.

Even if these sources were originally in oral form, however, they still must have originated with the patriarchs and their immediate families. Two lines of argument support this contention. First, only those personally involved in the events of the stories could have known the details that emerge in them. This argument will of course not satisfy those who are skeptical about the historical value of the narratives, but, whether or not one feels the stories have any historical value, a second piece of evidence demands consideration.

In reading the patriarchal narratives, it is noteworthy that although they are not in first-person, they reflect the perspective of the patriarch, or figure associated with a patriarch, and are not written from an omniscient perspective. In the stories of Jacob in Laban's household, the reader sees nothing of the internal discussions in Laban's family, discussions from which Jacob would have been excluded. For example, when Laban and his family took counsel to substitute Leah for Rachel in the wedding, how was it done? Was it Laban's own scheme? Did Leah object, or did she demand that she marry Jacob first? Did Rachel object? Of this the reader, seeing the action from Jacob's perspective, knows nothing. Indeed, the reader knows no more of what is going on than Jacob himself can be reasonably expected to have known. Similarly, the reader knows nothing of the personality or experiences of Esau apart from his encounters with Jacob.

With respect to Jacob himself, however, the situation is different. The reader experiences the most intimate moments of his life (his vision at Bethel, his discovery of Leah after his wedding night, his wrestling with the Angel of the Lord) in nearly the same perspective that Jacob himself experienced them. In whatever situation Jacob finds himself, the reader is given only minimal forewarning of what is to come next.

This should not all be attributed simply to the narrator's skill. It reflects rather a prehistory to the written narrative, a prehistory that is in the perspective of and comes from the patriarch himself. The transformation of the narrative from a first- to third-person style, therefore, probably came about in the oral stage, as the stories the patriarchs told to their children were retold by their children to their grandchildren and great-grandchildren. At some point (probably within a one-hundred-year period), the tales were written down for reliable transmission.

The same is true in the other narratives as well. As the reader follows Abraham through his journeys, he is never far from Abraham's own perspective. Even those details that are outside of his personal experience, moreover, are details about which he would have immediately known. Abraham did not personally experience Abimelech's vision (20:3–7), but without question the reader understands that Abimelech told him of it the next morning (20:8–9). Also, much of the material in the Abraham cycle, we will argue, originally was in separate sources derived from Hagar or Lot.

Joseph's rise to power in Egypt, similarly, consistently reflects his perspective. The moment Joseph is cast into the dungeon in Egypt, Potiphar and his wife disappear abruptly from the story, and the reader is told nothing of their fates. An omniscient narrator might have vindicated Joseph by describing some calamity that befell Potiphar's wife. Other characters appear and disappear with equal abruptness; nothing is said of them beyond what Joseph would have known. A significant exception is in 37:18–35, where the reader is told of the debate and uncertainty among the sons of Jacob over what to do with Joseph. Here, the narrative goes into considerable detail beyond what Joseph himself could have known: The brothers conspire to kill him, Reuben persuades them to put him in a cistern and plans to release him later, the brothers eat a meal, Judah persuades them to sell Joseph into slavery, Reuben discovers Joseph's absence, and Jacob falls into inconsolable mourning when the brothers tell him that Joseph has been killed by an animal. Much of this is well outside of Joseph's personal experience, and even in the description of Joseph's being sold to the Midianites, his perspective on the experience is conspicuously absent.

Yet this does not contradict the assertion that the narratives are from the patriarchal perspective, for the brothers are themselves part of the patriarchal tradition. Indeed, precisely in this narrative, evidence emerges for separate sources in their oral stages. In the first part of the Joseph narrative (37:2b–36), all the material presented would have been common knowledge to all the brothers (except parts of vv. 18–35, of which Joseph would have been ignorant). After the interlude of Judah and Tamar (chap. 38), the story of Joseph resumes strictly from his perspective (39:1ff.). A reasonable conclusion is that in the oral stage, after the reunification of the family in Egypt, the brothers told the story of how they sold Joseph into slavery (Reuben and Judah especially seem to have told their versions!), and Joseph recounted his adventures and rise to power (see 45:15b).

The question of when the individual stories of Genesis (and many other patriarchal narratives now lost to us) were reduced to writing cannot be answered with certainty. But it is valuable here to maintain Kitchen's distinction between the transmission and the dissemination of important information in the Near Eastern world. Among the ancients, material thought worth preserving (history, myth, law, contracts) was transmitted from generation to generation in written form. Since no means of mass communication yet existed (e.g., the printing press), this information was disseminated to the people of each generation orally.[30] This would indicate that, assuming the Israelites regarded the patriarchal stories to be of great significance, many oral traditions were reduced to writing at a fairly early stage.

This preliminary analysis of Genesis indicates that a set of *toledoth* sources can be isolated in the text. These are primarily genealogical in nature, and they were probably transmitted as written sources from earliest times. The bulk of Genesis, however, is narrative in nature. These sources were originally oral accounts from the patriarchs that were subsequently reduced to writing. Some narrative sources can be isolated as discrete units in the text. To appreciate fully the nature of these sources, however, it is necessary first to examine the structure of Genesis.

---

30. Kitchen, *Ancient Orient,* 135–36.

5

The Structure of Genesis

The recovery of ancient Near Eastern civilization through archaeology and linguistic research, in addition to the value of that enterprise for its own sake, has been of enormous importance for biblical studies. The meaning of biblical history, poetry, wisdom, and prophecy emerges with new clarity when read in the light of contemporary Mesopotamian, Canaanite, and Egyptian studies.

No longer are scholars forced to read the Old Testament through Western spectacles in a tradition that goes back only as far as Greco-Roman antiquity. Although the exact meaning of many biblical texts may be still in doubt and the precise importance of a particular ancient Near Eastern "parallel" may be disputed, it is beyond question that many layers of anachronistic interpretation have been stripped away by research in cognate languages and of historically contemporary societies.

Genesis, the Myth of Atrahasis, and the Structure of Ancient Epic

The study of ancient literary genres in particular has enhanced our understanding of biblical texts. A number of parallels are obvious and frequently pointed out in biblical studies (e.g., the *Enuma elish* and the biblical creation account, the law codes of Hammurabi and of the Bible, Ugaritic and biblical hymnody). The intricacies of ancient literary structure, however, are just beginning to be recognized. Scholars are now seeing, for example, that chiastic structuring of narrative and poetry is far more common than once was recognized.[1] We may safely say that a great deal more has yet to be done in the study of ancient genre and literary structure.

A significant advance here, however, is Isaac Kikiwada's and Arthur Quinn's recent analysis of Genesis 1–11, *Before Abraham Was*.[2] Kikiwada and Quinn begin with an examination of the ancient Mesopotamian cosmological myth of Atrahasis. In this myth, humanity was created after the laboring gods, the Igigi, rebelled against their status as servants of the higher gods, the Anunnaki. Humanity was in effect made to be the slaves of the gods in order to free the Igigi from their service.

Created at the request of the chief god Enlil by the mother goddess Mami and the god Enki, the human race multiplied rapidly and filled the earth. Distressed by the tumult made by the human race, Enlil tried to deal with them first with a plague, then a famine, and then a flood. The flood would have destroyed humanity entirely except that Enki had warned the man Atrahasis to build a boat.

At last, however, a resolution came about. The gods would no longer try to destroy humanity, but the population of the race would be held in check by barrenness among some women, infant mortality, and celibacy on the part of some priestesses. In other words, not all women would be fertile, and many of the babies born of fertile women would die.[3] Human life was of little value to most of the gods of this grim tale.

Kikiwada and Quinn, following the lead of earlier scholars, point out that the myth has a five-point structure composed of a creation narrative, three threats to human existence (the plague, famine, and flood), and a resolution. They note that the same basic structure of introduction, three threats, and a resolution is found in Genesis 1–11, in the ancient story of the Trojan War, and in an old Iranian flood story.[4] In addition, they show how this pattern was followed in Exodus 1–2 and Matthew 1–3.[5] Also, building on the work of Walter

1. See John W. Welch, ed., *Chiasmus in Antiquity* (Gerstenberg Verlag, 1981).

2. *Before Abraham Was: A Provocative Challenge to the Documentary Hypothesis* (Nashville: Abingdon, 1985).

3. Ibid., 39–47.

4. Ibid., 48–52.

5. Ibid., 111–18.

Figure 5.1

Parallels between the Myth of Atrahasis
and the Primeval History
(Gen. 1–11)

Creation	**1.1–351**	**1:1–2:3**
	Summary of work of gods	Summary of work of God
	Creation of man	Creation of man
First Threat	**1.352–415**	**2:4–3:24**
	Man's numerical increase	Genealogy of heaven and earth
	Plague, Enki's help	Adam and Eve
Second Threat	**2.1.1–5.21**	**4:1–26**
	Man's numerical increase	Cain and Abel
	1. Drought, numerical increase	1. Cain and Abel, genealogy
	2. Intensified drought, Enki's help	2. Lamech's taunt (in genealogy)
Final Threat	**2.5.22–3.6.4**	**5:1–9:29**
	Numerical increase	Genealogy
	Atrahasis' flood, salvation in boat	Noah's flood, salvation in ark
Resolution	**3.6.5–8.18**	**10:1–11:32**
	Numerical increase	Genealogy
	Compromise between Enlil and Enki, "birth control"	Tower of Babel and dispersion genealogy, Abram leaves Ur

This figure is a modified version of one that appears in Isaac M. Kikiwada and Arthur Quinn, *Before Abraham Was: A Provocative Challenge to the Documentary Hypothesis* (Nashville: Abingdon, 1985), 47–48.

Brueggemann,[6] Kikiwada and Quinn see a strong parallel between Genesis 1–11 and the history of the house of David with a somewhat similar structure.[7]

6. "David and His Theologian," *CBQ* 30 (1968): 156–81. Brueggemann argues that the J construction in Gen. 1–11 is dependent on the David story (p. 158). Kikiwada and Quinn, of course, reject the existence of J and reverse the sequence, so that the David story is dependent on the creation epic. That issue aside, the parallels Brueggemann is able to draw between the two biblical narratives are remarkable.

7. Kikiwada and Quinn, *Before Abraham Was*, 107–11.

This establishes an important pattern. In ancient literature, a particular type of narrative often had the structure (1) introduction, (2) three threats to the hero or party with which the epic is concerned, and (3) a resolution or conclusion. This pattern, which I call the ancestor epic pattern, is the dominant structure of Genesis. Genesis 1–11 and the myth of Atrahasis both follow the ancestor epic pattern. The parallels between the two are seen in figure 5.1.

Beyond the strong formal arguments they present, Kikiwada and Quinn further develop their analysis of the internal structure of Genesis 1–11. Most important is the observation that in the biblical narrative, a genealogy comes between each major segment of the overall structure. Thus, the stories of Adam and Eve, Cain's murder of Abel, Lamech, the flood, and the dispersion after Noah are all followed by genealogies. The creation narrative is not followed by a formal genealogy, but it is followed by the line, "These are the generations (*toledoth*) of heaven and earth."[8] The structure of Genesis 1–11 can be seen in figure 5.2. The parallel with the Atrahasis myth is remarkable; it even extends to the doublet of the second threat. As the threat of the drought is repeated twice in Atrahasis, there is a double account of violence in the Cain-Lamech section (C, C').

Kikiwada and Quinn also note some important thematic elements that Atrahasis and Genesis 1–11 have in common. The most important of these is a concern both share with the issue of population increase and the geographical expansion of the human race.

In Atrahasis, population increase is a major problem for the gods: The noise and commotion made by the prolific people were proving to be quite a nuisance to Enlil. The situation was resolved when the *pashittu* demon (infant mortality) and other restraints on human fertility established a check on population growth.

It is worth noting that in the Bible, God desires the human race to multiply and fill the earth. Human sin, not divine annoyance, is the threat. God must repeatedly take steps to see that people fill the earth as he desires. The problem is resolved at the tower of Babel when humanity, which had tended to cluster in one place (hindering the expansion of the race), is scattered abroad by an act of God.[9]

The question of whether people and their offspring can survive against various threats is therefore a dominant concept in the ancestor epic. The theological implication of reading Genesis 1–11 against

8. This supports the contention that the use of *toledoth* in Gen. 2:4 is artificial, that it is a *toledoth* line that does not represent an original *toledoth* source but is redactional.

9. Kikiwada and Quinn, *Before Abraham Was*, 80.

Figure 5.2

The Structure of the Primeval History
(1–11)

A   Creation
    Genealogy = Heaven and earth

B   Adam and Eve
    Genealogy = Eve's sons

C   Cain and Abel
    Genealogy = Cain's line

C' Lamech's taunt
    Genealogy = Adam/Seth

D   Noah's flood
    Genealogy = Nation table

E   Dispersion
    Genealogy = Shem's line

Isaac M. Kikiwada and Arthur Quinn, *Before Abraham Was: A Provocative Challenge to the Documentary Hypothesis* (Nashville: Abingdon, 1985), 60.

Atrahasis is clear: The gods of the nations regard people as an endurable nuisance at best, but Yahweh loves his creation and has even protected people from themselves.

This presents a strong case for the unity of Genesis 1–11 as opposed to the fragmentation of the text in the Documentary Hypothesis, which is indeed the conclusion drawn by Kikiwada and Quinn. It is worth noting, however, that Kikiwada's and Quinn's hypothesis does not establish that there were no separate sources for Genesis 1–11. It only implies that the sources behind the narrative must be compatible with the present structure and not slash across it in the way the Documentary Hypothesis does.

The Structure of Genesis

Early Attempts

Every commentator on Genesis has said something about its structure. In most traditional commentaries, these statements have amounted to little more than outlines of the book, prepared accord-

Figure 5.3

Rendsburg's Analysis of the Structure of the Jacob Cycle (25:19–35:22)

A	Oracle sought, struggle in childbirth, Jacob born	25:19–34
B	Interlude: Rebekah in foreign palace, pact with foreigners	26:1–34
C	Jacob fears Esau and flees	27:1–28:9
D	Messengers	28:10–22
E	Arrival at Haran	29:1–30
F	Jacob's wives are fertile	29:31–30:24
F'	Jacob's flocks are fertile	30:25–43
E'	Flight from Haran	31:1–54
D'	Messengers	32:1–32
C'	Jacob returns and fears Esau	33:1–20
B'	Interlude: Dinah in foreign palace, pact with foreigners	34:1–31
A'	Option fulfilled, struggle in childbirth, Jacob becomes Israel	35:1–22

Gary A. Rendsburg, *The Redaction of Genesis* (Winona Lake, Ind.: Eisenbrauns, 1986), 53–54.

ing to a Western scholar's reading of the text, which have paid little attention to ancient Near Eastern patterns.[10] Documentary critics, on the other hand, have been so obsessed with the documentary sources of Genesis that they have paid little attention to the structure of the whole.[11] Insomuch as they considered the final redaction to have come very late, they were not inclined to look for signs of ancient narrative technique.[12] Therefore, although scholars have come far in demonstrating ancient Near Eastern patterns in other biblical books, most notably Deuteronomy, the narrative structure of Genesis has only begun to be properly explored.

10. E.g., Derek Kidner, *Genesis*, TOTC (Downer's Grove: Inter-Varsity, 1968), 42; Harold G. Stigers, *A Commentary on Genesis* (Grand Rapids: Zondervan, 1975), 43–45.

11. E.g., John Skinner, *A Critical and Exegetical Commentary on Genesis,* 2d ed., ICC (Edinburgh: T. and T. Clark, 1930), xlii–lxvi; E. A. Speiser, *Genesis,* AB (New York: Doubleday, 1964), liii–lx.

12. On the other hand, George W. Coats, *Genesis: With an Introduction to Narrative Literature,* FOTL (Grand Rapids: Eerdmans, 1984), 27–34, does attempt to give the structures of the whole of Genesis and of the JE and P narratives.

This is not to say that nothing has been done. Indeed, several significant studies of narrative structure in Genesis have come forth this century. In addition to Kikiwada's and Quinn's analysis of Genesis 1–11, Michael Fishbane has done a significant analysis of the Jacob cycle (Gen. 25:19–35:22b), which he demonstrated to be chiastic in structure.[13] Fishbane's conclusions were accepted and further developed by Gary A. Rendsburg, who sets forth the chiasmus seen in figure 5.3.

Fishbane provides a good deal of evidence in support of this chiastic structuring of the text. The similarity between A and A', for example, is that the former, A, (1) tells of a prediction that the elder (Esau) should serve the younger (Jacob), (2) describes the suffering of Rebekah at the birth of the twins, and (3) gives an account of the naming of Jacob. The latter, A', includes (1) a blessing on Jacob (35:11–12), (2) an account of the death of Rachel in Benjamin's birth, and (3) mentions the changing of Jacob's name to Israel.

The sections B and B' correlate in that neither relates to its immediate context in the larger narrative; both deal with a story of one of the women of Jacob's family (his mother Rebekah, his daughter Dinah) in the palace of uncircumcised foreigners (Philistines, Shechemites), and both involve deception on the part of the patriarchs. Rendsburg has considerably added to the evidence first set forth by Fishbane, which indicates that these and other correlations occur in all the pairs of the chiasmus.[14] The chiastic structuring of the whole narrative is undeniable.

Two Caveats on Chiasmus

Two significant points need to be kept in mind, however, in any discussion of chiastic structuring. First, the existence of a chiastic structure does not prove that the whole narrative was composed at one time by one author, that is, that no separate, prior sources existed. Some scholars, particularly those writing polemics against the Documentary Hypothesis, tend to assume that any chiasmus is evidence against any source-critical work. A chiasmus does provide a

13. "Composition and Structure in the Jacob Cycle (Gen. 25:19–35:22)," *JJS* 26 (1975): 15–38. See also Michael Fishbane, *Text and Texture* (New York: Schocken, 1975), 40–62.

14. For a detailed demonstration of the evidence in support of this chiastic interpretation, see Gary A. Rendsburg, *The Redaction of Genesis* (Winona Lake, Ind.: Eisenbrauns, 1986), 53–69.

good basis for arguing that a particular subsection of a larger text is not a later interpolation, and it argues against a documentary source-critical approach to a text that radically cuts across the chiasmus. That is, if there is no plausible explanation of how a group of hypothetical sources were combined into an evident chiasmus, the hypothetical source documents probably never existed. But one cannot call a halt to source-critical work wherever a chiasmus is encountered.[15]

Second, chiastic (and parallel) structures should not dominate exegesis. Although chiasmi are sometimes significant, they are sometimes subtle demonstrations of the narrator's skill, which are interwoven well beneath the surface of the text. They do not always determine the narrative (or poetic) structure of a passage, nor do they always indicate where the climax of a text lies. The actual narrative structure, although it may correspond exactly to an underlying chiasmus, may be independent of it. A chiasmus, parallelism, acrostic, or other device may provide "background music" for the text but may not be the only determining factor in the shaping of the text.

For the ancient audience, these parallel elements worked on a deep level to bring out reversal, similarity, irony, and resolution. Chiasmus tends to bind a story together; parallelism in structure tends to show how two or more incidents were somehow similar. Nevertheless, these are stories, not mathematical equations. Indeed, the ancient writers handled their literary techniques with great freedom.

For example, in his analysis of the Book of Isaiah, R. K. Harrison, following the work of W. H. Brownlee, has shown that the book has a remarkable parallelism, chapters 1–33 being in many ways parallel to 34–66. One can agree with Harrison that this finding at least has negative implications for Deutero- and Trito-Isaiah[16] (although, by itself, it does not disprove the theory of multiple authorship).

But Harrison goes too far in trying to make this parallelism the dominant feature on the landscape of the text.[17] To the contrary, it is clear that in its literary structure the book reaches a climax at chapter 39, the prophecy that Jerusalem is doomed to exile in Babylon.

New Testament scholars, similarly, have long recognized that the Book of Acts to some degree sets the life of Paul in parallel with the

15. Neither Fishbane nor Rendsburg falls into this error. Rendsburg, *Redaction*, 99–106, does use the structure he sees in the Genesis text to argue against the Documentary Hypothesis, but he does so quite carefully, on the basis of sound linguistic evidence, not on the basis of chiasmi alone.

16. *Introduction to the Old Testament* (Grand Rapids: Eerdmans, 1969), 788–89.

17. Ibid., 764.

life of Peter.[18] However, it is not correct to draw the conclusion that this parallel controls the narrative structure of the book. Large-scale parallelism or chiasmus is significant, but it is not a grid that fixes the structure of a text when other, more conspicuous features point in another direction.

Rendsburg's Hypothesis

Rendsburg, in *The Redaction of Genesis,* builds on the work of Fishbane, Umberto Cassuto, J. M. Sasson, Nahum Sarna, and others, and attempts to show that Genesis is structured as a series of parallel and chiastic cycles (see fig. 5.4). Rendsburg uses many of the same type of arguments for the chiastic and parallel structures as those set forth by Fishbane in support of the chiastic structure of Genesis 25:19–35:22. In addition, Rendsburg especially cites verbal parallels between various texts to establish correspondence between them.

Figure 5.4

Rendsburg's Analysis of the Structure of Genesis

Section	Extent	Structure
The Primeval History	1:1–11:26	parallel
The Abraham Cycle	11:27–22:24	chiastic
Linking material	23:1–25:18	parallel with 35:23–36:43
The Jacob Cycle	25:19–35:22	chiastic
Linking material	35:23–36:43	parallel with 23:1–25:18
The Joseph Story	37:1–50:26	chiastic

Gary A. Rendsburg, *The Redaction of Genesis* (Winona Lake, Ind.: Eisenbrauns, 1986), 8, 28–29, 53–54, 71, 80.

THE ABRAHAM MATERIAL

A great deal of Rendsburg's work is helpful. Following Cassuto and Sarna, he sees a chiastic structure in Genesis 11:27–22:24 (see fig. 5.5). In addition to the chiastic elements of Rendsburg's presentation, he has demonstrated many verbal parallels that support the structure. For example, in B Abram is told to go "from your land, from your

18. See Donald Guthrie, *New Testament Introduction* (Downer's Grove: Inter-Varsity, 1970), 339.

homeland, and from your father's house" (12:1), and he journeys to
Moreh (12:6), whereas in B' he is commanded to sacrifice "your son,
your favorite, Isaac whom you love," and he goes to Moriah (22:2).[19]
Evidence for chiasmus in this text is strong.

Figure 5.5

Rendsburg's Analysis of the Structure of the Abraham Cycle (11:27–22:24)

A	Genealogy of Terah	11:27–32
B	Start of Abram's spiritual odyssey	12:1–9
C	Sarai in foreign palace; ordeal ends in peace and success; Abram and Lot part	12:10–13:18
D	Abram comes to the rescue of Sodom and Lot	14:1–24
E	Covenant with Abram; annunciation of Ishmael	15:1–16:16
E'	Covenant with Abraham; annuciation of Isaac	17:1–18:15
D'	Abraham comes to the rescue of Sodom and Lot	18:16–19:13
C'	Sarah in foreign palace; ordeal ends in peace and success; Abraham and Ishmael part	20:1–21:34
B'	Climax of Abraham's spiritual odyssey	22:1–19
A'	Genealogy of Nahor	22:20–24

Gary A. Rendsburg, *The Redaction of Genesis* (Winona Lake, Ind.: Eisenbrauns, 1986), 28–29.

THE JOSEPH MATERIAL

Other parts of Rendsburg's presentation, however, are not fully
convincing. His analysis of the Joseph cycle[20] is in some respects problematic. He asserts that 37:1–50:26 is a chiasmus (see fig. 5.6). This
analysis is questionable in some parts. For example, Rendsburg argues
that Genesis 38 (Judah and Tamar) corresponds to Genesis 49 (the
blessings of Jacob). This seems implausible at the outset, and his rationale, that Joseph was not present in the former and only nominally
present at the latter, does not help.

Following the work of earlier scholars, Rendsburg does note some
important links between Genesis 38 and 49:8–12. The "Shiloh" of
49:10 recalls "Shelah" of 38:5, 11, 14, and 26. The scepter of 49:10

19. Rendsburg, *Redaction*, 31.
20. Ibid., 79–97.

Figure 5.6

Rendsburg's Analysis of the Structure of the Joseph Cycle (37:1–50:26)

A	Joseph and his brothers, Jacob and Joseph part	37:1–36
B	Interlude: Joseph not present	38:1–30
C	Reversal: Joseph guilty, Potiphar's wife innocent	39:1–23
D	Joseph hero of Egypt	40:1–41:57
E	Two trips to Egypt	42:1–43:34
F	Final test	44:1–34
F'	Conclusion of test	45:1–28
E'	Two tellings of migration to Egypt	46:1–47:12
D'	Joseph hero of Egypt	47:13–27
C'	Reversal: Ephraim firstborn, Manasseh secondborn	47:28–48:2
B'	Interlude: Joseph nominally present	49:1–28
A'	Joseph and his brothers, Jacob and Joseph part	49:29–50:21

Gary A. Rendsburg, *The Redaction of Genesis* (Winona Lake, Ind.: Eisenbrauns, 1986), 80.

recalls the staff of 38:18, 25 and may also, in a reflection on the story of Judah's visit to Tamar, have a sexual connotation. The term *Shiloh* could allude to Shelah, the son whom Judah would not give to Tamar.[21] Also, the Hebrew words *donkey* and *she-ass* might play on the names *Er* and *Onan* of Genesis 38.[22]

All the significant parallels to Genesis 38 are in the blessing on Judah, not the rest of Genesis 49. Other attempts at verbal parallels between Genesis 38 and 49 are often forced or insignificant. It is difficult to see, for example, how it is important that 49:3 and 7 have the word `*oz* (strong), and 38:17 and 20 have `*izzim* (goats).[23] In addition, at some points the blessing on Judah appears to allude to texts that are outside the Judah-Tamar episode and thus outside the chiasmus Rendsburg sees. The washing of the coat in the blood of grapes (49:11) recalls the dipping of Joseph's coat in goat's blood (37:31).[24] The section about Simeon and Levi

21. Edwin M. Good, "The Blessing on Judah, Gen 49:8–12," *JBL* 82 (1963): 430.

22. Rendsburg, *Redaction*, 84.

23. Ibid., 85. Such a pun might be conceivable if the occurrences of the words were in proximity, but that is not the case here.

24. Good, "Blessing," 431.

(49:5–7) certainly alludes to Genesis 34[25] and not to Genesis 38. In summary, the only genuine parallels to Genesis 38 in Genesis 49 are in the section about Judah. The significance of this is explored in chapter 9.

This is not to say that Rendsburg's analysis has not brought forth valuable insights on the correspondence among passages of the larger text. Many chiastic elements in 37:1–50:26 function as Rendsburg describes. Elements from the earlier conflicts and tensions in 37:1–46:7 reverberate in 46:28–50:26. The deaths of Jacob and Joseph (50) recall the apparent death of Joseph in 37, the blessing on Judah (49:8–12) recalls ironically Genesis 38 (Judah and Tamar), and the wisdom of Joseph during the famine (47:13–27) recalls his display of wisdom in 40-41. All of this is brought to light in Rendsburg's study.[26]

Rendsburg notes that the story of Potiphar's wife (Gen. 39) has some noteworthy catchword parallels to Genesis 48 and that both play on the theme of reversal. Of the catchword links between the two texts that Rendsburg points out, perhaps the most significant are the repetition of "he resisted and said" in 39:8 and 48:19 and the ironic twists in the uses of the words *shakab* (to lie down, 39:7–14; 47:30), *yad* (hand, which occurs nine times in 39; cf. 48:14, 17) and *lehem* (bread). The latter is figuratively one's wife, as implied by a comparison of 39:6 to 39:9. This usage accounts for the mention of Bethlehem in 48:7, as Rendsburg notes.[27]

But an important parallel not observed in Rendsburg's analysis is that between the story of the two brothers Perez and Zerah, in which the one who would be first-born loses his place (38:27–30), and the story of the two brothers Ephraim and Manasseh, in which the younger is placed ahead of the elder (48:13–22). In addition, the unfair treatment Joseph received at the hands of Potiphar in chapter 39 is contrasted with the "unfair" favorable treatment he receives from his father in being singled out among the twelve for a special blessing in 48:1–12. Two reversals are thus set against each other. The first is the reversal of the positions of the younger and elder brothers and the second is the unfavorable/favorable treatment received by Joseph.

Genesis 42–45 also to some degree contrasts with 46:28–47:12 in a way Rendsburg does not note. In the former, Jacob sends Joseph's brothers down to Egypt but has to send them a second time with Benjamin after Joseph accuses them of being spies. They are then

25. See Calum M. Carmichael, "Some Sayings in Genesis 49," *JBL* 88 (1969):435–37.
26. *Redaction*, 79–92.
27. Ibid., 86–88.

tricked by Joseph, arrested by his Egyptian subordinate, but saved when he reveals himself to them. Then Jacob himself departs for Egypt.

In the latter, Jacob sends Judah ahead to make arrangements (as he had sent Benjamin in Judah's charge), is welcomed by Joseph (not threatened, as the brothers were) and introduced to the Pharaoh of Egypt, Joseph's superior, instead of being arrested by his Egyptian subordinate. Finally, Jacob moves to the prized district of Rameses, having departed for Egypt at the end of the previous section.

The genealogical material of 46:8–27 works as a division marker between the two major sections (37:3–46:7 and 46:28–50:26). Note that the center of this chiastic structuring is 46:8–27 (the offspring of Jacob), not 44:1–45:28, as Rendsburg has it. A number of chiastic elements, therefore, are present in 37:1–50:26 (see fig. 5.7). These chiastic elements do not dominate the structure of the narrative but work underneath it. They are background music. This conclusion is confirmed by taking note of where the actual climax of each of the two major divisions occurs.

In 36:1–46:8, the Joseph story, the climax clearly comes at the breaking of the extreme tension of 42:1–44:34 (the visits of the brothers) in the self-revelation of Joseph to his brothers (45).[28] The departure of Jacob for Egypt with divine assurance of safety (46:1–7) serves as an anticlimax to return the tale to a zero-tension level. Genealogical data then forms a boundary to indicate the termination of the drama (46:8–27).

In 46:28–50:26, the dominant feature of the narrative is the blessings of Jacob on his sons (48–49). The Israelites have settled in Egypt for a prolonged stay, and the aged patriarch of the small band is soon to die. What does the future hold for this little band of outsiders? Do they have a future at all? The blessings of Jacob serve to resolve these questions, end the story of the patriarchs, and look ahead to the story of the nation.

In short, the two climactic texts are not set in a chiastic parallel. Nevertheless, the chiastic elements discovered here are significant, as chapter 9 will demonstrate.

THE "LINKING MATERIAL" AND THE PRIMEVAL HISTORY

The "linking material" of Rendsburg's analysis is an even greater problem.[29] He argues that the two sets of linking material (23:1–25:18

---

28. Cf. Robert E. Longacre, *Joseph: A Story of Divine Providence* (Winona Lake, Ind.: Eisenbrauns, 1989), 22, 28. The importance of the self-revelation of Joseph (45) would seem to support Rendsburg's contention that it is the center of a large chiastic construction. But this is misleading, since Rendsburg also makes chapter 44 part of the center of the chiasmus. Gen. 44 is part of the gradual heightening of the tension in 42:1–44:34; it is not part of the resolution.

29. *Redaction*, 71–77.

Figure 5.7

The Structure of the Joseph Cycle
(37:1–50:26)

A	Hostility of brothers to Joseph	37:3–11
B	Apparent death of Joseph, Jacob mourns	37:12–35
C	Judah and Tamar	38:1–26
D	Unfair reversals	38:27–39:23
	Da Perez and Zerah	38:27–30
	Db Potiphar's wife and Joseph	39:1–23
E	Wisdom of Joseph	40:1–41:57
F	Movement to Egypt	42:1–46:7
	Fa Jacob sends brothers, brothers threatened, Jacob sends Benjamin on a second trip	42:1–43:34
	Fb Brothers tricked by Joseph, arrested by Egyptian subordinate, Joseph reveals self	44:1–45:28 46:1–7
	Fc Jacob sets out for Egypt	
G	Genealogy	46:8–27
F'	Settlement in Egypt	46:28–47:12
	F'a Jacob arrives in Egypt, but sends Judah ahead	46:28
	F'b Joseph welcomes Jacob, introduces him to Pharaoh	46:29–47:10
	F'c Jacob moves to Rameses	47:11–12
E'	Wisdom of Joseph	47:13–26
D'	"Unfair" reversals	48:1–22
	D'a Jacob favors Joseph	48:1–12
	D'b Ephraim and Manasseh	48:13–22
C'	Irony in blessing on Judah	49:8–12
B'	Death of Jacob, Joseph buries him	49:29–50:14
A'	Joseph reassures brothers	50:15–21

and 35:23–36:43) are arranged "along parallel lines." But even in Rendsburg's analysis, the two sections are not even remotely parallel in structure: The first section he divides into five segments (A, B, C, D, and E, in that sequence) whereas the latter is in four segments in a different order (C', D', B', and E'; A' being missing). Rendsburg admits that there are "imperfections," but such inadequacy begs the

question whether to call this parallelism at all. Furthermore, the individual segments do not always really correspond.[30]

Similarly, although Rendsburg has certainly shown that there are parallel elements in the primeval history,[31] the text is hardly dominated by a parallel structure. It functions well beneath the surface of the text and reflects the narrator's multiple skills as a storyteller, but it does not determine the shape of the text.

Perhaps the most telling weakness of Rendsburg's presentation, however, is this: In his thesis, although each of the major segments of Genesis is set up in careful and often extremely subtle parallel or chiastic fashion, the whole of Genesis has no such structure whatsoever. Instead, the major chiasmi and parallel narratives are simply set one after the other with no transitions, except for the two jumbled "linking" segments, and have no overall structuring. The redactor, in other words, who is said to have been profoundly concerned to include verbal clues to the chiastic or parallel intertwining of each major section, was totally indifferent to the structure of the whole and merely lined up the major narratives in a chronological sequence. This is unlikely.

Nevertheless, Rendsburg brings together some significant evidence for correspondence and literary parallel throughout all fifty chapters of Genesis. The subtle interweaving of the text on multiple levels only serves to heighten our appreciation of the magnitude of Genesis as a literary accomplishment. As Rendsburg points out, this should make us skeptical about source and redactional theories that treat Genesis as a patchwork of documents.[32] In addition, Rendsburg produces significant arguments for a redaction during the early monarchy.[33]

A New Hypothesis: Genesis as Ancestor Epic Literature

The question of the structure of Genesis, therefore, is still unresolved and in need of a fresh examination. In light of the work of Kikiwada and Quinn, moreover, it is worth considering whether the whole of Genesis has the same structure as the Atrahasis myth and Genesis 1–11. They have already done preliminary work in this area.

---

30. E.g., Rendsburg tries to match the narrative in Gen. 24 with the genealogical data in 36:1–5, but this is not convincing.
31. *Redaction*, 7–25.
32. Ibid., 99–106.
33. Ibid., 107–20.

They observe that Genesis follows the sequence of primeval history, three patriarchs (Abraham, Isaac, and Jacob), and a conclusion (the Joseph stories). They also observe an *inclusio* pattern, Genesis 1 having elements that correspond to the final chapters of the book. They also detect a similar structure for the entire Pentateuch (Genesis and Deuteronomy serving as introduction and conclusion and Exodus–Numbers serving as the triadic center of the work). Like Rendsburg, they have brought out striking evidence of the narrator's skill.[34]

Nevertheless, the structure Kikiwada and Quinn propose for the Book of Genesis is not satisfactory. While it may be significant that there are three patriarchs prior to the twelve, from a literary standpoint the three figures who dominate Genesis are Abraham, Jacob, and Joseph.[35] This is not just because very few verses are devoted to Isaac, but because Isaac only slightly figures in the major literary theme of Genesis. That theme, as will be argued later, is alienation.

As we have seen, the ancestor epic pattern includes (in its full form) a prologue, a triadic narrative which describes some threat to the central characters, and a conclusion, with transitional material between each major section. Each of the major characters of Genesis—Abraham, Jacob, and Joseph—is driven far from home. Alienated and often in danger, these figures dominate the story. Isaac, however, never wanders from the land of his birth. One story does describe Isaac in a hostile environment, the palace of Abimelech, but, as will subsequently be demonstrated on formal grounds, Genesis 26:1–16 originally belonged to a separate epic structure. From the standpoint of narrative structure, therefore, Isaac is not a major figure.

In addition, the *toledoth* material, that is, the genealogies, have been set between each of the major cycles of Genesis exactly as they have been set between the major divisions of the primeval history. The pattern, in fact, is exactly the same as that of Atrahasis and Genesis 1–11. The primeval history serves as the prologue, the three patriarchal cycles (of Abraham, Jacob, and Joseph) make up the heart of Genesis, and the story of Israel in Egypt after the arrival of Jacob is the conclusion.

The overall structure of Genesis is seen in figure 5.8. It is noteworthy, moreover, that just as the threat to humanity is repeated twice in the second cycle of both Atrahasis and Genesis 1–11, Jacob is twice threatened by Esau (27:42; 32:6–8) in his (the second) cycle. The

---

34. Kikiwada and Quinn, *Before Abraham Was,* 119–25.

35. Cf. Speiser, *Genesis,* lviii; Rendsburg, *Redaction,* 1. See also Robert L. Cohn, "Narrative Structure and Canonical Perspective in Genesis," *JSOT* 25 (1983): 3–16.

Figure 5.8

The Structure of Genesis

Prologue	Primeval History	1:1–11:26
Transition	Genealogy	11:27–32
Threat	The Abraham Cycle	12:1–25:11
Transition	Genealogy	25:12–18
Threat	The Jacob Cycle	25:19–35:22b
Transition	Genealogy	35:22c–36:40
Threat	The Joseph Cycle	37:1–46:7
Transition	Genealogy	46:8–27
Resolution	Settlement in Egypt	46:28–50:26

validity of this approach is shown by the way that the five major cycles each function separately as part of the structure of the whole.

The prologue, Genesis 1–11, serves as a guide and pattern to the larger narrative. It shows how the God who brought humanity through their difficult early days would do the same for the fathers of the special covenant people. But Genesis is primarily concerned with the issue of how the nation (Israel) was threatened even before it really began, and this comes out in the three major cycles of the book.

The three major figures of the narrative often stand alone in hostile lands with little hope of having or preserving offspring. Only the protection of the covenant God enables them to survive, prosper, and see their children. Abraham is commanded to sojourn in the strange land of the Canaanites, but it is precisely that land which God promises Abraham's offspring will fill. Jacob flees to the treacherous Laban, but it is there, because of Laban's schemes, that Jacob becomes the prosperous father of the twelve. Joseph is sold into slavery by his own brothers and ultimately, through no fault of his own, finds himself abandoned and forgotten in an Egyptian dungeon. Yet it is precisely from there that he is able to rise to a position beside Pharaoh himself and provide deliverance for his family when its survival is threatened by famine.

Genesis, like Atrahasis, is an ancestor epic of human survival, but it is more than that. It is an account of how the God of the fathers, Yahweh, was himself the true father of the human race.

The composition of the Abraham cycle will be explored in more detail in subsequent chapters, but it is worth noting here that the chiasmus uncovered by Cassuto, Sarna, and Rendsburg (11:27–22:24) in no way invalidates the contention that the Abraham cycle extends from 12:1 to 25:11. The chiastic structure functions beneath the larger structure of the text. The report of the offspring of Nahor (22:20–24) at the end of this chiasmus is in fact a minor stop; it is not a *toledoth* text of the sort that establishes the major divisions of Genesis. More than that, one can hardly deny that 23:1–25:11, although outside of the chiasmus that ends in 22:24,[36] is part of the larger cycle of Abraham. The cycle does not end until Abraham dies.

The unity of the chiastic section is important. It implies that the various sources that made up the Abraham account must have been of a kind which, when gathered together, were suitable for redaction into a chiastic narrative. The source narratives themselves may have contained parallel episodes that could become components of chiastic parallelism. A theory such as the Documentary Hypothesis, however, which fragments even individual narrations and is hostile to parallel doublets in a single source, is incompatible with the chiastic structure of the Abraham cycle.

The cycle of Jacob proposed here, coincidentally, corresponds exactly to the extent of the chiasmus proposed by Fishbane (25:19–35:22).[37] This reinforces the validity of the conclusion, since it was attained by an altogether different method.

The Joseph cycle (37:1–46:7) also has a symmetry of its own, and this symmetry is independent of the chiastic structure of 37:3–50:26. The story line begins with Joseph on a high level but, despite his wisdom and capability, his fortunes sink step by step. Then, when he is at the very bottom, a series of divine acts reverses his fortunes and brings him back to the height of glory. He begins as his father's favorite in a richly ornamented robe, but he loses prestige before his father not because of any sin but because of the frank telling of a revelation he received (37:1–11). He is sent out by his father to observe his brothers, but because of their treachery he is almost killed and finally enslaved (37:12–36).

36. In chap. 7 I also point out that Gen. 23 and 24 are from sources formally distinct from the rest of the Abraham cycle.

37. "Composition," 15–38. I call the correspondence between Fishbane's conclusion and my own coincidental because I had reached my conclusion about the extent of the Jacob cycle before I was aware of Fishbane's study. Also, my methods of analysis are quite different.

The story of Judah and Tamar does not directly concern Joseph, but it shows Judah to have been a man of character after what had been a poor showing on his part in the selling of Joseph (38:26). Joseph then becomes chief steward of Potiphar's house, but the lust of Potiphar's wife lands Joseph in a dungeon (39). He rises to prominence in the Egyptian prison and does a favor requiring great wisdom for two of Pharaoh's staff, the cupbearer and baker, but that act seems forgotten (40). The very lowest point of Joseph's career is told in 40:23: "The chief cupbearer did not remember Joseph but forgot him."

At that point, however, the reversal begins. Pharaoh has a dream, and the reader understands that behind that dream is the work of God to release Joseph from prison (41). His fall into the dungeon has been reversed. In the next major reversal, God brings the brothers down to Egypt by means of the famine, and they bow to Joseph as the dream had predicted. Joseph deceives them and demands to see their younger brother, just as they had earlier deceived Jacob by saying their younger brother was dead. When they bring Benjamin to Egypt, Joseph frames Benjamin as Potiphar's wife had framed him. Here, too, there is a reversal: Joseph does not imprison his brothers but welcomes them after Judah proves his character at the end (44:33), as he had in the story about Tamar.

At last, in a reversal of Jacob's decision to send out Joseph, Jacob himself sets out to join Joseph, and he is given divine assurance as he does so. Jacob does not bow to Joseph, as the dream seemed to predict (37:10), but God tells him that Joseph's hand will close his eyes (46:4). This is not in all points neat and tidy, but it is a subtle and free yet remarkably careful intertwining of all the major strands of the cycle. This is what one would expect from a master narrator.

The final resolution of Genesis (46:28–50:26) describes no threat to the tiny, emerging people. They are secure in the choicest region of Egypt (47:11), and are given every courtesy as honored guests. Nevertheless, like the resolutions of Atrahasis and Genesis 1–11, the ending does not have an entirely happy resolution. They are still aliens and strangers living in a land that is not their own. The potential of threat, in light of 15:13, is certainly present. The complete resolution of the problem is to be found in the next act of God, the exodus.

6

The Ancestor Epics

Having examined the overall structure of Genesis, it is now necessary to isolate the sources behind this structure. To do this, we must define a few terms. Our choice of terms will be somewhat arbitrary, but this is unavoidable. When we move into a new area, old terminology must be redefined or new terms invented. Sometimes this leads to confusion,[1] but these difficulties can be minimized if the method is simple and consistent.

Terminology

The best place to begin is with a term we have already used and to some extent defined, *ancestor epic*. The full ancestor epic is a narrative with the pattern found in the myth of Atrahasis, Genesis 1–11, and the full text of Genesis. It contains a prologue, three major stories of threat, and a resolution. Between each of these elements, in the full ancestor epics of Genesis, is a transitional section composed of *toledoth* source material.

Content, however, and not merely form, helps to define the full ancestor epic. At the center of the ancestor epic is the question of the

---

1. This is nowhere more apparent than in the confusion over the use of the word *saga* in Genesis studies. I have found it best to avoid the term altogether rather than add my own special meaning.

survival of the race. All of the three threats, therefore, are especially significant not as simple threats to individual persons but as challenges to the existence of the whole people. In Atrahasis and Genesis 1–11, the survival of the human race is in doubt; in Genesis (the full text) the survival of Israel, the people, is in doubt.

For this reason, the matter of reproduction and offspring figures prominently in the stories. In Atrahasis, the prolific reproduction of the race is an annoyance to the gods, and checks placed on this capacity form the resolution. In Genesis 1–11, God desires humanity to fill the earth, but sin, violence, and other distortions threaten the race.[2] A resolution comes in the confusion of tongues and the scattering of the people. In Genesis, the threats come in the form of the wanderings of the patriarchs and the dangers they face. Infertility, the threat of violence, treacherous hosts, famine, and other perils combine to put in doubt the likelihood that the seed of Abraham will ever fill the land of Canaan. The *toledoth* transitional material serves to prove that the people are multiplying in spite of these threats. The story is resolved by giving the offspring a shelter in which they can grow, the fertile delta of Egypt.

Within the text of Genesis, a number of *parallel epics* exist. These are not full ancestor epics: that is, they do not possess all the epic elements already described. In particular, they do not have the prologues, epilogues, or transitional material in their present states. Whether some of them were originally much larger and had all these elements is impossible to say; a good deal could have been lost in the Mosaic redaction of Urgenesis. On the other hand, as is implied in the name, the major cycles (episodes) of a parallel epic are set up in a parallel structure. In the full ancestor epic, the major threats do not always parallel each other structurally.

Nevertheless, parallel epics are related to the ancestor epic. From the standpoint of formal structure, these narratives are built around a triadic or (in one case) binary threat structure. The community, in the person of its eponymous or maternal head, is three times (or twice) threatened. The question of whether he or she will survive is at the center of each triadic ancestor epic, and each threat to the ancestor is understood to threaten his or her offspring. The matter of reproduction again figures heavily.

---

2. Important here is the danger to the human race posed by the cohabitation of humans with the demigod figures, the "sons of Elohim," in Gen. 6:1–3.

In the previous chapter, the three major sections of Genesis (those of Abraham, Jacob, and Joseph) were called *cycles*. A cycle, as the term is used here, relates a major threat within an ancestor epic.

The *tale* is distinct from the ancestor epic in that it follows a single story line and does not employ a triadic or binary structuring of parallel incidents.[3] Sometimes a threat to the family line may be described. However, the purpose of the tale is not to describe how the line survived some major threat. Instead, it recounts incidents, be they threatening or not, which are important to the nation and its subsequent history.

Other forms of literature are also present in Genesis, but it is not the purpose of this chapter to name them all. For example, the carefully structured heptad in Genesis 1:1ff. is a type unto itself. The story of Joseph is also a special category. These texts are examined in more detail later in this study.

The Ancestor Epics of Genesis

The Primeval History

Genesis 1–11 has already been described as an ancestor epic in the previous chapter. All the major elements of the ancestor epic are present here, and the dominant theme of threats to the community (all humanity) in the persons of the ancestors is obvious. The question of the redaction history of Genesis 1–11 is examined in chapter 10.

The Ancestor Epic of Jacob

The ancestor epic of Jacob is both the most complete and easiest to discern of the patriarchal epics beneath the text of Genesis. This, like all the other epics, is a national and not just a personal story. It is the story of how the Israelites came to exist as a unified people.

The ancestor epic of Jacob is of particular significance because it is the story of the nation of Israel, not of some other tribe or nation. The cycle of Abraham concerns not just Israel but also Ishmael, Moab, Ammon, and the tribes from Keturah. Isaac's story concerns both Israel and Edom. The story of Joseph is important to all of Israel, but is not an ancestor epic for Israel since Joseph is ancestor only to

---

3. The term *tale* does not in any sense imply that the material is fictional.

Ephraim and Manasseh. The Jacob cycle, standing at the center of Genesis, is distinctively the story of Israel.

Within the larger Jacob cycle of the present text (25:21–35:22b), the ancestor epic of Jacob is the major source document. In addition to the epic, the Jacob cycle has two other major source documents, the third section of the wife-as-sister ancestor epic with additional material about Isaac (Gen. 26) and the tale of Dinah (Gen. 34). That material being excluded from the cycle, what remains is a full ancestor epic. The structure of the ancestor epic of Jacob is seen in figure 6.1. The ancestor epic of Jacob is complete with prologue, three cycles (27:1–28:22, 29:1–31:55, 32:1–33:20), a resolution, and even a dual structure in the middle of the second cycle, as is found in Atrahasis and Genesis 1–11. The resolution, as is common, is partially tragic.

Figure 6.1
The Structure of the Ancestor Epic of Jacob
(25:21–35:22b)

Prologue	Birth of Esau and Jacob; conflict begins	25:21–34
Threat	Jacob gets Esau's blessing and flees for his life	27:1–28:22
Threat	Jacob at Paddan Aram	29:1–31:55
1.	Laban cheats Jacob	29:15–27
2.	Laban hates Jacob	31:1–2
Threat	Jacob faces Esau	32:1–33:20
Resolution	Jacob returns to Bethel, Benjamin born, Rachel dies	35:1–22b

The divine blessings on Jacob play an important role at each stage of the epic narrative. The first of these comes at Bethel (28:10–22), as Jacob is fleeing Esau and moving into unknown territory alone. A second blessing is related in Genesis 31:10–13, where Jacob tells his wives of a dream he had. God shows him that divine providence (and not Jacob's peculiar attempt at genetic engineering) brought about the increase in Jacob's flock in his conflict with Laban. The third major blessing is described in Genesis 32:22–32, where Jacob wrestles with the angel just before he meets Esau. Each of these three blessings appears in connection with one of the threats to Jacob. They stand in the ancestor epic as counters to the threats and as proof of the supernatural origin of Israel.

The Parallel Epics

The Triadic Epics

When examined formally and in light of the definitions provided (pp. 127–29), a significant amount of the Genesis material is seen to have been originally in the form of triadic epics. These epics, although they once existed separately, were broken up in order to weave them into the present text of Genesis. In the course of inserting these epics into the larger redaction (Urgenesis), a good deal of material may have been omitted from the triadic epics. It is possible that they were originally full epics, but this assertion is beyond any verification.

THE WIFE-AS-SISTER TRIADIC EPIC

No reader of Genesis can fail to be struck by the threefold repetition of the story of a patriarch sojourning in the land of an alien king and there, fearing for his life, passing off his wife as his sister (12:10–20; 20:1–18; 26:1–17). Scholars, too, have long puzzled over this repetition and have developed various theories to account for it.[4] The triadic structure, however, strongly indicates that these stories once circulated together, separate from other material, as a story in the ancestor epic pattern.

Formal and material indications reinforce the probability that this approach to understanding the wife-as-sister deception stories is valid. The first cycle appears in Genesis 12:10–20 (see fig. 6.2). This cycle, we might note, is self-contained in that the reader needs no prior understanding of any of the elements of the cycle.

The second cycle, Abraham in the territory of Abimelech, is found in Genesis 20:1–18 (see fig. 6.2). This cycle, although almost twice as long as the previous one, is in at least one respect incomplete and reliant upon the former for information to make it comprehensible. No motive whatsoever is given for Abimelech's taking of Sarah. If he had to take one of his guest's women, why not choose one of the younger women? The reason, of course, is in the earlier narrative,

---

4. The older Documentary Hypothesis scholars regarded these stories as three variants of the same story, with the first being J, the second E, and the third P. Cf. John Skinner, *A Critical and Exegetical Commentary on Genesis*, 2d ed., ICC (Edinburgh: T. and T. Clark, 1930), 251, 315, 363; Gerhard von Rad, *Genesis*, trans. John H. Marks (Philadelphia: Westminster, 1961), 226, 270; E. A. Speiser, *Genesis*, AB (New York: Doubleday, 1964), 150–52. More recently, the second narrative has been argued to be an expansion of the first. See George W. Coats, *Genesis: With an Introduction to Narrative Literature*, FOTL (Grand Rapids: Eerdmans, 1984), 151.

Figure 6.2

A Triadic Ancestor Epic
(12:10–20; 20:1–18; 26:1, 7–17)

First Cycle (12:10–20)

Section	Text	Content
Migration	10	Abram goes to Egypt because of a famine
Deception	11–13	He sees Sarai is beautiful so tells her to say she is his sister
Abduction	14–16	Pharaoh takes Sarai and rewards Abram
Deliverance	17	The Lord afflicts Pharaoh
Confrontation	18–19	Pharaoh rebukes Abram
Conclusion	20	Abram leaves with wealth

Second Cycle (20:1–18)

Section	Text	Content
Migration	1	Abraham goes to Gerar
Deception	2a	He tells Abimelech that Sarah is his sister
Abduction	2b	Abimelech takes Sarah
Deliverance	3–7	The Lord rebukes Abimelech in a dream
Confrontation	8–16	Abimelech rebukes Abraham but rewards him
Conclusion	17–18	Abraham prays for Abimelech (departure understood)

Third Cycle (26:1, 7–17)

Section	Text	Content
Migration	1	Isaac goes to Gerar
Deception	7	He says that Rebekah is his sister when men of Gerar ask about her
Abduction	—	No abduction
Deliverance	8	Abimelech sees Isaac caressing Rebekah
Confrontation	9–13	Abimelech rebukes Isaac but protects him; the Lord blesses Isaac
Conclusion	17	Isaac separates from Abimelech when rivalry develops

where both Abraham and the Egyptians speak extravagantly of Sarah's beauty. Also, in the second cycle, the discussion of the abduction is considerably abbreviated and explicit mention of Abraham's departure at the end is omitted.

The third cycle concerns Isaac and Rebekah, again with Abimelech of Gerar, and is found in Genesis 26:1, 7–17 (see fig. 6.2). The third cycle, in its present form, contains two elements not present in the two previous accounts: the blessing (26:2–6), which appears to have come from another source, and an account of a rivalry with the local population (14–16), which relates to the story that follows. More will be said about this.

Nevertheless, the similarity in form and content with the two previous wife-as-sister deception stories is obvious.[5] Most remarkably, the three stories are bound by a pattern in which a narrative element is consistently present in two out of the three accounts (in this discussion A = the first, B = the second, and C = the third). A begins with a famine which C, also beginning with a famine, explicitly mentions. B refers to no famine. In A and B, the patriarchal couple is Abraham and Sarah, but in C, it is Isaac and Rebekah. In A, the location is Egypt and the host Pharaoh; but in B and C, the location is Gerar and the host is Abimelech. A and C explicitly mention the beauty of the wife, but B does not. In A and C, the host's servants first notice the beautiful woman, but not in B. In A and B, the wife is taken into the harem, but not in C. In A and B, deliverance comes by direct intervention of God, but in C, deliverance comes by the providential accident of Abimelech seeing Isaac with Rebekah. The host rewards the patriarch in A and B, but God blesses the patriarch in C. God is called Yahweh in A and C, but in B, he is Elohim.[6] In A and C, the patriarch explicitly departs, but in B, his departure is implicit. Thus, both in obvious, formal characteristics and in the remarkable two-out-of-three pattern found throughout the triad, the unity of the whole is clear.

In addition, the dominant concern of the triad is that of the full ancestor epic narrative—the survival of the race in the face of a three-

5. Contrary to Thomas L. Thompson, *The Origin Tradition of Ancient Israel,* JSOTSS 55 (Sheffield: JSOT Press, 1987), 56–59, who argues that Gen. 26 is not parallel to Gen. 12:10–20 and Gen. 20 on the grounds the only real parallels are the common motifs of the famine and the wife-as-sister deception. But the formal parallels are clear.

6. God is once called Yahweh at the end of B, in 20:18. The use of Elohim in B may be because in B God is dealing directly with the Gentile Abimelech, not the covenant figure Abraham or Isaac. See Umberto Cassuto, *The Documentary Hypothesis and the Composition of the Pentateuch,* trans. Israel Abrahams (Jerusalem: Magnes, 1941), 40.

fold threat. The patriarchs in these stories are far less than heroic. In each case they told a half-truth or an outright lie in order to save themselves. The real impact of the epic, however, is not to point out the character weaknesses of Abraham and Isaac but to show how their actions placed the matriarchs, and thus the offspring, in great danger.[7] In each case, the reader shudders at what could have happened and sees that only divine intervention preserved the family. Indeed, not only does God save the family, he makes it richer each time he does so! Nevertheless, this does not detract from the conclusion that materially this is an ancestor epic narrative in that it deals with the ancestor epic theme, the threat to the family line in the person of an ancestor.

This is, therefore, a true triadic ancestor epic and not just three stories that are form-critically the same. James G. Williams, in his study of conventions in biblical literature, has argued that these three stories simply follow the literary convention of the wife-as-sister deception. Williams has pointed out other literary conventions in the Bible, such as that of the betrothal to a woman at a well (as in Gen. 24 and 29, Exod. 2) and that of the beloved but barren woman finally bearing children (e.g., Sarah, Rachel, Hannah).[8]

One must distinguish, however, between common literary motifs and formal indications of the unity of a narrative. Literary motifs or conventions occur throughout literary history and do not imply literary dependence of one text on another. Williams has isolated the example of the woman-at-the-well motif in the biblical texts. Outside the Bible, common motifs include Cinderella, the evil twin, the flawed hero, and the disguised lover. An entirely different matter, however, is the formal indication of structural unity of several texts within a single book of the Bible. Here, we are dealing not with separate stories that share a common motif, but with three passages whose structure and contents indicate that they could be read as a single, unified narrative in several parts and that they may have originally existed in that form. The precise structural parallels, the peculiar two-out-of-three pattern, and the dependence of 20:1–18 on 12:10–20 (in the detail that Sarah was beautiful) confirm this in respect to the wife-as-sister stories of Genesis. By contrast, while Genesis 24 and 29, and Exodus 2

7. See Coats, *Genesis*, 109, 149, 188, who refers to each incident as a "tale of a threat to the ancestress."

8. "The Beautiful and the Barren: Conventions in Biblical Type-Scenes," *JSOT* 17 (1980): 107–19. Williams includes John 4 as a deliberate play on the betrothal-at-the-well motif.

all contain the motif of meeting the wife-to-be at a well, Kenneth T. Aitken has concluded, after a detailed study of the structure of Genesis 24, that "aside from the marriage itself, therefore, the basic structure of the plot in Genesis 24 has no parallel in either [Genesis 29 or Exodus 2]."[9] Williams himself admits that the "differences are great" among these narratives.[10] But the wife-as-sister narratives are not only uniform in structure; they all concern the same set of characters, are set in the same locations, and have the same results (the pattern of variations already noted). Moreover, all three are recorded in the same book instead of being scattered across the pages of the Bible. There is more here than a common literary convention. Williams's conclusion that the wife-as-sister deception stories are built on a mythological motif is also highly suspect.[11]

Certainly no one would advocate that every time two or more texts are found to be form-critically similar those texts must have once stood together in a separate source. But here, close formal correspondence combines with both the material use of the ancestor epic theme of threat to the family line and the additional binding of the three stories together by the two-out-of-three pattern. What is most important is that these stories together form the same structure as that which makes up the heart of the full epics in Genesis 1–11 and the whole of Genesis, the triadic threat narrative. It is reasonable, therefore, to conclude that these three once stood together as a separate triadic ancestor epic of threats to the maternal ancestors.

No direct evidence indicates how this triad came together, but hypothesis is possible. According to the material, Abraham tried to pass off his wife as his sister not just twice but many times (20:13). Many of the stories of these incidents must have been known to the earliest Israelites, but three, those that have been preserved in Genesis, were apparently drawn out of that pool and shaped in the ancestor epic pattern. The epic of the wife-as-sister deceptions was subsequently broken up and used in the redaction of Urgenesis.

The insertion of 26:2–6 and apparently verses 14–16 into the third cycle of the triad also appears to have taken place in the Urgenesis redaction. Isaac stayed in Gerar a long time (26:8, 12), and a number of stories of his activities there can be assumed to have been passed down to the Israelites. In the earliest oral transmission of these sto-

9. "The Wooing of Rebekah," *JSOT* 30 (1984): 11.
10. "Conventions," 112.
11. Ibid.

Figure 6.3

Parallels between the Abraham and Isaac Stories

Abraham

A	12:1–3	Receives God's call and promise
B	12:10–20	Wife-sister deception episode
C	13:1–12	Quarrel with Lot's men; Abram takes lesser land
D	15:1–21	Divine reassurance and a sacrifice
E	21:22–34	Treaty with Abimelech at Beersheba

Isaac

A'	26:2–6	Receives same call and promise from God
B'	26:7ff.	Wife-sister deception episode
C'	26:14–22	Quarrel with Abimelech's men and other local men; Isaac moves rather than fight
D'	26:23–25	Divine reassurance and a sacrifice
E'	26:26–33	Treaty with Abimelech at Beersheba

ries, the various incidents and accounts would have traveled together as "things that happened to Isaac in Gerar" until they were compiled and written as formal narratives and individual records. The cycle of the threat to Rebekah must have been drawn from this pool of sources in the formation of the wife-as-sister deception ancestor epic.

The record of the divine call and promise to Isaac (26:2–6), on the other hand, was once written separately (as George W. Coats observes, the theophany has no direct connection with the story that unfolds),[12] even though originally it came out of the same quarry of remembrances of Isaac in Gerar. It may have once stood with 26:23–25a as a record of divine promises to Isaac. The parallel of 26:2–6, with the call and promise of Abraham (12:1–3), moreover, is self-evident.

The story of the quarrel of Abimelech's men with Isaac and his clan also appears to have come out of the same set of recollections from Gerar and afterwards, in the first formal recording and arrangement of the material, was in a separate record. In addition, 26:25b–33 appears to have once been circulated with 21:22–34 as a pair of Beersheba stories.

12. *Genesis*, 189.

What is remarkable is how these accounts were redacted into Urgenesis. Isaac's legitimacy as the promised line of Abraham (over the claims of Ishmael or the sons of Keturah) is reinforced by setting elements of his life in parallel with many of the details of Abraham's life (see fig. 6.3).[13]

Also, note that just as Hagar secured an Egyptian wife for Ishmael (21:21) while Abraham sent his servant to Aram-Naharaim for a wife for Isaac (24), even so Esau took Hittites for his wives (26:34–35) while Jacob went to Haran for his wives. The parallel is unquestionably deliberate, but it is part of the redactional structure of Genesis.

Nevertheless, it is clear that the structure of Genesis 26 was to some extent determined by the narrative purpose of setting Isaac's life in parallel to that of Abraham. This accounts for the integration of the third cycle of the wife-as-sister ancestor epic into the other episodes now found in Genesis 26 of the present text. The appearance that the third cycle in the triad is formally unlike the first two is misleading; it is the result of subsequent redaction.

The Epic of Lot

The ancestor epic of Lot, as the present text witnesses to it, is a large and complex narrative. It contains material that functions in significant ways apart from the epic of Lot, which is to say that some episodes, which formally are part of the structure of the ancestor epic, may have been described in other sources as well. That is, just as both a history of Persia and a history of Greece would devote attention to the story of Alexander the Great, albeit from different perspectives, both the epic about Lot and other sources concerning Abraham would have shared material in common. This material would naturally be merged at the redaction of Urgenesis. On one level, the common material functions as part of the present ancestor epic of Lot, but on another level, when read as part of the whole of Genesis, this material functions as part of the story of Abraham and Isaac.

Evidence for these conclusions will be given subsequently, but first it is necessary to examine the larger epic of Lot. The epic is found in 13:1–14:24 and 18:1–19:38.[14] The triadic structure of the whole is seen in figure 6.4.

---

13. Genesis sets up other parallels among the lives of the patriarchs as well. See Peter D. Miscall, "The Jacob and Joseph Stories as Analogies," *JSOT* 6 (1978): 28–40.

14. Coats, *Genesis*, 113–15, also sees what he calls an "Abraham-Lot novella," except that he adds 11:10–12:9 to the novella but does not allow 18:1–15. The method Coats uses to arrive at his conclusions regarding the extent of the proposed novella are not clear to me; no recognizable form-critical pattern is present in his outline of the structure.

Figure 6.4

**The Structure of the Epic of Lot
(13:1–18; 14:1–24; 18:1–19:38)**

First Cycle (13:1–18)

Section	Verses	Formal Content
A	1–4	Initial setting
B	5–7	Crisis
C	8–13	Abram saves Lot; Sodom very wicked
D	14–18	The Lord blesses Abram

Second Cycle (14:1–24)

Section	Verses	Formal Content
A'	1–11	Initial setting
B'	12	Crisis
C'	13–16	Abram saves Lot
D'	17–24	Melchizedek blesses Abram; Sodom very wicked

Third Cycle (18:1–19:38)

Section	Verses	Formal Content
A''	18:1–15	Initial setting
B''	18:16–21	Crisis
C''	18:22–19:29	Abraham/the Lord saves Lot; Sodom very wicked
D''	19:30–38	Lot's accursed end

This is perhaps the most intriguing, if also the darkest, epic narrative in Genesis. Each of the three cycles begins with an initial setting. In the first, Abram moves to the region of Bethel and Ai, and emphasis is on his wealth (13:2) and piety (13:4). In other words, this is an ideal situation for Lot; he is attached to a godly and prosperous man (13:1c).[15] The crisis comes in the quarreling of their men over pasture. This is the first threat to Lot. As the weaker party, he, not Abram, is the one in jeopardy. Abram, however, in an act of

15. It is possible, as argued by Larry R. Helyer, "The Separation of Abram and Lot," *JSOT* 26 (1983): 77–88, that Lot was even Abram's heir at this time and that Lot's departure from Canaan meant his removal from that position. The text, however, does not indicate heirship as an issue. Abraham's subsequent efforts to save Lot (Gen. 14, 18) and the importance attached to those episodes, make little sense if Lot had abandoned the position of heir.

grace, saves Lot from the dilemma (13:8–13). He allows the younger Lot to take whatever he wants, but Lot, against propriety, greedily seizes what looks best to him. The text then sounds an ominous warning: "The men of Sodom were wicked. . . ." The Sodomites do not actually figure in the story of chapter 13, but this verse forebodes disaster for Lot. The cycle ends with a promise that all the land, as far as Abram can see, will belong to his offspring (13:14–18).[16]

The initial setting of the second cycle is a war (14:1–11). All the information here is historical, and Lot does not appear at all. In verse 12, however, the crisis is declared: Lot has been taken prisoner! This is the second threat. Abram saves Lot by military action (14:13–16). Melchizedek then appears as suddenly as the Lord had in the first cycle and blesses Abram.[17] Nevertheless, once again, the wickedness of Sodom emerges, even though it does not yet really figure in the story: Abram does not want to give even the appearance of accepting money from the king of Sodom (14:21–23). The second cycle is not an alien insertion into the text of Genesis but is an integral and original part of the Lot ancestor epic.[18]

The epic comes to a climactic conclusion in the third cycle. The stage is set in 18:1–15, the annunciation of Isaac. Lot is entirely

16. Although it was written in conjunction with the second and third cycles and looks forward to them, the first cycle does have a symmetry of its own. Von Rad, *Genesis*, 225, rightly sees the unity of chapters 13, 18, and 19, but he is wrong to see 13 as an exposition to 18–19. The triadic unity of the form of the narrative indicates the real balance in the structure.

17. The Melchizedek episode is often regarded as an interpolation, but the formal structure of the Lot epic speaks against that conclusion. The Melchizedek story is ancient; it is not from the Davidic monarchy. See Robert Houston Smith, "Abram and Melchizedek (Gen 14:18–20)," *ZAW* 77 (1965): 129–53, especially 130–31. Smith argues the Melchizedek tradition should be separated from its context, but his interpretation is most suspect and builds too much on questionable parallels to the Keret epic.

18. Von Rad, *Genesis*, 175, excludes Gen. 14 as a text that has no connection to any of the hexateuchal sources. See also Speiser, *Genesis*, 105–6. Contrast Coats, *Genesis*, 118–21. The nature and origin of the material in Gen. 14 has been a matter of scholarly debate. Scholars have claimed that Gen. 14 was originally poetry, that it has an Akkadian background, and that it is derived from the Spartoli texts, which allegedly told of four foreign kings who invaded Babylon. A number of scholars separate the somewhat annalistic account in vv. 1–11 from the account of the heroic deed of Abram, and the incident involving Melchizedek (vv. 18–20) is often regarded as an interpolation. No real consensus exists concerning the purpose or *Sitz im Leben* behind the narratives. For a good survey of various views, see J. A. Emerton, "Some False Clues to the Study of Genesis XIV," *VT* 21 (1971): 24–47, and "The Riddle of Genesis XIV," *VT* 21 (1971): 403–39.

absent, just as he is in the setting of the second cycle (he is briefly mentioned in the setting of the first cycle). But the annunciation of Isaac plays an important role here; in addition to providing the setting for Abraham's intercession, it also anticipates in an ironic way the sordid story of the origin of Moab and Ammon. The crisis is set up after the visitors finish their business with Abraham. In an ominous manner, they look off toward Sodom (18:16) and after dramatic hesitation, tell Abraham what they intend to do: investigate the sin of Sodom. Abraham, knowing by intuition what lies ahead, lingers to intercede with the Lord. The reader recognizes concern for Lot behind this intercession,[19] and the Lord fulfills the intention although not the letter of the intercession in delivering Lot. As the angels enter Sodom, the wickedness of the city, to which the earlier cycles had proleptically alluded, is laid bare to the reader in all its ugliness. The angels' encounter with the men of Sodom is thus something of a climax in the Lot ancestor epic because it is there, above all, that the folly of Lot's decision dramatically strikes the reader. In 19:27–29, Abraham looks toward Sodom and sees the smoke rising. This poignant moment in the narrative serves an important form-critical function. It closes off section C" ("Abraham saves Lot"), but in a way that contains a sad reversal. As far as Abraham can tell, he has not managed to save Lot, although in fact he did.

Then Genesis 19:31–38 closes the ancestor epic with a dramatic reversal and resolution. Instead of concluding with a promise of blessing to Abraham (D, D'), it finishes with Lot meeting a terrible, accursed end. Lot has offspring—in that sense it resolves the threat to the race that is intrinsic to the ancestor epic narrative—but their incestuous origin leaves no doubt that a curse hangs over the family line. Instead of a blessing on the seed of Abraham, there is a curse on the seed of Lot.

In addition to the form-critical evidence for the unity of this material, therefore, material evidence also plainly shows it to be epic in character. The epic follows Lot, ancestor of Moab and Ammon, through a series of three threats to the epic's resolution, the birth of

19. It is insensitive to the narrative to interpret the text as only serving to point out the wickedness of Sodom, simply because Lot is not explicitly named (see Coats, *Genesis,* 141). The discussion concerns Sodom, where Lot is, and not one of the other cities. Coats's contention that the text does not assert Lot to be righteous fails to account for the significance of the hospitality of Lot (19:1ff.), which parallels that of Abraham (18:1–8). See T. Desmond Alexander, "Lot's Hospitality: A Clue to his Righteousness," *JBL* 104 (1985): 289–91.

the eponymous heads of the two nations.[20] This is a bleak resolution, to be sure, but such is more the rule than the exception (as in Atrahasis or Genesis 1–11).

As indicated, however, some material in the present triad about Lot functions in the current text of Genesis as part of another story, the story of Abraham and Isaac. The narrative of the annunciation of Isaac (18:1–15) is the specific case in point. Some of the details of this story may have come from another source on the birth of Isaac. In the redaction of Urgenesis, that material was evidently redacted into the already extant third cycle of the Lot ancestor epic, which was in turn redacted into the larger text of Urgenesis. From the present text, an attempt to distinguish the original material of the third cycle of the Lot ancestor epic from an independent source on the annunciation of Isaac would be futile. One can only state that another source is implied, and that from it a redactor correlated additional information. Thus it may be called an "implied correlative source."

In analysis of historical documents, it cannot be regarded as strange that two different sources would mention the same event from different perspectives. Each source has its own purpose and direction, but if both discuss the same or related historical figures (in this case, one discussing Abraham and Isaac, the other discussing Abraham and Lot), it is inevitable that overlap will occur. They will sometimes both mention the same incident, but from different perspectives, for different reasons, and with different amounts of detail. The redactor, in producing a larger history that includes both the sources will not set down the two accounts side by side (as if ignoring the fact that they talk about the same thing), but will merge the two sources where they overlap. If the redactor is skillful and creative, the merge will be seamless. A later reader may suspect that two sources are behind the unified account, but it is most unlikely the reader will be able to assign portions of the unified text to one source or another. Therefore, one cannot conclude that Genesis 18 does not have the ancestor epic of Lot as its source on the grounds that the story of the annunciation of Isaac would not have been placed in the structure of the Lot epic.

It is clear, in fact, that in the Genesis text the annunciation of Isaac, although it is obviously important to the story of Abraham and Isaac, is structurally part of the Lot ancestor epic. Evidence for this is

20. Coats, *Genesis,* 115, considers the purpose of the narrative as presenting Lot as a "comic foil" to Abraham. This interpretation misses the ancestor epic nature of the narrative. Lot's role as ancestor of Moab and Ammon is not an addendum to the narrative; it is the direction in which the whole is moving.

twofold. First, the structure of the third cycle is the same as the first two cycles, and the annunciation is part of that structure. Second, the story of the annunciation structurally parallels (with some significant reversals) the story of the angels' visit to Sodom, which implies that the two visitations are to be read as a single narrative strand.

The parallels and reversals between the two chapters are as follows (in this discussion, A refers to Genesis 18:1–15, the visitation to Abraham, and L refers to Genesis 19, the visitation to Lot): In A, the angels arrive in the heat of the day, and Abraham is at the tent entrance. In L, the angels arrive in the evening, and Lot is at the city gate. Both men arise and bow to the ground before the visitors, and both invite them to a meal. It is precisely in this one parallel, the hospitality of both men, that Lot is like Abraham and different from the rest of Sodom. This is indicative of the righteousness by which he is saved.[21] After the meal in A, the angels ask where Sarah is; in L, after the meal and the interruption from the Sodomites, the angels ask if Lot has any relatives in addition to those in the house, and Lot gets his sons-in-law.

Sarah laughs when she hears that she is to bear a child in A, and the sons-in-law, when told in L that the Lord is about to destroy the city, think he is joking. But in A, Sarah realizes the danger of laughing at the words of God and tries to extricate herself with a lie—she claims she did not laugh. She receives a firm but not harsh rebuke: "Yes, you did laugh." Beyond that, she receives no punishment. The family of Lot, on the other hand, does not awaken to the serious nature of the situation. The sons-in-law are lost altogether, while Lot, his wife, and daughters are removed from the city by force.

An especially stark reversal in the L section is the fate of Lot's wife. Part A concludes with Sarah humbled but promised a son; L ends with Lot's wife turned to salt. It is appropriate to conclude, therefore, that the structure of 18:1–15 places it in the framework of the Lot ancestor epic, even though the annunciation of Isaac has importance beyond the Lot ancestor epic.

The texts concerning Lot and Sodom thus have the form of a triadic epic. Both structure and content demonstrate the text to be of the same larger ancestor genre as Genesis 1–11, the wife-as-sister triad, and the whole of Genesis. The Lot epic is one of the major sources of Genesis.

21. See Alexander, "Lot's Hospitality."

The Binary Epic of Hagar

Genesis contains one narrative which, although it is binary rather than triadic in structure, is also best described as a parallel epic. It too is related to the ancestor epic genre, as we have defined it, because of its thematic similarity (threats to the ancestor). This is the ancestor epic of Hagar.

Hagar's story is found in two places in Genesis, 16:1–16 and 21:1–21. These two texts are formally the same, and they are arranged in parallel (see fig. 6.5). The epic of Hagar is properly designated an ancestor epic because it is primarily concerned with the question of the survival of the race (Ishmael) in the person of the maternal ancestor and her son (Hagar and Ishmael) in the face of severe danger.[22]

The binary, rather than triadic, character of this epic may be the result of redaction into the present text. A good deal of the original ancestor epic could have been deleted in the redaction. More probably, however, it was originally binary in structure. The early narrators simply told it as a binary structure on the basis of the information they had, instead of artificially making it into a triad. But the formal unity of the whole, combined with the ancestor epic theme, establish it as an ancestor epic structure.

Once again, however, not everything in the present text was necessarily unique to the original epic of Hagar. Other sources probably described some of the same events as does the Hagar epic, but not in the same detail or with the same emphases. The details of the pregnancy of Sarah and the birth of Isaac, in particular, probably came from an "implied correlative source," which dealt more particularly with the story of Abraham, Sarah, and Isaac. When 21:1–8 is read by itself, it strikes the reader as part of the whole of the Abraham story, but when all of chapter 21 is read together, the major emphasis is not on Isaac but Hagar and Ishmael. The original epic of Hagar probably gave a more abbreviated account of Isaac's birth. Many details of 21:1–8, therefore, may have come from another source more directly concerned with Abraham and Isaac. In the redaction of Urgenesis, the brief account of Isaac's birth in the Hagar ancestor epic was expanded with material from the other source. Nevertheless, the present text

22. Coats, *Genesis*, 127ff., designates all of 16:1–21:21 the "Sarah-Hagar Novella," but this is not satisfactory. It is difficult to see how 18:16–19:38 fits under that heading, and how 20:1–18 alone, and not its form-critical parallels (the wife-as-sister epic), found its way into the novella.

Figure 6.5
The Structure of the Epic of Hagar
(16:1–16; 21:1–21)

First Cycle (16:1–16)

Section	Verses	Formal Content
A	1	Sarai's infertility
B	2–3	Sarai's response: "Sleep with Hagar"
C	4	Hagar pregnant, abuses Sarai
D	5–6	Sarai complains and drives out Hagar
E	7–9	Angel of the Lord speaks, sends Hagar back
F	10	Promise: "I will increase your descendants"
G	11–14	Second word from Angel: Ishmael will be a lone wanderer in the desert
H	15	Ishmael born to Abraham
I	16	Ishmael born of Hagar

Second Cycle (21:1–21)

Section	Verses	Formal Content
A'	1–5	Sarah's fertility
B'	6–8	Sarah's response: praise and laughter
C'	9	Ishmael older, abuses Isaac
D'	10	Sarah complains: "Drive out Hagar"
E'	11–12	God speaks: "Send Hagar out"
F'	13	Promise: "I will make the son of your maid a nation"
G'	14–18	Hagar and Ishmael alone in the desert; second word from God
H'	19–20	Ishmael saved
I'	21	Hagar gets Ishmael a wife

witnesses to the presence of the ancestor epic of Hagar and to the fact that the ancestor epic determined the shape of 21:1–21.

The source of this material is the early Ishmaelites, with whom the early Israelites had contact (Gen. 37:28). It does not have an anti-

Ishmaelite purpose: although not all the details are flattering to Hagar and Ishmael, the stories of the Israelite patriarchs are not always flattering to them either. If anything, Hagar emerges as a heroic figure who received mercy from God in the face of great adversity. The real purpose is to describe the genesis of the race of Ishmael.

Besides the fact that the whole of Genesis is an ancestor epic, it contains a number of smaller ancestor epics and analogous parallel epics. The two complete ancestor epics are the primeval history and the ancestor epic of Jacob. The parallel epics include the wife-as-sister epic, the epic of Lot, and the epic of Hagar. Other source narratives, those concerning Abraham and Joseph, are in some ways similar to the ancestor epics, but enough differences exist to indicate that they belong to different genres. More will be said of this later, but first it is necessary to examine the tales of Genesis.

7

The Negotiation Tales

All the narrative material in Genesis 12–50 in one way or another concerns the ancestors of the people of Israel. Nevertheless, a great deal is not in the formal structures we have called ancestor epics but are individual stories about various events. These stories are not triadic in form, and they often lack the characteristic threat to the ancestor that the ancestor epics possess. They do, however, contain important family traditions.

One particular group of stories about the ancestors is of a form that may be called the "negotiation tale." The term *tale* is here used because all the stories of this type are short, simple narratives. The action generally follows only a small number of characters and there are no subplots.[1] A particular feature of the negotiation tale is that it includes a fairly detailed account of negotiations between two parties. The structure of the negotiation tale, as it appears in Genesis, is seen in figure 7.1.

The crisis setting is an incident that begins the negotiation tale. It is a crisis in that it is in some way calamitous to one party, the central character(s), and that party must take immediate steps to deal with the situation. This is followed by a development of circumstances in which the nature of the situation is more clearly defined. These circumstances set the parameters in which the central character(s) must act. After

---

1. Cf. the definition of the term *tale* in George W. Coats, *Genesis: With an Introduction to Narrative Literature,* FOTL (Grand Rapids: Eerdmans, 1984), 7–8.

Figure 7.1

The Structure of Negotiation Tales in Genesis

1. A crisis setting

2. Development of circumstances

3. Decisive action by the central character(s)

4. Result of the action

5. Aftermath of the incident

---

this, the central character makes some decisive action, which becomes the turning point of the narrative. The immediate results of the decisive action are then described, and a short aftermath follows. The aftermath is almost an epilogue. It brings out the larger ramifications of the decisive act and its immediate results. A detailed account of negotiations between two parties, from which this genre gets its name, occurs either as part of the decisive action or the result of the action.

A Ugaritic story with strong analogies to the biblical negotiation tale is the negotiation account in the legend of Aqhat. This is a story of the hero Aqhat and the goddess Anath. The tablets are broken and incomplete, but the main details of the portion of the legend that concerns us here are clear. The crisis that initiates the story is Anath's coveting of Aqhat's bow, a gift to him from the craftsman god, Kothar wa-Khasis. Hoping to get it from him by trade, she enters into intense negotiations.

First, Anath tries to buy the bow from Aqhat: "Hearken, I pray thee, [Aqhat the youth! / A]sk for silver, and I'll give it thee; / [For gold, and I'll be]stow't on thee; / but give thy bow [to me; / Let] Yabamat-Liimmim[2] *take* thy *darts*." Aqhat is willing to give her the means to secure her own bow, but will not give up his: "*I vow yew trees* of Lebanon, / *I vow* sinews from wild oxen; / *I vow* horns from mountain goats, / tendons from the hocks of a bull; / *I vow* from a *cane-forest* reeds: / Give (these) to Kothar wa-Khasis. / He'll make a bow for thee, / *Darts* for Yabamat-Liimmim."[3]

Anath then raises the stakes and offers Aqhat eternal life: "Ask for life, O Aqhat the Youth. / Ask for life and I'll give it thee, / For deathlessness, and I'll bestow't on thee. / I'll make thee count years with Baal, / With the sons of El shalt thou count months." The negotiations

---

2. I.e., Anath.

3. *ANET*, 151.

come to a decisive ending as Aqhat turns her down flat: "Fib not to me, O Maiden / For to a youth thy fibbing is *loathsome*. / Further life—how can mortal attain it? / How can a mortal attain life enduring? / . . . / And I'll die as everyone dies / I too shall assuredly die."[4] He knows that, being a mortal, he will never have eternal life. Thus he not only accuses her of negotiating in bad faith (of lying, in fact), but he goes on to mock her femininity: "Moreover, this will I say: / My bow is [*a weapon for*] warriors. / Shall females now [*with it*] to the chase?"[5] The text then reads ominously, "[Loud]ly Anath doth laugh, / While forging (a plot) in her heart."[6]

The immediate result of this is that Anath murders Aqhat through her henchman Yatpan. The legend then goes on to give the aftermath of the incident. A drought ensues, and Paghat, sister of Aqhat, realizes that her brother has been murdered. She then plots vengeance against Yatpan, but the final tablet of the story is missing.

The full legend of Aqhat, is, of course, more complex than the simple negotiation tales found in Genesis, but the immediate context of the negotiations between Anath and Aqhat and the outcome of those negotiations both follow the pattern of the negotiation tale and have some remarkable parallels to the tales in Genesis, to which we now turn.

Genesis contains three negotiation tales. These are The Death and Burial of Sarah (Gen. 23), The Betrothal and Marriage of Isaac (Gen. 24), and Dinah and the Shechemites (Gen. 34).

The Death and Burial of Sarah

Scholars agree that Genesis 23 constitutes a single unit, but attempts to categorize this unit form-critically have been imprecise and dominated by the Documentary Hypothesis. Gerhard von Rad only remarks that it is part of P, but he is somewhat perplexed at its "narrative graphicness," a quality that seems unusual for P.[7] George W. Coats regards it as a "death report." He notes that it frames a dialogue and is in a P setting.[8] While it is true that Sarah's death is

4. Ibid.
5. Ibid., 151–52.
6. Ibid., 152.
7. *Genesis,* trans. John H. Marks (Philadelphia: Westminster, 1961), 241.
8. *Genesis,* 165. Claus Westermann, *Genesis 12–36: A Commentary,* trans. John J. Scullion (Minneapolis: Augsburg/Fortress, 1985), 371–72, also regards it as a dialogue in a P setting.

reported and that there is a dialogue, neither the term *death report* nor *dialogue* is helpful as a formal designation; they are only descriptions of content.

By contrast, recognition of Genesis 23 as a negotiation tale is both more precise as a formal designation and provides a structural pattern by which the account can be examined. This approach helps to elucidate the theological point of the text. The structure of the narrative is seen in figure 7.2.

Figure 7.2
The Structure of One Negotiation Tale
(23:1–20)

Crisis setting	1–2	Sarah's death
Circumstances	3–5, 10–11	Abraham must obtain a burial place from the Hittites; Hittites offer to give it
Decisive action	7–9, 12–13	Abraham insists on paying
Result of action	14–16	Agreement concluded
Aftermath	17–20	The cave is legitimately owned by Abraham's line

Against the assertion that this is an example of a dialogue contract from the neo-Assyrian period,[9] note that this account is in the form of a narrative; it is not a contract at all.[10] It lacks four formal characteristics of the dialogue contract (title, seals, quitclaim clauses, and witnesses). Moreover, since every significant purchase includes the other formal parallels between the dialogue contract and Genesis 23 (negotiation of price, payment, transfer of property), these elements are not formally significant.

Also, although the story of Sarah's death is of obvious historical interest to the Israelites, the text can hardly be designated a "death report." To the contrary, her death is only the initial crisis that sets

9. Gene M. Tucker, "The Legal Background to Genesis 23," *JBL* 85 (1966): 77–84.

10. A point made by K. A. Kitchen, *Ancient Orient and Old Testament* (Chicago: Inter-Varsity, 1966), 155, and in fact conceded by Tucker, "Genesis 23," 84. See my chap. 3.

the story in motion. Nothing is said of how she died, her legacy, or her last words. In short, her death is the occasion of the story but not its subject matter.

The circumstances confronting Abraham are then developed. He must find a proper place to bury his wife in the land of the Hittites, among whom he is sojourning. He owns no real property, however, and must enter into negotiations with them. The situation confronting him then takes an unexpected twist: Ephron the Hittite offers to give the land to Abraham (v. 11). He has only to take it and bury his wife.

From the historian's standpoint, it is an open question whether Ephron's offer was genuine or a mere formality spoken in extreme politeness out of deference to the fact that Abraham was in mourning. The price that is finally set, four hundred shekels, is high indeed. On the other hand, Ephron's declaration before all present that he will give the land reads like a genuine offer, and it appears that legally he would have been bound by his words had Abraham taken the gift. Unanswered questions about what laws and customs would have had a bearing on this case are also of historical interest.

As a literary text, however, the passage must be read as a genuine offer. Abraham must bury his wife, and an easy solution is ready at hand. He can accept the land that is offered to him. But Abraham takes the decisive step of insisting on paying the full price: "I will pay the price of the land! Take it from me! Then I will bury my dead there!" (v. 13). This is to be the resting place for his wife and himself, and he wants it to be clear to all that the land is rightfully and legally his. He will not be the owner as the result of having caught a man in his words.

The immediate consequence of Abraham's action, of course, is that he must pay the high price Ephron then sets. But the aftermath is that Abraham indisputably owns the land. Although a stranger and an alien, he now owns property that is beyond question his own, and that property is in the land of promise—Canaan.

This leads to the question of what may have been the intention of this negotiation tale. Considering the emphasis on Abraham's determination to pay for the land, it cannot be so mundane as "simply a report of acquisition of burial property" on the grounds that it does not "develop theological intentions" or contain theological language.[11] A text need not use explicit theological language to have more than a surface meaning.

---

11. Coats, *Genesis*, 165. So also Westermann, *Genesis 12–36*, 376.

Closer to the mark is Walter Brueggemann's comparison of Genesis 23 to Jeremiah 32, in which Jeremiah buys property in Anathoth in the face of the devastation of the land by the Babylonians. Jeremiah's purchase acts as a sign that the land has a future; it will yet be restored. Brueggemann wonders if Jeremiah 32 may be an interpretation of Genesis 23.[12] But one must also note the real difference between Genesis 23 and Jeremiah 32. Jeremiah 32 is a theological promise of restoration and economic revival in the land (vv. 42–44). Genesis 23 does not have the slightest hint of any of this.

Genesis 23 asserts that there was one place on earth where Abraham finally owned property. That place was in Canaan. For the Israelites, therefore, no other place could rightly be called home. No theological language is needed to make this point, for it is not really a theological point. The purchase of the land does complement the promises about the land, but the text itself is concerned with the very earthly matter of property ownership.

No setting could be more appropriate to the tale than that of Israel in Egypt. To a homeless group of aliens with no real tie to any other place in the world, the story says that there is one place to which they must be irresistibly drawn: they must return to where Abraham bought land.

The Betrothal and Marriage of Isaac

The story in Genesis 24 is probably the most beautiful, and certainly the most pleasant to read, of all the Genesis tales.[13] It recounts how the servant of Abraham faithfully discharged his duty of finding a wife for his master's son. Recent critics, apparently for no other reason than the length of the story, have given it the meaningless designation *novella*[14] or *novelette*.[15] Westermann's designation, *guidance narrative*,[16] is ad hoc and has no real value as a form-critical analysis.

---

12. *Genesis: A Bible Commentary for Teaching and Preaching* (Atlanta: John Knox, 1982), 196. The linking of Jeremiah to this text is in keeping with the critical tendency to regard it as a part of P. But Brueggemann is also troubled by the lack of theological language (195).

13. Von Rad, *Genesis*, 248, calls it "the most pleasant and charming of all the patriarchal stories."

14. Coats, *Genesis*, 166–71. It is not clear to me why Coats asserts that this story has a "complex plot" (170).

15. Von Rad, *Genesis*, 248. The only reason he gives for this designation is the length of the story.

16. Westermann, *Genesis 12–36*, 382.

The story contains the literary convention of meeting the wife-to-be at the well. Two other stories that have this motif are that of Jacob meeting Rachel at a well (29:1–14) and Moses meeting Zipporah at a well (Exod. 2:15–18). As James G. Williams notes, the same motif reappears, with a number of major differences, in John 4.[17] Still, each of these stories is distinct and unlike the other woman-at-a-well accounts in many points.[18] Thus, one should not allow the motif of the well to dominate exegesis.

A significant difference is that Jacob and Moses each met their respective wives at a well in person. In the case of Genesis 24, it is a servant, not Isaac himself, who meets Isaac's future wife at a well. The narrative gives the reason for this: Abraham is unwilling to allow his son to return to Mesopotamia. This is not to be interpreted as overprotectiveness on Abraham's part. To the contrary, he is determined not to allow his offspring to return to the security of the old country. He believes the promise that his offspring will inherit the land of Canaan (24:7). The servant, and not Abraham or Isaac or any other character, is the central figure in the narrative. The structure of the narrative is seen in figure 7.3.

The opening crisis is that Abraham knows that he does not have long to live and wants to secure a wife for Isaac before he dies. But this crisis for Abraham becomes a crisis for the servant when Abraham has him swear an oath to find her.

The circumstances confronting the servant are further developed when he asks if he might be allowed to take Isaac with him. His reasoning is that this may make the negotiating go a little more smoothly. For the reasons described, Abraham absolutely refuses. The servant now must face the task of finding the right woman without the woman or Isaac ever seeing each other prior to their engagement.

The servant is a devoted Yahwist. He responds to the crisis by voicing a decisive, specific prayer for a sign from God. He has cast the future of the offspring of Abraham into God's hands.

The result of the servant's prayer is described in great detail, and it includes the lengthy account of negotiations between the servant and Rebekah's family. Just as he had prayed, the girl of whom the servant asks a drink of water not only gives it but offers to give water to the camel as well. When he asks her identity, she is none other than the granddaughter of Nahor!

17. "The Beautiful and Barren: Conventions in Biblical Type-Scenes," *JSOT* 17 (1980): 114–15.

18. Cf. Kenneth T. Aitken, "The Wooing of Rebekah," *JSOT* 30 (1984): 10–14. Aitken also notes some parallels between Gen. 24 and the epic of Keret.

Figure 7.3

The Structure of a Second Negotiation Tale
(24:1–67)

Crisis setting	1–4	Abraham near death, Isaac unmarried, oath
Circumstances	5–9	Servant must not take Isaac back
Decisive action	10–14	Prays for a sign
Result of action	15–61	Sign given; negotiations successful
Aftermath	62–67	Isaac married

The prayer and its fulfillment are central to the story. In verse 26, the servant bows and worships Yahweh for the answer to his prayer. Laban then greets him as one "blessed of Yahweh" (v. 31). In the negotiations for Rebekah, the servant makes the miraculous answer to his prayer the crux of his case (vv. 42–47). Laban can hardly resist the obvious will of God (v. 50). Rebekah's mother and brother naturally desire to detain her for a few days before they lose her forever (v. 55), but the servant once again appeals to divine intervention as evidence that they should go at once (v. 56). She is willing, and they depart.

The aftermath is that when Rebekah and Isaac marry, she becomes a comfort to him, and he truly loves her (v. 67). The servant's prayer has as its outcome a marriage that is in all respects successful.[19]

The purpose of the tale, therefore, is not to give an example either of devotion to duty on the servant's part or of marital obedience on Rebekah's part, although both play a role in the tale. It is rather the account of the faithfulness of God to provide for Abraham, the one who had accepted alienation and loss of home and kindred for the sake of his God. God did this by answering the prayer of Abraham's servant.

---

19. It is impossible to follow Aitken in treating this theological perspective as the result of later redactional activity. Aitken argues that an original marriage story, meant to portray the bride's willing departure for her husband's home, was reworked to give the story a stronger theological impact. This conclusion is unusual, considering that Aitken states: "To bracket out the elements expressing or reflecting divine guidance would result in the destruction of narrative continuity and leave only an unintelligible residue" ("Rebekah," 17). Aitken suggests that the theological reflections were substituted for an earlier, more complete account of the negotiations with Laban. This is not only unlikely, it is contrary to the formal structure of the narrative, which makes the prayer of the servant the decisive moment of the story. The account is theological from beginning to end.

Figure 7.4

**The Structure of a Third Negotiation Tale
(34:1–31)**

Crisis setting	1–2	Dinah raped
Circumstances	3–12	Shechem loves Dinah; negotiations for marriage
Decisive action	13–17	Jacob's sons negotiate deceitfully
Result of action	18–29	Hamor and Shechem fall into trap; town slaughtered and plundered by Simeon and Levi
Aftermath	30–31	Jacob rebukes Simeon and Levi

Dinah and the Shechemites

Traditional source criticism, as illustrated by John Skinner's analysis, has assigned Genesis 34 to two distinct sources called simply "I" and "II" because neither source appears to belong exclusively to the J, E, or P schools.[20] Von Rad similarly speaks of the "extraordinary difficulty of literary analysis" but concludes that the two sources are a J document and parallel variant.[21] By contrast, Martin Kessler notes that "a careful analysis of the inner structure of the pericope" militates against division into two sources.[22]

The latter conclusion is borne out by the present study. Not only does the chapter follow the pattern of the negotiation tale, but also it has the closest biblical parallels to the negotiation segment in the legend of Aqhat. The structure of the narrative is seen in figure 7.4.

The text begins tragically with the rape of Dinah, the crisis that sets the whole narrative in motion. As in the case of the imminent death of Abraham in Genesis 23 and the death of Sarah in Genesis 24, however, this functions on a literary level primarily as the catalyst to the narrative. This is not a text about rape per se.

The developing circumstances then blunt the initial shock of Dinah's rape. Shechem, who committed the crime, is profoundly in love with her and wants to marry her. The negotiations that follow are not concerned with the matter of what penalty is to be extracted from Shechem but whether or not a marriage can be arranged. Wisely,

20. *Genesis,* 417–18. Cf. Westermann, *Genesis 12–36,* 535, who detects sources "A" and "B" here.

21. *Genesis,* 325.

22. "Genesis 34—An Interpretation," *RefR* 19 (1965): 3–8.

Jacob is willing to talk the matter through before seeking a particular course of action (v. 5).

But Jacob's sons are in no mood to discuss the matter rationally. Instead, they make the fateful decision to negotiate under false pretenses (v. 13). From that point on, the text moves steadily toward a violent outbreak. When they declare that all the men of the city must be circumcised before the marriage can occur, it can only be a trap.

Hamor and Hamor's son, Shechem, fall headlong into the snare set for them. Shechem's willingness to undergo circumcision to gain Dinah is a testimony to his love for her. At the same time, Hamor and Shechem are themselves to be seen negotiating in bad faith with their own citizens. Their promise, "[The Israelites'] cattle, property, and beasts will all be ours" (v. 23), if only the men will submit to circumcision, is more than they can deliver.

The result of the brothers' false negotiation is the slaughter of an entire community (vv. 15–29). Simeon and Levi are expressly declared to be the principal culprits. Any sympathy the reader may have had for the brothers' sense of outrage is completely obliterated by the full account of what they did: they not only slaughtered all the men but also plundered the community and took the women and children for themselves. In return for the rape of one girl, they take the wives of a whole community for themselves.

The aftermath of the incident, an aftermath unforeseen by Simeon and Levi, is Jacob's absolute censure of their act. He specifically points out that their deed has made his situation all the more precarious, but in the context of the story, the main point is not that he is now in greater danger but that Simeon and Levi are rejected by Jacob.

The text is well worth comparing to the legend of Aqhat. In both, wrongful negotiation is the antecedent to disaster. In Genesis 34, both the brothers and Hamor and Shechem are guilty of dishonesty in negotiation. In Aqhat, Anath is guilty of negotiating in bad faith, in that she offers what she cannot give (eternal life), and Aqhat is guilty of tactlessness and rudeness in negotiations. His behavior particularly contrasts with the attention Abraham gives to protocol in Genesis 23. Also, both Genesis 34 and Aqhat turn decisively when one party begins to plot a crime. In Aqhat, it is, "[Loud]ly Anath doth laugh, / While forging (a plot) in her heart".[23] In Genesis 34, it is when the brothers "answer deceitfully" and use the covenant sign as a cover for their crime (vv. 13–17). Both Aqhat and Genesis 34 culminate in a

23. *ANET*, 152.

carefully planned and executed murder. Finally, both deeds have repercussions beyond what the murderers could have imagined. In Aqhat, it is the drought that follows and the avenging work of Paghat. In Genesis 34, it is Jacob's rejection of Simeon and Levi.

Kessler has attempted to show that the intention of the narrative is to warn against intermarriage with the Canaanites.[24] While it is true that Hamor and Shechem are far from being guiltless in this story, that interpretation is not possible. Far too much is made of the enormity of the brothers' crime, and Shechem is, by the end of the story, made into a sympathetic character. Coats has some justification in calling this passage "The Rape of Shechem."[25]

In the context of Genesis, a developing story is that of which one of the twelve sons should have the right of the first-born. There should be no question about this; Reuben is clearly the first-born. But Reuben is never in his father's favor after he sleeps with Jacob's concubine (35:22), and everything he does subsequently only makes matters worse. After Reuben, the next in line are Simeon and Levi.

It is precisely here that the intention of Genesis 34 comes to light. The story tells us that Simeon and Levi have so offended their father by their crimes that nothing can erase their deeds. Judah Goldin, who has examined the issue of the right of the first-born among Jacob's sons in detail, correctly remarks that "on his deathbed he still could not forget their violence."[26]

Genesis 34 is therefore the permanent record of what was, to the Israelites, an unforgettable crime. It was preserved among the tribes as a permanent bar against Simeon or Levi becoming the leader in Israel. They above all others could not take the position of first-born.

---

24. "Genesis 34."

25. *Genesis,* 233.

26. "The Youngest Son or Where Does Genesis 38 Belong," *JBL* 96 (1977): 27–44; the quote is from p. 41.

8

The Gospel of Abraham

Abraham is appropriately called the father of many nations. The Ishmaelites, Edomites, Israelites, and the offspring by Keturah all come from him. Two other nations, Moab and Ammon, come from Lot, a nephew whose life history was closely intertwined with Abraham's. Unlike Jacob, Esau, or Ishmael, Abraham is not the ancestor of a single national group, and therefore no single, simple ancestor epic is possible for him as it is for Jacob (the epic of Jacob) or Ishmael (the epic of Hagar).

This is highly significant for the present source analysis of Genesis. It implies that, despite Abraham's obviously central position in the book, no ancestor epic is likely to exist for him. Instead, a great deal of the Abraham cycle is derived from the ancestor epic sources of Lot and Hagar rather than an "Abraham source." The wife-as-sister epic also contributes material to the Abraham cycle, and some information on the life of Abraham is from separate tales (e.g., Gen. 23, Gen. 24). In summary, a great deal of the story of Abraham, as it now appears in Genesis, is from sources other than what may be called the distinctive Abraham source.

We are left with the question of whether there was a body of material that primarily concerned Abraham himself, or whether what we know of him is simply a composite of material from other sources and narratives. This question can be answered only by examining the material that remains to Abraham after the other source material has been removed. If what remains is a broken, confused narrative with no real beginning or end, then either no separate Abraham source existed or the actual shape and content of that source is hopelessly lost. On the other hand, if a unified narrative arises from what is left, then it may be assumed that the Abraham source has been discovered.

The Structure of the Abraham Source

The latter is in fact the case. When the *toledoth* source material, the ancestor epics, the tales, and other extraneous pieces of material are removed from the Abraham cycle, what remains is a structurally and thematically unified piece in four sections. The texts are Genesis 12:1–9; 15:1–21; 17:1–27; and 22:1–19.

These four texts are arranged chiastically, with 12:1–9 (A) corresponding to 22:1–19 (A') and 15:1–21 (B) corresponding to 17:1–27 (B'). The structure of the whole is set out in figure 8.1. In the figure, individual units of texts A and B are numbered consecutively. Units of texts A' and B' are numbered according to their correspondence with units of A and B. Units in A' and B' that have no correspondent in A and B are marked with an *x*.

Each of the four sections of the narrative leads into the next. The promise that Abraham will have offspring (A) is followed by a picture of Abraham vexed by his childless state (B). A chapter in which he assumes a servant will be his heir (B) is followed by a chapter in which he assumes that Ishmael will be his heir (B'). The covenant signified in circumcision (B') is confirmed by an oath after the "sacrifice" of Isaac.[1]

General knowledge of many of the facts of Abraham's life is presupposed in the narrative (e.g., the birth of Ishmael by a woman other than Sarah). This only implies that the source circulated in a community that had general knowledge about Abraham through other sources. It does not mean that these four texts could not have existed together as a separate source.

The whole is held together by the chiastic structure in figure 8.1. First (A), Abram hears the command to leave his father's household and the promise of divine favor for himself and his offspring. He

---

1. T. Desmond Alexander, "Genesis 22 and the Covenant of Circumcision," *JSOT* 25 (1983): 17–22, demonstrates that Gen. 22:15–18 is built upon chap. 17.

Figure 8.1

The Structure of the Abraham Source
(12:1–9; 15:1–21; 17:1–27; 22:1–19)

A *Initiation of the Promise (12:1–9)*

	Content	Text
1	Command	1
2	Promise for offspring	2–3
3	Obedient departure	4–6
4	Promise of land	7a
5	Two altars	7b–8
6	Departure	9

B *Covenant Sacrifice (15:1–21)*

	Content	Text
1	Divine self-identification	1
2	Heir suggested	2–3
3	Suggestion rejected, son promised	4
4	Promise of many offspring	5
5	Abraham believes	6
6	Promise of land	7
7	Covenant sacrifice demanded	8–9
8	Covenant sacrifice performed	10–11
9	Abraham's terror	12
10	Prophecy concerning Israelites	13–16
11	Covenant ceremony ratified	17
12	Promise of foreign lands	18–21

B' *Covenant Circumcision (17:1–27)*

	Content	Text
1	Divine self-identification	1–2
5	Abram worships	3
x	Abram renamed	5
4	Promise of many offspring	4–7
6	Promise of land	8
7	Covenant circumcision demanded	9–14
x	Sarai renamed, son promised	15–16
9	Abraham's laughter	17
2	Heir suggested	18
3	Suggestion rejected, son promised	19
10	Prophecy concerning Ishmaelites	20
x	Promise reiterated, concluded	21–22
8	Covenant circumcision performed	23–26
2	Foreigners circumcised	27

A' *Vindication of the Promise (22:1–19)*

	Content	Text
1	Command	1–2
3	Obedient departure	3–5
5	Altar, "two" sacrifices	6–14
2, 4	Promise of land and offspring	15–18
6	Departure	19

obediently departs, is promised Canaan as his inheritance, builds two altars, and moves on as a sojourner.

Next (B), God calls upon Abram and identifies himself as Abram's "shield" and "reward." Abram is in a state of anxiety over his childlessness and laments that his inheritance must go to his servant. God corrects his wrong assumption—his servant will not be his heir—and promises him offspring more numerous than the stars. Abram believes God. Then he is told to make a sacrifice as a sign both of the certainty of the promise and of the covenant agreement between the two parties. Dread comes over Abram, and he learns that his offspring will be for four hundred years in an alien land. But God ratifies the covenant between himself and Abram and then promises Abram dominion over many nations.

Another story of covenant ceremony follows (B'). Once again, it begins with a divine self-identification ("I am El-shaddai") and a promise. Abram falls down and worships in response, just as he had earlier believed God. A new element enters the story—Abram is renamed Abraham. He again is promised many offspring and Canaan as his inheritance. God commands Abraham to undergo circumcision as a sign of covenant identification, just as he had previously required a sacrifice for the covenant ceremony. God then renames Sarai, as he had earlier renamed Abraham, and promises that she will be the mother of Abraham's offspring. Bewildered unbelief overtakes Abraham, and he laughs at this suggestion, just as he had earlier fallen into dread of the future. He then suggests Ishmael as an heir in the same way that he had earlier assumed that a servant would be his heir. God rejects the suggestion, just as he had corrected the earlier assumption, but he makes a promise concerning the Ishmaelites, which is analogous to the previous promise concerning the Israelites. The promise concerning Sarah is repeated, and Abraham carries out the circumcision. Finally, the foreigners in Abraham's household undergo the rite of circumcision as a proleptic fulfillment of the promise in the previous text of dominion over foreign lands.

The story ends with a profound vindication of the promise in a climactic test of Abraham (A'). Like the corresponding text (A), it begins with a bare command—there is no divine self-identification. And once again the text describes in the most stark terms how Abraham simply sets out in obedience to God. An irony is that A told how Abraham made two altars to God, but now Abraham builds a single altar but offers two sacrifices. The first is the happily aborted sacrifice of Isaac, and the second is the actual sacrifice of a ram. In response to

Abraham's obedience, God reaffirms the promise of many offspring and an inheritance. The ceremony complete, Abraham departs as he had done at the end of A.

The isolation of these four texts as a single source does not deny that links exist between it and texts outside these four. They have, after all, been redacted into the unified Book of Genesis. Nor does it imply that the tradents of this material were unaware of other aspects of the life of Abraham as described in the other texts. All that is indicated is that these four texts witness to a single source and that this source had a recognizable structure and message. It is to the message of the source, its intention and its genre, that we now turn.

Earlier Critical Analyses

The single Abraham source has no real analogy in the extrabiblical literature of the ancient world. In fact, it has no real counterpart anywhere else in the Old Testament. There are, to be sure, analogies to this material in the Old Testament. Perhaps the closest is the "oracle of salvation" found in the prophets, in which the nation is promised deliverance after judgment. This text is a four-episode historical account; it is not an oracle.

Earlier attempts to account for this material are not satisfactory. The Documentary Hypothesis treats it as collection of fragments and stories from sources J, E, and P. In this approach, Genesis 12:1–9 is a collection of J and P fragments, 15:1–21 is a composite of E and J material, 17:1–27 is a P narrative, and 22:1–19 is an E text with some J material. It beggars the imagination to suppose that three such disparate documents (J, E, and P) could have been redacted in such a way that the four separate texts that came from them would together display such structural unity. Indeed, the integrity of these four texts as representing a single source renders the documentary approach impossible.

More recent form-critical study of these four texts has also been unsatisfactory. George W. Coats, for example, correctly notes that there is some connection between 15:1–21 and 17:1–27, but he classifies both as dialogues.[2] Both texts include dialogue between Yahweh and Abraham, but neither are true dialogues in a formal sense (e.g.,

2. *Genesis: With an Introduction to Narrative Literature,* FOTL (Grand Rapids: Eerdmans, 1984), 122–27, 132–36.

the Platonic dialogues). It is also hard to see how the term *dialogue* carries any real meaning. It does not illuminate the intention or setting of the text. Claus Westermann, similarly, refers to chapters 15 and 17 as *promise narrative*.[3] It is again beyond question that these chapters include promises, but this term is not helpful as a formal designation.

In fact, the terms *dialogue* and *promise narrative* miss the crucial, central themes of the four passages—Abraham's need for an heir and the covenant between God and Abraham. The analysis of Genesis 22 by Coats is particularly weak on this point. He gives it the designation *legend* (i.e., a story of a heroic act), and it is meant to celebrate the importance of obedience.[4] Genesis 22 is for Coats a "story about Abraham's obedience, not Isaac's near sacrifice," and the use of the term *test* signals that Isaac "is not in any real danger."[5] To be sure, the obedience of Abraham is an important aspect of the story, but Coats's analysis obscures the enormous tension that is at the heart of the story. If Abraham obeys God and Isaac dies, the heir is lost. And if the heir is lost, the covenant itself becomes meaningless. The word *test* in verse 1 does not reduce this tension; one cannot know in advance if the test involves the actual slaying of Isaac.

The Gospel of Abraham

The Abraham source thus focuses above all on the covenant between Abraham and God and, as part of that covenant, the promise of a son and heir. In examining these themes in this context, I come to the inescapable conclusion that the source can only be called the Gospel of Abraham.

In designating this source a gospel, I am of course not implying that it is in all respects parallel to the four Gospels of the New Testament. It plainly has no parallels to many features of those books (for example, the teachings and miracles of Jesus). Nevertheless, the resemblance between the Abraham source and the New Testament gospel is striking.

3. *Genesis 12–36: A Commentary,* trans. John J. Scullion (Minneapolis: Augsburg/Fortress, 1985), 216, 254–55. He also calls 17 a "dialog" and an "appearance of God."

4. "Abraham's Sacrifice of Faith," *Interp* 27 (1973): 389–400.

5. Ibid., 392.

A Promise Founded on the Birth of a Son

The New Testament is dominated by the conviction that the promises of God can be fulfilled and salvation can come only through the birth of God's Son (John 1:14, 18; Rom. 8:3). All is predicated on this event. For this reason, joy permeates the text—the Son has come (Luke 2:28–32). This conviction reinforces the idea that until the Son came, there could be only waiting and hope.

In the Gospel of Abraham, similarly, the promises of God to Abraham all hinge upon the question of whether or not he will ever see a son born to him. It is not going too far to say that the promises are really of little value if he remains childless (Gen. 15:2).

The Miraculous Birth of the Son

The New Testament teaches that Jesus was born by miracle. Through an act of God, Mary became pregnant while yet a virgin. The Gospel of Abraham also takes great pains to show that Isaac's birth was a supernatural event. Sarah was not a virgin, but she had long passed the menopause and in fact had been barren all her life. Abraham's initial incredulity (Gen. 17:15–18) emphasizes this. Both the New Testament and Genesis show that the birth of the son was impossible without divine action.

Note that the Gospel of Abraham, as outlined here, does not describe the actual birth of Isaac (21:1–7; note the reference to laughter). Nor does it include the announcement to Sarah, which later has the same motif of incredulous laughter (18:10–11). In chapter 6, it was pointed out that 18:1–15 is formally part of the ancestor epic of Lot and that 21:1–7 is part of the epic of Hagar. But it was also noted that frequently several historical sources mention the same event. Therefore, it is possible that the Gospel of Abraham was much larger than what remains of the present text, and that it too contained reference to Isaac's birth. The matter of laughter in the narratives is a motif associated with the birth of Isaac (a pun on his name) but is not significant for formal analysis.

Even so, it is not essential to assume that the original Gospel of Abraham, to which the present text witnesses, explicitly mentioned either the annunciation to Sarah or Isaac's birth. All that one need assume is that the community that heard the account knew that Isaac was born. The miraculous nature of his conception is fully indicated in the present Gospel of Abraham.

A Covenant Sacrifice

The New Testament regards the crucifixion of Jesus, portrayed as a sacrificial act, as the initiation of the new covenant between God and the redeemed community. Jesus anticipated the sacrificial and covenant-making importance of his death in declaring the cup to be the "new covenant in my blood" (Luke 22:20). It was a singular act and was recognized by God himself in his tearing of the temple veil (Matt. 27:51).

In Genesis 15, Abraham makes a sacrifice to God at his command. Nevertheless, this was a sacrifice like no other, for the Angel of the Lord himself, in the form of a flaming torch, passed between the pieces of the sacrifice and, as the text reads, "That day the Lord made a covenant with Abram" (Gen. 15:18).

A Covenant Memorial

In the New Testament, the community reminds itself of its covenant bond to Christ every time it partakes of the cup and the bread. The communion ceremony is decreed by Christ as a ritual to be carried out in perpetuum as a function of covenant solidarity with Christ himself and other members of the community. In addition, baptism serves as a sign of admission to the community.

The sign of circumcision in Genesis 17 is also declared to be the "sign of the covenant" (v. 11). It is initiatory (like baptism) but also perpetual (like communion) in that the sign of circumcision never disappears. For the Israelites, it declared both their identity and their relationship to God.

Alienation of the Covenant Community

Genesis 12 opens with a command for Abraham to leave his homeland. This edict immediately establishes the covenant community as a group of aliens and sojourners. Their identity is not with their homeland but with the God who called them out of their homeland. The same theme is developed in the New Testament. The new community is not of this world; citizenship is of heaven. In this world believers have tribulation. They are content to be in any place but are nowhere at home.

A Promise of Trials for the Covenant Community

At the initiation of the covenant relationship, God predicts four hundred years of alienation and trial for the community (15:12–14). It is a dark, apocalyptic moment for Abraham but, as in apocalypse, punishment is predicted for the enemies of the community (v. 14).

The New Testament gospel is also replete with apocalyptic images. When the whole world is shaken, the disciples will then know that their redemption is drawing near (Luke 21:25–28). Persecutions, antichrists, upheavals, and martyrdom are all anticipated, but the beast that opposes the church will be destroyed.

An Eschatological Hope for the Covenant Community

It hardly need be said that the New Testament is founded on eschatological hope. The resurrection, the new heaven and earth, and the hope of eternal life permeate the text. But an eschatology is present in the Gospel of Abraham as well. It is not an eschatology of a resurrected world but the promise of the land and nationhood. Someday God would give the community greater Canaan as its inheritance, and its members would then be a great nation (Gen. 15:18–21; 22:15–18). This is the hope on which they leaned.

The Inexplicable Death of the Son

Nothing could seem more incongruous than that God would ask Abraham to sacrifice his son. Apart from the revulsion at such an idea and the natural affection of Abraham for the son whose coming was so long awaited, the son is the very heart of the covenant promise. If he dies, the covenant is empty and the promises meaningless. The highest paradox is that God himself demands the sacrifice.

For the followers of Jesus, the coming death of Jesus was equally enigmatic. Surely they did not await a Messiah so long just to see him die with his work unfulfilled (Matt. 16:22)! But in the hindsight of the New Testament texts, Jesus' death is realized to be not a disaster but an essential element of the messianic task. In the same way, the "sacrifice" of Isaac is realized to have been a test. But it was a test Abraham had to face. It was the climactic moment at which Abraham's position as the father of the people of faith was forever established.

The Resurrection of the Son

The New Testament celebrates the triumph of Christ in his resurrection. Death is conquered, and the eschatological hope has been secured. He is himself the first-fruits, and because he is risen the community members can be certain that they too will rise.

The Gospel of Abraham also contains something of a resurrection. To be sure, Isaac is not really killed; the dramatic intervention of God breaks the sentence of death that hangs over his head. That moment is the assurance that the offspring of Abraham will survive despite all the hardships they confront. It is also the earnest of a glorious future: "Since you have done this and have not held back your son, your only son, I will indeed bless you and make your offspring as countless as the stars in the sky" (Gen. 22:16–17). Because Isaac faced death and was delivered, the community knows that it too shall be delivered.

Intention and Setting

From this, the intention and setting of the Gospel of Abraham is clear. It is the evangel, the kerygma, in which Israel in Egypt placed its hopes. In this sense, it is very much a gospel. The covenant, the promises, and the sacred history together form a message of hope for a people awaiting deliverance.

The notion that a Genesis source could formally parallel a New Testament Gospel may seem prima facie absurd. What is implied here, however, is not literary dependence but a theological statement of hope, a gospel, in the context of the canon of Scripture. Such a possibility presupposes that after all has been said for extrabiblical parallels to individual texts in the Bible, the Bible itself remains more than just a collection of ancient genres and literary types. It is a single book, a canon of Scripture, and it has an internal theological dynamic that allows for internal theological parallels. These parallels may show themselves to be formally parallel as well, as is the case observed here.

It is clear, moreover, that the texts are meaningful only in a setting of Israel in Egypt. The prediction of four hundred years in Egypt can hardly have had value to the nation of Israel after the conquest or even to the community of the Babylonian exile, for whom this was ancient history. A gospel gives comfort and hope for the future, not curious *vaticinia ex eventu*. More than that, the promise of offspring as numerous as the stars are most significant to a people who have not yet achieved nationhood.

The work is thus an evangel and not an etiology. We may study the material with any number of historical or theological interests, but for them, it was the Gospel of Abraham.

9

The Migration Epic of Joseph

Much attention has been given in studies of Genesis to the question of the sources of Genesis 37–50. Most of this work has been done along the lines of the Documentary Hypothesis, although the Migration Epic of Joseph does not readily yield to traditional documentary analysis. The criterion of divine names fails completely—texts that ordinarily would be assigned to J often use *elohim*.[1] Documentary analyses are therefore inconsistent. They treat the narrative either as a mass of J, E, and P fragments[2] or as a JE redaction with P fragments.[3] Others try to separate E and J.[4]

New Theories for the Sources of the Joseph Narrative

Recent critics have tended to abandon the Documentary Hypothesis as a guide to the Joseph narrative. Donald B. Redford, for example, in

1. John Skinner, *A Critical and Exegetical Commentary on Genesis,* 2d ed., ICC (Edinburgh: T. and T. Clark, 1930), 438–39. *Yahweh* occurs only eleven times in Gen. 37–50: 38:7 (twice), 38:10, 49:18, and seven times in chap. 39.

2. Thus Skinner, *Genesis,* 438–540. Cf. S. R. Driver, *An Introduction to the Literature of the Old Testament* (1897; reprint, Gloucester, Mass.: Peter Smith, 1972), 17–19, and Robert H. Pfeiffer, *Introduction to the Old Testament* (New York: Harper and Brothers, 1941), 154–55, 169–70, 189.

3. Thus Gerhard von Rad, *Genesis,* trans. John H. Marks (Philadelphia: Westminster, 1961), 343. See also Georg Fohrer, *Introduction to the Old Testament,* trans. David E. Green (Nashville: Abingdon, 1968), 147, 153.

4. E. A. Speiser, *Genesis,* AB (New York: Doubleday, 1964), 287–360, assigns a large portion of Gen. 37:2b–48:22 to J, except that 40–42 are given primarily to E.

his major study, has concluded that the Joseph stories came about in four stages, all distinct from the documents of the Documentary Hypothesis.[5]

The first is an original story, in which (1) Reuben alone tries to save Joseph from the brothers, (2) Midianites chance upon Joseph in a pit and take him away as a slave, (3) Joseph is raised to power when he interprets Pharaoh's dream, and (4) the brothers come to Joseph to buy grain during the famine. In this version, Reuben, not Judah, makes the appeal for Benjamin's life.

A "Judah-expansion" was then added to the original story. This expansion either places Judah alongside Reuben or replaces Reuben altogether with Judah as the "good brother" of the story, and adds a few other details (e.g., the Ishmaelites).

As a third stage of the growth of the work, several other additions found their way into the story. Most significant is Genesis 39, the story of Potiphar's wife. Finally, the editor of Genesis redacted the whole into the present form and made some significant additions, including Genesis 38 and 49.

Because Redford has used the same methods as those employed by documentary critics, his conclusions are no more satisfactory than the Documentary Hypothesis. He must at times invent details to fill lacuna in his hypothetical sources (e.g., that in the original story Midianites chanced upon Joseph in the pit, and Reuben interceded for Benjamin's life before Joseph). Other aspects of the story, which appear to be integral to the narrative, are regarded by Redford as later additions (e.g., Gen. 39). More to the point, the arguments he sets forth in behalf of a source division between the "Reuben" and "Judah" texts are simply not persuasive, as has been pointed out by George W. Coats,[6] and his reconstructed sources do not have any discernible structure that corresponds to ancient Near Eastern patterns or forms.

5. *A Study of the Biblical Story of Joseph (Genesis 37–50)* (Leiden: Brill, 1970), 106–86. Redford uses the same criteria for detecting sources (onomasticon, plot details, style) as those used in the Documentary Hypothesis, but he rejects the theory as a working hypothesis for the Joseph narrative, calling it an "albatross," and undercuts many of its arguments, particularly as it relates to separating J from E (he allows for a P redaction).

6. Redford's arguments that Reuben originally stood as the good brother in the tale (*Story of Joseph,* 132–35) are particularly strained. Equally doubtful is the supposition that the doublet Jacob/Israel is significant for source-critical purposes. See Coats, *From Canaan to Egypt* (Washington, D.C.: Catholic Bible Association, 1976), 69–72.

Coats argues that the original kernel of the Joseph stories was Genesis 39–41, and suggests that these chapters be identified as a "political legend." He further states that they have the didactic function of demonstrating "to future administrators the proper procedure for using power." The *Sitz im Leben* of the political legend, he contends, is the royal court.

Coats suggests that the political legend of 39–41 was later incorporated into the larger Joseph narrative, which he classes as a novella. He does not explain how or why this occurred, but he does argue that although Joseph is the archetype of wisdom in 39–41, he is tactless and deceptive in the other chapters. This further implies that some source division is indicated.[7]

Coats's analysis is problematic. First, it is hard to see how 39–41 could serve as an example story for future administrators. The particular elements of the story (imprisonment on a false accusation of rape and promotion to high office through a phenomenal ability to interpret dreams) are too idiosyncratic to Joseph to serve as examples for the young bureaucrat-to-be.

In addition, the Joseph outside of 39–41 is not nearly as unwise as Coats argues. From the outset, Joseph's superior moral and administrative qualities are implied in his father's trust in him over his brothers (37:13). Also, Joseph's deception of his brothers in Egypt would have been regarded by the ancients as an act of wisdom, not unwisdom. It was a precautionary testing of his brothers to determine if their character had improved.[8] The text makes clear that it was not done out of spite (45:1–15).

Finally, Coats does not establish that either of the terms *political legend* or *novella* are legitimate genres of ancient literature. A great deal of wisdom literature from Egypt celebrates the work of the scribe and gives advice to future rulers, but there is nothing that can be classed as a "political legend" as Coats defines it for Genesis 39–41. The term *novella* for the Joseph narrative, a term preferred by many scholars, also should be jettisoned.[9]

7. Coats, "The Joseph Story and Ancient Wisdom: A Reappraisal," *CBQ* 35 (1973): 285–97. See also Coats, *From Canaan to Egypt,* 19–32, and *Genesis: With an Introduction to Narrative Literature,* FOTL (Grand Rapids: Eerdmans, 1984), 276–84.

8. See Robert E. Longacre, *Joseph: A Story of Divine Providence* (Winona Lake, Ind.: Eisenbrauns, 1989), 50–51.

9. See chap. 2.

Figure 9.1

The Structure of the Joseph Narrative
(37:3–50:21)

A	Hostility of brothers to Joseph	37:3–11
B	Apparent death of Joseph, Jacob mourns	37:12–35
C	Judah and Tamar	38:1–26
D	Unfair reversals	38:27–39:23
	Da Perez and Zerah	38:27–30
	Db Potiphar's wife and Joseph	39:1–23
E	Wisdom of Joseph	40:1–42:57
F	Movement to Egypt	42:1–46:7
	Fa Jacob sends brothers, brothers threatened, Jacob sends Benjamin on a second trip	42:1–43:34
	Fb Brothers tricked by Joseph, arrested by Egyptian subordinate, Joseph reveals self	44:1–45:28
	Fc Jacob moves to Rameses	46:1–7
G	Genealogy	46:8–27
F'	Settlement in Egypt	46:28–47:12
	F'a Jacob arrives in Egypt, but sends Judah ahead	46:28
	F'b Joseph welcomes Jacob, introduces him to Pharaoh	46:29–47:10
	F'c Jacob moves to Rameses	47:11–12
E'	Wisdom of Joseph	47:13–26
D'	Unfair reversals	48:1–22
	D'a Jacob favors Joseph	48:1–12
	D'b Ephraim and Manasseh	48:13–22
C'	Irony in blessing on Judah	49:8–12
B'	Death of Jacob, Joseph buries him	49:29–50:14
A'	Joseph reassures brothers	50:15–21

The Unity and Genre of the Joseph Narrative

The Joseph narrative contains a number of chiastic elements (see fig. 9.1). The account of Joseph's death (50:22–26) is outside the chiastic structure but appears to be part of the Joseph story and can be regarded as an epilogue. The text, as it stands, exhibits clear unity. This is not only because of the chiastic structure but because of the organic cohesion of the whole narrative.

Genesis 38 and 49

Few would agree that the text exhibits clear cohesion and unity. Many regard Genesis 38 in particular as an obvious interpolation, which has no relationship to its context.[10] Indeed, the strange tale of Judah and Tamar does appear to be quite alien to the movement of the Joseph narrative and something of an interruption. But it is not an alien intrusion. It is rather a digression (not an interpolation) meant to give background information, which is taken up later in the narrative.

An important subplot of Genesis 37–50 is the question of which of Jacob's sons will have the right of the first-born. After all, he did have twelve sons, and the issue of who is to be regarded as first among the twelve is of no small importance. This theme is analyzed in detail by Judah Goldin, and what follows here is to a great extent dependent upon his work.[11]

The obvious son to receive the right of the first-born is Reuben, the actual first-born, but Reuben does the unpardonable. In an effort to prove to his brothers that he will indeed rule them, he sleeps with Jacob's concubine Bilhah (35:22).[12] The plan backfires, as the text cryptically indicates: "but Israel heard about it." From that time forward, Jacob never favors him. This may be not only because of Reuben's detestable act, but also because Reuben is the son of Leah, the woman Jacob never wanted. Instead, Jacob gives every indication that he will bestow the right of the first-born on Jospeh (37:3), his first son by his beloved Rachel.

10. Thus von Rad, *Genesis,* 351: "Every attentive reader can see that the story of Judah and Tamar has no connection at all with the strictly organized Joseph story at whose beginning it is now inserted."

11. "The Youngest Son or Where Does Genesis 38 Belong," *JBL* 96 (1977): 27–44.

12. Sleeping with his father's concubine implies that he has supplanted his father. It was not an act of sexual passion. Cf. 2 Sam. 16:21–22 and 1 Kings 2:20–22, and see Goldin, "The Youngest Son," 37–38.

Having to submit to the very young Joseph is intolerable for all the brothers, but especially for Reuben, who is being displaced. Nevertheless, when the brothers finally vent their hatred on Joseph and plan to kill him (37:12–20), Reuben sees it as an opportunity to get back into his father's good graces. He will rescue Joseph and "take him back to his father" (22b). It is important to see, however, that this is not an act of goodness on Reuben's part (contrary to Redford) but a ploy to insure that he will become first among the brothers.[13]

The ploy fails. Judah persuades the brothers, in Reuben's absence, to sell Joseph to a band of Ishmaelite/Midianite[14] traders and thus robs Reuben of his chance to look heroic. It is not clear whether Judah detected Reuben's strategy and proposed the sale in order to thwart him (as Goldin argues),[15] or whether it was simply an act of mercy. Regardless, his words in verses 26–27 do imply feelings of guilt and mercy. If all he had wanted to do was ruin Reuben's plan, he could have rescued and restored Joseph to Jacob himself, or he could have killed Joseph outright.

Reuben's dismay at Joseph's disappearance is complete. When he cries out, "What will I do?" (37:30), the implication is that he has lost his opportunity to gain Jacob's favor. Thereafter, Reuben is a pitiful character. He reappears in 42:22, where he weakly casts an "I told you so" at his brothers. Then, in 42:37, he tries to persuade Jacob to allow the brothers to take Benjamin to Egypt on a second journey. His offer, that Jacob may kill his sons (Jacob's grandsons) if he does not return Benjamin safely, is outrageous. Goldin rightly comments that "only a man in desperation uses such language."[16] Jacob dismisses the appeal out of hand.

13. The rabbinic literature understood this to be the reason behind Reuben's apparent compassion. See Goldin, "The Youngest Son," 40.

14. The problem of whether the traders were Ishmaelite or Midianite is well known, and it has become a linchpin in the Documentary Hypothesis analyses. It must be pointed out that only a foolish editor would have left such an obvious inconsistency unless there is some meaning we do not perceive. The notion that "Ishmaelite" and "Midianite" represent two different sources but that the editor was unwilling to choose one name or the other in redaction will not hold. On any kind of documentary analysis of the text, the redactor did an enormous amount of selection and suppression of material. This may be no more than an early textual corruption, but K. A. Kitchen, *Ancient Orient and Old Testament* (Chicago: Inter-Varsity, 1966), 119–20, 123, contends that there is semantic overlap between the two terms.

15. "The Youngest Son," 42.

16. Ibid., 41.

Finally, Jacob rebukes Reuben from his deathbed in his "blessing." Reuben was indeed the first-born and should have inherited all the honor that went with it, but his impetuous power-grab in the detestable act of sleeping with his father's concubine could not be overlooked. Reuben is rejected (49:3–4).

Simeon and Levi are the next two brothers in line after Reuben, but they are already excluded (49:5–7) because of their actions in the affair of Genesis 34. Judah is the next in line.

The text gradually moves from a less favorable to a more favorable portrayal of Judah. His role in the selling of Joseph, if not above reproach, does at least show some sense of pity on his part (37:26–27). His two sons, Er and Onan,[17] are both so evil that Yahweh puts them to death (38:7–10), but Judah wrongly ascribes their deaths to Tamar and refuses her the right of raising up children by Judah's third son, Shelah. Yet after Judah himself impregnates Tamar, he admits that he and not she was at fault (38:26).

After this, Judah begins to emerge as the leader of the brothers. In 43:3–10, Jacob listens to Judah, after he had ignored Reuben, and allows the brothers to take Benjamin on the second journey. This is not all; Judah willingly risks his status as the one who would receive the right of the first-born in his pledge that he would bear his blame before Jacob all his life should harm befall Benjamin (43:9). After Joseph frames Benjamin, Judah pleads for Benjamin's release and offers himself as a substitute (44:16–34). Finally, when Jacob himself moves to Egypt, he trusts Judah with the task of going ahead to prepare the way (46:28). Judah has assumed the position of first-born.

What is the place of Genesis 38 in this story? The key is in the account of the birth of Tamar's twin sons, Perez and Zerah. In the story, Zerah put his hand out first and naturally would have been the first-born. A red thread was tied around his wrist. Yet to the surprise of all, his brother, Perez, was actually born before him and was thus first-born of the two.

This strange event is a sign of the divine election of Perez to that position. It follows the pattern of Isaac and Jacob, neither of whom

17. An important sideline is that the story of Onan also concerns the matter of the right of first-born. Onan's sin is not that he engaged in strange sex or practiced a primitive birth-control technique, but that he attempted to seize the right of first-born for himself. After the death of Er, Onan knew that the inheritance was his only if no "son" was born to Er. Although the child by Tamar would biologically be Onan's, the legal fiction that it would be Er's was of enormous significance. The inheritance would bypass Onan and be in Er's name (38:9).

were first-born but both of whom obtained that position by God's choice. This phenomenon, divine preference for the younger son, reappears repeatedly in the Bible, as in the election of David (1 Sam. 16:11–12).

The significance of the Perez-Zerah episode is implied by its parallel to the story of Jacob and Esau. In both cases, twins are involved and the one who is expected to gain the birthright, but loses it, is associated with the color red (Gen. 25:25; 38:30). Like his grandfather Jacob, Perez rushes ahead and supplants his brother.

The importance of Genesis 38 for the Joseph narrative, therefore, is that it contributes materially to the story of how Judah achieves the status of first-born. The strange births of Perez and Zerah, following the pattern of special favor on the younger son, is a sign that the miraculous history of the chosen line has now come to Judah alone among the twelve.

This is confirmed both in Jacob's blessing on the sons of Joseph (Gen. 48) and in his blessing on Judah (49:9–12). Out of his profound love for Joseph, Jacob desires to pass a special blessing on to him. He knows that this can be accomplished only if the pattern of divine favor going to the younger son is followed. Thus, he crosses his hands in the blessing and confers special favor on the younger Ephraim.

But when Jacob comes to his blessing on each of his twelve sons (Gen. 49), he cannot go against the sign of divine choice in the unusual births of Perez and Zerah. The true position of first-born is given to Judah. His brothers will praise Judah, they will bow to him, and the scepter will belong to him (49:8, 10). A special bounty is promised to Joseph (49:22–26), but the right of first-born is not. It is therefore indisputable that both Genesis 38 and 49 are integral to the story of Genesis 37–50. Without these two chapters, a major subplot of the Joseph narrative is left hanging.[18]

It was earlier remarked that the blessings on all the brothers except Judah (49:1–7, 13–28) have no counterparts in the first part of the chiasm. The reason for this is now apparent. Both Genesis 38 and 49:8–12 relate to the story of how Judah obtained the position of first-born. One would not expect parallels to Genesis 38 to appear in 49:1–7, 13–28.

18. For other indications of how Gen. 38 fits into its context, see Coats, *Genesis,* 273. Coats correctly notes that chronologically Gen. 38 could fit only where it is, and that it shares catchwords with the Joseph narrative. This seems to be a shift from his earlier study, *From Canaan to Egypt,* 18 n. 3, where he comments, "It is, of course, clear that Gen. 38 is not an intrinsic element in the Joseph story."

Other Possible Extraneous Material

The unity of Genesis 37–50 is evident elsewhere also. Besides Genesis 38 and 49, other episodes that could be taken as secondary are found to be integral to the story, albeit as subplots. Genesis 47:1–27, for example, would appear to be extraneous to the narrative because it involves the meeting between Pharaoh and Jacob and an account of Joseph's administrative success.[19]

Brian Alexander McKenzie has demonstrated that this chapter develops the theological theme (first encountered in Genesis 12:3a) of God blessing those who bless his elect. In particular, Jacob pronounces a blessing on Pharaoh, his host (47:10), and Joseph, through his capable management, greatly enriches Pharaoh (47:13–26). This theme is not isolated to this chapter; Genesis 39:3 had already noted that God prospered Potiphar for promoting Joseph to a high position in his house.[20] The narrative thus develops a second subplot, that of divine favor on those who favor the patriarchs.

Genesis 37–50 as a Migration Epic

If Genesis 37–50 is to be treated as a single unit, there remains the question of whether it has an identifiable genre. The answer to this question is found in the main story line of the narrative, the migration of Israel into Egypt.

Several travel narrations come from the ancient world. Among these, at least three distinct types are apparent. The first is the "voyage and return," in which the hero leaves on a voyage, encounters dangers, sees and hears strange things, and makes his way home. Examples of this type include the Egyptian Middle Kingdom "Tale of the Shipwrecked Sailor"[21] and the late Egyptian "Report of Wenamun."[22] A sub-genre of the voyage and return is the "quest," as in the quest for the plant of eternal life in the *Epic of Gilgamesh* and the heroic quests of Greek mythology. The voyage and return can be

---

19. See von Rad's perplexity over the source of vv. 13–26. He suggests that it may be "subsequently added growth," *Genesis,* 403.

20. Brian Alexander McKenzie, "Jacob's Blessing on Pharaoh: An Interpretation of Gen 46:31–47:26," *WTJ* 45 (1983): 386–90.

21. See Miriam Lichtheim, *Ancient Egyptian Literature,* 3 vols. (Berkeley: University of California Press, 1973), 1:211–15, for the text.

22. Ibid., 2:224–30.

mythical and fictitious, as are *Gilgamesh* and the "Tale of the Shipwrecked Sailor," or historical, as the "Report of Wenamun" apparently is.[23]

A second type is the "narrative of the voyage home." This is like the first except that it begins with the hero already far from home. He and his comrades must struggle against natural or supernatural obstacles to make their way back. Examples are the *Odyssey* of Homer and the *Anabasis* of Xenophon.[24] In the former, the obstacles facing the hero are for the most part mythical and supernatural. The latter is legitimate history.

A third category is what may be called a "migration epic." It tells the story of how a people came to be in the land where they find themselves. Although the story involves the migration of a group of people, a single heroic figure is at the center of the epic. The migration occurs because some calamity has forced the people out of their former home, and various dangers threaten the successful completion of the migration. Two examples are the Joseph narrative in Genesis and the *Aeneid* of Vergil.

The *Aeneid* is far removed from the Joseph narrative, but both accounts describe how a people came to be in their present environment (the Romans in Italy, the Israelites in Egypt). In other words, although no historical lines of influence or dependence can be drawn between the two works, they are related in that in one respect they belong to a common literary category.[25]

The two works actually share a number of features. In both, calamity initiates the migration. In the *Aeneid,* that calamity is the fall of Troy. In the Joseph narrative, it is both the selling of Joseph into slavery and later the worldwide famine. In both, threats to the successful migration are described. In the *Aeneid,* these are direct threats and temptations (e.g., Dido) to Aeneas and his followers. In the Joseph narrative, the threats are twofold. The first is the direct threats and temptations (e.g., Potiphar's wife) to Joseph himself. The audience knows that if Joseph is lost, any hope of a migration to Egypt dies with him. The second is the ironic threats to the brothers—ironic in that they are not real but contrived by Joseph to test them.

23. This is not to deny that "Wenamun" contains exaggeration. See the introduction in *ANET*, 25.

24. The *Anabasis* could also be classed as a report from a military expedition. Cf. the report of the expedition to Syria, the Lebanon, and the Mediterranean Sea by Tiglath-Pileser I, *ANET*, 274–75.

25. In many other respects they are of course quite different.

Curiously, in both works there are indications of what the future holds for the people of the story. Jupiter explicitly predicts a glorious future for Rome in the *Aeneid* (1.278–91) and Aeneas's father, Anchises, shows Aeneas a pageant of future Roman heroes (6.752–83). The Joseph narrative culminates in the blessings by Joseph's father, Jacob (Gen. 48–49), in which Judah receives the right of the first-born. Also, in both works, episodes in the hero's life forebode troubles to come, and both works end on rather bleak notes. The broken love affair between Aeneas and Dido (book 4) augurs the grim history of the Punic Wars, and the false accusation of Joseph by Potiphar's wife presages the unfair hostility the Israelites are to experience in Egypt. The *Aeneid,* in an indictment on the cruelty of Roman history, ends with Aeneas's brutal slaying of Turnus: *hoc dicens ferrum adverso sub pectore condit / fervidus. ast illi solvuntur frigore membra / vitaque cum gemitu fugit indignata sub umbras.*[26] The Migration Epic of Joseph, however, ends with a tomb in Egypt, a symbol of the entombed condition of the Israelite people.

Finally, both the *Aeneid* and the Migration Epic of Joseph have elaborate poetic structuring. The *Aeneid* can be read as two major halves (books 1–6 and 7–12) set in parallel,[27] while the Joseph narrative has the chiastic structure already described.

The genre itself is neither historical nor mythical and fictitious by definition. As in the other types of voyage narration, it can be either. The Migration Epic of Joseph cannot be dismissed as nonhistorical on literary grounds.

If anything, the Joseph narrative appears to be the historical counterpart to the mythical *Aeneid.* Not only is it utterly free of the mythological history presented in the *Aeneid,* but it lacks the *vaticinium ex eventu* found in Vergil's work. The prophecy of the rise of Rome in the latter is detailed and explicit (1.266ff.). The pageant of book 6 not only alludes to the Alban and Roman kings, as well as the heroes of the republic, but explicitly names or clearly refers to Romulus, Augustus, Caesar, Brutus, and Pompey.[28]

Nothing remotely like this appears in the blessings of Jacob. In fact, explicit predictions are few.[29] To the contrary, Jacob's blessings are at

26. *Aeneid* 12.950–52. From R. D. Williams, ed., *The Aeneid of Virgil* (Glasgow: St. Martins, 1973). The lines may be rendered, "Saying this with burning rage he plunged the sword direct beneath the breast. / But the limbs grow cold and slacken / as the offended spirit flees with groaning to the shades below."

27. See Williams, *The Aeneid,* xix–xx.

28. E.g., 6.792: *Augustus Caesar, divi genus, . . .*

29. Gen. 49:13 is one example of an explicit prediction.

times more retrospective than prospective[30] and cannot be read as *vaticinia ex eventu* from an Israel already settled in Canaan. Many of the blessings are no more than descriptions of the general characteristics of the sons of Jacob and by extension of their eponymous tribes, but they can hardly be called predictive.[31] Even where some kind of prediction is present, the language is often too general for these to be defined as *vaticinia ex eventu*. The blessing on Judah gives no indication of being a pro-Davidic polemic. It is simply a pronouncement that Judah has the right of first-born and contains no allusion to David.

Historical questions aside, it is evident that the travel account, be it a voyage and return, a narrative of the voyage home, or a migration epic, had a place in the types of ancient literature, and that the material about Joseph may be classed as a migration epic. This leads to the question of how the Migration Epic of Joseph functions as a story to convey its particular message to its original audience.

The central plot is that of how Israel came to be in Egypt.[32] The brothers sell Joseph to slave traders, and he in turn, after a series of mishaps, rises to a high government position in Egypt and prepares Egypt to face a coming famine. The brothers then have to deal with Joseph when they come to Egypt to buy grain, and he tests them to determine if their character has changed. Profoundly moved by a selfless speech by Judah, he reveals himself and invites all the family to migrate to Egypt. Jacob and Joseph are reunited, and before he dies, Jacob makes a final patriarchal pronouncement over all the sons. Then he, and Joseph after him, die.

But the epic also indicates that the Israelites are indeed aliens and that Egypt cannot be their permanent home. Jacob's refusal to be buried in Egypt and the solemn pledge to take Joseph's bones along when Israel finally leaves (50:24–25) serve to show that they are foreigners who can never assimilate into the population.

At the same time, the migration epic tells the Israelites that as long as they sojourn in Egypt, they have a right to be there. They are not refugees who furtively crept into Egypt. They were welcomed by Pharaoh himself and given a land grant (47:11), and their ancestors received the highest honors (41:41–43; 50:7–9). The Egyptians have no right to treat them as intruders. To the contrary, the subplot of

---

30. E.g., Gen. 49:5–7 on Simeon and Levi.

31. Cf. especially the blessings on Issachar, Dan, Asher, Naphtali, and Benjamin.

32. This is not to deny the importance of the theme of divine providence in the book, a theme described in Longacre, *Joseph*, 42–56.

God blessing those who bless his people means that Egypt would be far better off if she continued to treat Israel with hospitality and kindness.

Another subplot of the epic is the story of how Judah gained the right of first-born. Given the importance of this question in their culture, it was a story that had to be told.

Possible Sources behind the Migration Epic

The Migration Epic of Joseph is a lengthy and complex work. A question that must be considered is whether or not individual sources may be detected within the epic. It goes without saying that at some stage in its history sources for this material must have existed, but it is another matter to establish with confidence what those sources were. The unity of the migration epic is such that it is nearly impossible to dissect it.

If one wishes to remove from the ancestor epic material that is most likely to have once existed independently, the genealogy (46:8–27, a *toledoth* source) can be considered secondary. Other than that, Genesis 38–39 and the blessings (48–49), are possible candidates. One may also speculate that the accounts of Joseph's administrative wisdom (47:13–26) and of the deaths of Jacob and Joseph once existed as some kind of independent stories. All of this can be only speculation. Otherwise, the text is so closely bound together that further attempts to separate sources are meaningless. All one can really say is that at some stage sources for the epic must have existed.

Another subject of speculation is that of when the migration epic was edited into (more or less) its present form. Did the Mosaic redaction take over a fully formed migration epic and simply add it to the text of Urgenesis, or did Moses himself redact a mass of individual sources into the migration epic and then incorporate the whole into Urgenesis? It is impossible to say, but I prefer to believe that the migration epic existed in some recognizable form prior to the time of Moses, but that he did substantial re-editing and writing before including the whole history in the text of Urgenesis.

One significant item is that the migration epic makes up two parts of the larger structure of Genesis. It includes both the Joseph cycle (37:1–46:7) and the resolution (46:28–50:26).

The question of what stories of Genesis 37–50 once existed as separate sources can be answered only with guesswork. What is extraordinary is that Genesis 37–50 is a tightly woven unity and has so clear a purpose that it can be designated a migration epic. Even more extraordinary is how the entire work merges perfectly into the rest of Genesis to complete the ancestor epic structure of the whole book.

The Authorship
and Composition of Genesis

10

Genesis 1
and the Primeval History

The Structure of and Implications of the Primeval History

As described in chapter 5, the text of Genesis 1–11 is in the ancestor epic pattern found in the myth of Atrahasis as well as in several other texts of Genesis. It contains the full form of prologue, three major threats (with a double threat in the middle position), and a resolution. Like other ancestor epics, it tells how the ancestors of a given race were threatened with destruction but managed to survive, although the resolution ends on a somewhat bleak note. It fits the form-critical criteria both of displaying an identifiable form and intention and of having meaningful formal analogies both in the biblical text and in other ancient Near Eastern literature. For the reader's convenience, the structural outline of Genesis 1–11 is reproduced here (see fig. 10.1).

The mere fact that Genesis 1–11 has an identifiable form does not mean that it has no sources or came into existence as a single block. It does imply that any source-critical work that slashes across the structure of the text is prima facie unlikely. This brings us back to the Documentary Hypothesis. Following this method of analysis, Genesis 1–11 can be divided as shown in figure 10.2.

Figure 10.1

**The Structure of the Primeval History
(1:1–11:32)**

A	Creation	1:1–2:3
	Summary of work of God	
	Creation of man	
B	First threat	2:4–3:24
	Genealogy of heaven and earth	
	Adam and Eve	
C	Second threat	4:1–26
	Cain and Abel, genealogy	
	Lamech's taunt (in genealogy)	
D	Final threat	5:1–9:29
	Genealogy	
	Noah's flood, salvation in ark	
E	Resolution	10:1–11:32
	Genealogy	
	Tower of Babel and dispersion, genealogy,	
	Abram leaves Ur	

This figure is a modified version of one that appears in Isaac M. Kikiwada and Arthur Quinn, *Before Abraham Was: A Provocative Challenge to the Documentary Hypothesis* (Nashville: Abingdon, 1985), 47–48.

The inadequacy of the Documentary Hypothesis was demonstrated in chapter 1. At this point, I only want to observe the fundamental incompatibility of the Documentary Hypothesis with the formal structure of Genesis 1–11 as an ancestor epic. That incompatibility is seen most clearly in source P.

The ancestor epic is built upon a triadic pattern (the three threats). In J, the three threats (the fall, Cain and Abel, the flood) do appear, but only the flood appears in P. The importance of this is that if J had established the triadic pattern, it is difficult to see how P, written after J, would abandon it. The P writer must have been aware of J, and yet he had no interest in preserving the pattern by mentioning the stories of the fall and Cain's murder of Abel. And yet the redaction of J and P, done soon after P, returned to the triadic pattern. Others have also noted that P is a structural anomaly.[1] Indeed, it is hard to see how a

---

1. W. M. Clark, "The Flood and the Structure of Pre-patriarchal History," *ZAW* 83 (1971): 210, attempts to account for structure of P on the grounds that P is influenced by the King List tradition. But Clark himself admits that this proposal is problematic (186).

Figure 10.2
The Sources of Genesis 1–11:
The Documentary Hypothesis

J	E	D	P
			1:1–2:4a
2:46–3:24			
4:1–26			
			5:1–28
5:29			
			5:30–32
6:1–4			
6:5–8:22*			6:5–8:22*
			9:1–17
9:18–27			
			9:28–29
			10:1–7
10:8–19			
10:21			
			10:22–23
10:24–30			
			10:31–32
11:1–9			
			11:10–27
11:28–30			
			11:31–32

*Genesis 6:5–8:22 is regarded as a merging of J and P flood accounts.

This version of the Documentary Hypothesis analysis is given by E. A. Speiser, *Genesis*, AB (New York: Doubleday, 1964), 3–81. Similar analyses can be found in Georg Fohrer, *Introduction to the Old Testament*, trans. David E. Green (Nashville: Abingdon, 1968), 147–79; J. Alberto Soggin, *Introduction to the Old Testament*, OTL (Philadelphia: Westminster, 1976), 99ff.; S.R. Driver, *An Introduction to the Literature of the Old Testament* (1897; reprint, Gloucester, Mass.: Peter Smith, 1972), 11–15; Robert H. Pfeiffer, *Introduction to the Old Testament* (New York: Harper and Brothers, 1941), 142–88; Gerhard von Rad, *Genesis*, trans. John H. Marks (Philadelphia: Westminster, 1961), 43–158; and Claus Westermann, *Genesis 1–11*, trans. John J. Scullion (Minneapolis: Augsburg/Fortress, 1984), 18. A number of critics divide J into two separate sources, J^1 and J^2 (J^1 is often called L [lay] or N [nomadic]). Pfeiffer argues for a source S (Seir).

work as late as R^P would have any interest in seeking to preserve an ancient literary pattern found in Atrahasis.[2] In short, the Documentary Hypothesis cannot be incorporated into the present approach.

Possible Sources behind Genesis 1–11

Nevertheless, the question of what sources are behind Genesis 1–11 is still open. In examining this question, we must emphasize that the present texts of Genesis can only be regarded as *witnesses* to the sources and not necessarily as the sources themselves. We have no reason to assume that whole documents were simply incorporated into Genesis in the fashion the Documentary Hypothesis claims.

The simplest approach is to remove what may be identified as source witnesses one by one. The *toledoth* sources can be removed, which eliminates all of chapters 5 and 10 as well as 11:10–32 and small portions of chapters 6, 7, and 9.[3] This leaves the bulk of chapters 2–4 and 6–9, the creation (1:1–2:3), and the account of the tower of Babel (11:1–9).

Genesis 2:4–4:26 is a tightly interwoven text. Although two threats are described (the fall and Cain's act of murder), it reads as a single narration. At the very least, the two were joined at an early stage. Two lines of evidence support this.

First, W. M. Clark has demonstrated that the two texts contain the same formal structure.[4] Slightly modifying his analysis, one notices that both begin with a decree or judicial decision by Yahweh (2:16–17, Yahweh forbids eating from the tree of knowledge of good and evil; 4:4b–5a, Yahweh accepts Abel's sacrifice but rejects Cain's). An entrapment ensues. In 3:1–5, the snake deceives the woman, and in 4:7, sin lurks at the door waiting to capture Cain. The actual event of transgression follows (3:6, eating the fruit; 4:8, murder).

Yahweh then interrogates the guilty parties and they attempt to conceal, excuse, or deny their shame or guilt (3:7–13; 4:9–10). They are then accursed by God (3:14–19; 4:11–12) and respond to the curses laid upon them (3:20; 4:13–14). A significant difference is that

2. The latest recension of Atrahasis extant is the neo-Assyrian, but the legend itself is at least a millennium older. Only deliberate archaizing could account for R^P taking up its formal structure. Other biblical texts from the postexilic period do not exhibit archaizing tendencies.

3. The *toledoth* sources are 5:1–32; 6:9a–10; 7:6; 9:18–19; 28–29; 10:1–32; 11:10–26; 11:27–32.

4. "The Flood," 196–97.

Cain responds by protesting that his punishment is too severe, whereas Adam responds by naming his wife Eve. Yahweh then mitigates the effects of the curses (3:21, garments of animal skins; 4:15, the mark of Cain). Finally, both guilty parties are exiled (3:22–24; 4:16).

Notice that this formal pattern covers the story of the first threat (2:17–3:24) and the first part of the second threat (4:4b–16). The first threat is immediately followed by "Adam knew his wife" (4:1) and goes on to tell of the births of Cain and Abel. The first part of the second threat is followed by "Cain knew his wife" (4:17), and the genealogy down to Lamech, the second part of the second threat, is given. This is followed by, "And Adam knew his wife again" (4:25), and the story concludes.

Second, the whole text (2:4–4:26) is highly interdependent. For example, in 2:5, it is said that there was no man to work the ground; in 2:7 man is formed from the ground; in 2:15, he is given the task of keeping the garden; and in 3:17–19, man's work in the fields is cursed. In 4:2–5, the produce of the fields is rejected as an offering.

In 2:17, the eating of the tree of knowledge of good and evil is prohibited, and 3:6ff. tells of the eating of the fruit and its consequences. But 3:15 promises deliverance in the form of a man born of the woman. In 4:1, Eve declares that she has given birth to a manchild "with the help of the Lord"[5] apparently in hope that 3:15 is now being fulfilled.

As Alan J. Hauser points out, the verb *know* in 4:1 points back to 3:5–7. The conception and bearing in 4:1 recalls 3:16, and the name *Abel* (fleeting breath) contrasts with the "breath of life" in 2:7. Also, the "fruit" of 4:3 alludes to the fruit of the tree in 3:2–6.[6] Genesis 2:4–4:26 is thus a single unit and has the pattern seen in figure 10.3.

The flood account is also a single unit and cannot be dissected. It is structurally chiastic and formally a flood narrative in the same category as the flood narrative in Gilgamesh.[7] This leaves us with four potential sources of Genesis 1–11. These are Genesis 1:1–2:3; 2:4–4:26; 6:1–9:29 (minus *toledoth* material); and 11:1–9. Most significantly, 2:4–4:26 and

5. Perhaps more boldly, "I have gotten a man, even the Lord." See the discussion in Walter C. Kaiser, Jr., *Toward an Old Testament Theology* (Grand Rapids: Zondervan, 1978), 37.

6. Hauser, "Linguistic and Thematic Links between Genesis 4:1–16 and Genesis 2–3," *JETS* 23 (1980): 297–305. Hauser develops other parallels as well in more detail than I have described here.

7. See chap. 1.

Figure 10.3

The Structure of Genesis 2:4–4:26

A	Introduction to first threat	Creation = "births" of Adam and Eve	2:4–25
B	First threat	The fall = "death" (2:17)	3:1–24
A'	Introduction to second threat	Births of Cain and Abel	4:1–3
B'	Second threat, part 1	Murder of Abel	4:4–16
A''	Introduction to second threat, part 2	Genealogy to birth of Lamech	4:17–18
B''	Second threat, part 2	Murders by Lamech	4:19–24
A' ''	Introduction to concluding line	Birth of Seth and Enosh	4:25–26a
B' ''	Conclusion	People call on Yahweh	4:26b

6:1–9:29 contain the three major threats of the ancestor epic and may be regarded as the original core of Genesis 1–11.

From this, one may suggest a possible history of the sources. First, the sources behind 2:4–4:26 and 6:1–9:29 were joined to form the basic triadic core of the narrative. The original core of Genesis 1–11 may have looked something like figure 10.4 (*toledoth* material has been excluded; the *toledoth* heading, 2:4a, is treated as a later redaction, as described in chap. 4).

If this was the original core of the primeval history, it has exactly the same pattern, the full ancestor epic, as found in the present structure. This explains why 2:4–25 includes an extended introduction; this was the original introduction to the ancestor epic. It also explains the inclusion of the sad tale of 9:20–27. As noted earlier in this study, the ancestor epic generally ends on a semi-tragic note (e.g., the conclusion of Atrahasis, the tomb in Egypt as the conclusion to Genesis). In Genesis 9:20–27, an ancestor epic pattern concludes with one of the three ancestors of the renewed human race under yet another curse, and this functions formally as the resolution.

Genesis 11:1–9 probably once existed as an independent source and may be related to the history of the collapse of Sumerian civilization at the fall of the Third Dynasty of Ur.[8] It and the rest of the

8. Dale S. DeWitt, "The Historical Background of Genesis 11:1–9: Babel or Ur," *JETS* 22 (1979): 15–26. See my chap. 3.

Figure 10.4

The Structure of the Original Core of Genesis 1–11

Introduction	2:4–25
First threat	3:1–24
Second threat	4:1–26
Third threat	6:1–8, 9b, 11–22; 7:1–5, 7:7–9:17
Resolution	9:20–27

sources (1:1–2:3 and the *toledoth* material) were at some point added to the original ancestor epic core, which gave the primeval history its present shape. When the primeval history was redacted into the larger ancestor epic pattern, the enlarged text was given a new introduction (1:1–2:3) and resolution (10:1–11:32). The old introduction and resolution were incorporated into the first and third triadic threats and no longer served their original structural purposes. To signal this altered structure, the *toledoth* material was used to delineate the bounds of the new structure. Thus the primeval history came to have the structure described at the beginning of this chapter.

But who is responsible for this redaction of Genesis 1–11 and when might it have taken place? Genesis 1 is the key to the problem, and it implies that the present shape of Genesis 1–11 is due to Mosaic redaction.

Genesis 1 and the Mosaic Redaction

Documentary critics have long contended that 1:1–2:3 and 2:4ff. appear to be from different sources.[9] Conservatives, eager to rebut the Documentary Hypothesis, have resisted this.[10] This is a questionable position. It indeed appears that we do not have a simple, continuous narrative. This does not mean that the two texts are incompatible (contrary to the Documentary Hypothesis), nor is there any awkwardness in the juxtaposition of 1:1–2:3 and 2:4ff. As described in the

9. Such critics nonetheless strangely attach 2:4a to what precedes on the grounds that it appears to be a P text.

10. For an example of a defense of the unity of Gen. 1–2, see Gleason L. Archer, Jr., *A Survey of Old Testament Introduction* (Chicago: Moody, 1973), 127–28.

excursus that follows, the *unity* of Genesis 1–2 is remarkable. Nevertheless, the two texts appear to be from different sources. By insisting that the whole of Genesis 1–3 is a single narrative, opponents of the Documentary Hypothesis have only played into the hands of its advocates.

As outlined (fig. 10.3), 2:4–4:26 is an ancient source, which is at the core of the history. But the question of the source of 1:1–2:3 remains. The parallel structure of this passage (days 1–3 paralleled by days 4–6, with day 7 as an epilogue) is so well known that it hardly needs mentioning. Interesting as the parallelism is, however, it does not give the reader any clue regarding the origin of the text.

It is easy to imagine how ancient traditions and stories concerning the earliest human history could have been passed down. To be sure, these stories relate to events at the very limits of human history, but it is after all *human* history. It concerns events in the lives of people. But Genesis 1 does not. It is utterly outside the realm of human experience. Even the creation of man and woman is presented abstractly rather than as a matter of historical process (contrast Genesis 2).

In addition, Genesis 1 has no parallel anywhere in the ancient world outside the Bible. The creation myths from Egypt and Mesopotamia can hardly be set alongside Genesis 1 as parallel in any meaningful sense.[11] It must be regarded as an example of a genre unique to the Bible.

The most obvious formal aspect of Genesis 1:1–2:3 is its heptadic structure. More precisely, it has a 6 + 1 structure, the seventh day being set apart by the fact that on that day God rested. As a literary form, this structure reappears in only one other place. Remarkably, this place is the Book of Revelation in the New Testament.

These parallels are the three 6 + 1 heptads of Revelation 6:1–8:1; 8:2–11:19; and 16:1–21. In each of the three, the pattern is of six related events followed by a seventh, which is somehow significantly different. In 6:1–8:1, there are the seven seals, and the fury of the

---

11. See *ANET*, 3–10, 60–72, for examples of ancient creation myths. Incidental similarities to Genesis 1 are well known, but they do not make for true formal parallels, and the differences are far more profound. A useful discussion of similarities is by W. G. Lambert, "A New Look at the Babylonian Background of Genesis," *JTS* n.s. 16 (1965): 287–300. For a thorough and provocative challenge to the widely held assumption that a dragon/chaos myth is behind Gen. 1:2, see David Toshio Tsumura, *The Earth and the Waters in Genesis 1 and 2: A Linguistic Investigation*, JSOTSS 83 (Sheffield: JSOT Press, 1989).

first six is followed by the silence of the seventh. In 8:2–11:19, the judgments unleashed by the first six trumpets are followed by the doxology following the seventh. And in 16:1–21, the torments poured out of the first six bowls are followed by the cataclysm of the seventh.

Revelation is apocalyptic and visionary. Can there be any formal relationship between this and Genesis 1? The obvious parallel is in the 6 + 1 heptadic structure. Instead of seals, trumpets, or bowls, there are seven days. But there is more in parallel here than form alone. Both are alike in intention because both give the divine view of the outer limits of history. Revelation gives the heavenly view of human history with a view toward its *culmination*. In Genesis 1, the focus is the *initiation* of the world and its history. I suggest that Genesis 1:1–2:3 is visionary and revelatory and that Moses, the premier prophet of the Old Testament, is the direct author of this material.

The 6 + 1 pattern does appear in one other place, in Exodus 24:16ff., not as a literary form but as a reference to a historic event. In Exodus 24:16, we read of Moses being called up to the mountain of God. For six days the cloud covered the mountain, but on the seventh Moses went up the mountain into the cloud and remained for forty days. In addition, the text tells us that Moses was for a long time alone with God on Sinai. If we may draw all this together, while in God's presence Moses may have received direct visions and revelations, and one of these revelations was of creation in the 6 + 1 pattern already established at Sinai.

The seven days of Genesis 1, therefore, are neither the actual length of time of the creation event nor a mere anthropomorphism. They are the seven days of divine revelation to Moses. Genesis 1 may thus be regarded as revelatory, as in the formal structure of apocalyptic vision, and as having the intention of giving the divine view of the initiation of human history.[12]

What does this say for the redaction of Genesis 1–11? If Genesis 1:1–2:3 is directly from Moses, it implies that the whole ancestor epic pattern of Genesis 1–11 was not complete until he composed the prologue, 1:1–2:3. Also, if the *toledoth* sources were maintained as inde-

12. P. J. Wiseman suggested that Genesis 1 represents revelatory days in *Creation Revealed in Six Days* (1948), reprinted in his *Clues to Creation in Genesis*, ed. D. J. Wiseman (London: Marshall, Morgan and Scott, 1977), 109ff. His presentation was somewhat confused, however, and did not persuade many. The suggestion I pose, by contrast, is based on form-critical parallels.

pendent sources in the Egyptian sojourn, it is impossible to imagine that the material of Genesis 1–11 had anything like its present form until the whole was redacted. A possible solution, therefore, is that Moses took the triadic core sources, the story of Babel, the *toledoth* material, and the revelation of Genesis 1, and brought the whole together as the ancestor epic we now call the primeval history, Genesis 1–11.

Excursus: Jacques Doukhan's Analysis of Genesis 1–2

Jacques Doukhan has proposed that Genesis 1:1–2:25 is structurally unified and that it is made of two separate heptads, each having an introduction and a conclusion. He identifies the two major sections as C (1:1–2:4a) and C' (2:4b–25). The results of his analysis are outlined in figure 10.5. The division C' is not explicitly set forth as a heptad, but Doukhan argues that, in 2:4b–25, vav consecutive imperfect forms, which have *yhwh elohim* (the Lord God) as subject, delineate the seven divisions of C'. Thus, for example, C'1 (2:7) begins, "and the Lord God formed" (*wayyetser*), C'2 (2:8) begins "and the Lord God planted" (*wayitta'*), and C'3 (2:9) begins "and the Lord God caused to grow" (*wayyatsmach*). He also points out that the number of *yhwh elohim* phrases in C' (a total of nine) parallel the nine occurrences of the phrase *and God said* (*wayyomer elohim*) in division C. The parallel phrases occur one time each in sections 1, 2, 4, and 5, two times each in sections 3, and three times each in sections 6.

In addition, Doukhan observes, as many have, that days 1–3 of Genesis 1 parallel days 4–6. But he also argues that sections 1–3 and sections 4–6 of C' parallel each other. He asserts that the formation of man from dust in 2:7 parallels the concern with death in 2:17, that the garden for man in 2:8 parallels the companion for man in 2:18, and that the dominion of man over earth in 2:15 parallels the dominion of man over animals in 2:19.[13]

Doukhan's proposal must be evaluated on two levels. First is the question of whether or not, or the degree to which, his ideas can be regarded as valid, and second is the question of what implications they have for the source analysis of this material.

13. *The Genesis Creation Story* (Berrien Springs, Mich.: Andrews University Press, 1978); see especially pp. 35–80.

Figure 10.5

Doukhan's Analysis of the Structure of Genesis 1:1–2:25

C	C'
Introduction (1:1–2)	Introduction (2:4b–6)
1. Light/darkness (1:3–5)	1. Man/dust (2:7)
2. Firmament in heaven (1:6–8)	2. Garden on earth (2:8)
3. Water and land, plants (1:9–13)	3. Plants, water, and land (2:9–15)
4. Luminaries separate days and seasons (1:14–19)	4. Tree of knowledge of good and evil separated from other trees (2:16–17)
5. First creation of animal life (1:20–23)	5. First concern for a companion for man (2:18)
6. Concern for a companion for man continued (2:19–22)	6. Creation of animals and man continued (1:24-31)
7. Pattern (2:1–3):	7. Pattern (2:23–24):
a. end of process	a. end of process
b. divine involvement	b. divine involvement
c. separation of Sabbath	c. separation of couple from parents
d. blessing of Sabbath	d. unity of couple
Conclusion (2:4a)	Conclusion (2:25)

Jacques B. Doukhan, *The Genesis Creation Story* (Berrien Springs, Mich.: Andrews University Press, 1978), 35–80.

Certainly Doukhan's theory (of which only the most abbreviated outline is given here) has great merit. He has demonstrated a degree of unity in the structure and message in Genesis 1–2 never previously established. The parallels he has pointed out between the two introductions to C and C' are particularly strong.[14] In addition, the parallel he describes between the two sections 7 is striking, although it appears to me that one modification is needed. Nevertheless, thanks especially to Doukhan's work, any reading of Genesis 1–2 as two unrelated texts juxtaposed to one another is impossible.

At the same time, a few questions must be raised. First, it is quite artificial to set 2:4a alongside 2:25 as a parallel conclusion. The one (the generations of heaven and earth) has nothing to do with the other (the man and woman were naked).[15] I have already argued that

14. Ibid., 53–73.

15. Doukhan's arguments here (pp. 73–76) are not persuasive to me.

Genesis 2:4a should be regarded as the heading of 2:4b–25 (on the analogy of all the other uses of the formula in Genesis) and that 2:4a has been inserted into the text as a literary parallel to the other *toledoth* passages. As the heading or title to what follows, it serves the purpose of marking a new division in the ancestor epic pattern of Genesis 1–11. It does not conclude 1:1–2:3. In terms of Doukhan's analysis, it should be regarded as the heading of the new division (C'), with 2:4b–6 being the introduction. Also, 2:25 should not be treated as a separate conclusion to C'. Rather, it should be read with 2:24 as a description of the unity and even holiness of the relationship between the man and woman and as part of the parallel to 2:3. In short, the two sections' number 7 should be regarded as the conclusions to the two divisions, and 2:25 should be regarded as part of C'7.

Second, it is impossible to avoid noticing that while the heptad of 1:1–2:3 is both explicit (the seven days are numbered) and formally constructed, the heptad Doukhan sees in C' has few formal markers (only the uses of *yhwh elohim* [p. 194] which by themselves do not delineate a heptadic pattern) and is nothing if not highly subtle. One would expect the markers that set off parallels between two major divisions to be equally explicit, and it is odd that this is not the case. In addition, although the parallels between the events of days 1 and 4, days 2 and 5, and days 3 and 6 are conspicuous, those that Doukhan sees in the respective sections of C' are quite faint. This does not invalidate Doukhan's work, which appears to be fundamentally valid, but it does have implications regarding the composition of Genesis 1–2.

First, it appears that the heptad of Genesis 1:1–2:3 was composed prior to the heptadic structuring of Genesis 2:4ff. This is because it is more reasonable to assume that the explicit heptad of Genesis 1:1ff. formed the pattern for the subtle heptad of Genesis 2:4ff. than it is to suppose the opposite. Indeed, if it were not for the explicit heptad of Genesis 1:1ff. it would be impossible to discover any heptadic pattern in 2:4ff. That is, the heptadic structure of Doukhan's C' is totally dependent on parallels to C. The structure of 2:4ff. is a deliberate imitation of 1:1ff.

The second conclusion, paradoxically, is that the source material behind Genesis 2:4ff. existed prior to the composition of Genesis 1:1ff. The reason is that if the material behind 2:4ff. was composed at the same time or after Genesis 1:1ff. was already in existence, that is, if there were no prior sources to Genesis 2:4ff., one might reasonably suppose that Genesis 2:4ff. would be as explicit a heptad as Genesis

1:1ff. In other words, if the author had wanted to set up two parallel heptads, *and if his freedom of composition were not restricted by any prior source material for 2:4ff.*, the two heptads probably would display the same degree of explicitness. If, on the other hand, the sources behind Genesis 2:4ff. already existed, the author could not structure his material as an explicit heptad without artificially imposing explicit heptad markers (such as seven days) on that material. If he was unwilling to make such a dramatic addition to his sources, he would have to structure the material of 2:4ff. into an implicit heptad (i.e., without explicit markers) in imitation of 1:1ff. Genesis 2:4ff. is a rewrite of already extant source material in deliberate imitation of the heptadic structure of 1:1ff.

This conclusion has two further implications, both of which support my position. First, it further indicates that what we see in Genesis now is not so much the sources as the *witnesses* to the sources. That is, the sources were edited to support the structure and purpose of the whole book. Second, it indicates that this redaction was done by an individual who already possessed Genesis 1:1–2:3, whether that person was the author of Genesis 1:1ff. or someone later. I have indicated my reasons for thinking that Genesis 1:1–2:3 is in fact a direct revelation to Moses, and I see no reason to doubt that he not only wrote that text but also edited the sources behind Genesis 2:4ff. into the present form.

11

Tradents of the Sources and the Israelite Priesthood

Having examined the nature and development of the pre-Mosaic *tole-doth* and narrative sources, it is now necessary to turn to the matter of how these sources were preserved and transmitted prior to their redaction into the Book of Genesis. This concerns the period between the patriarchal age and the exodus, the sojourn in Egypt. Unfortunately, we know next to nothing about the Israel of that time. It is nevertheless necessary to ask who might have transmitted these sources and how they came to be in Moses' possession. The answer to this question, I am convinced, is tied to the problem of the Levites.

The Problem of the Levites: The Traditional View

The Levites and the Levitical laws pose a major problem in Pentateuchal studies. The traditional view is that originally the Levites were a secular tribe in Israel; but because they so distinguished themselves in the affair of the golden calf, they were given sacral responsibilities (Exod. 32:29; Deut. 10:8; 33:8–11). Aaron and his family received the priestly role, and the other Levitical clans were made assistants. All non-Aaronites were excluded from the priesthood on pain of death (Num. 3:10). The Levitical families then more or less continued in their roles until the end of the Old Testament period.

The basic difficulty with this traditional view is that the Old Testament does not use the term *Levite* in a uniform manner. Certain passages, those assigned by the documentary critics to P, clearly distinguish between the Aaronite priests and the Levites (Exod. 28:1, 43; Lev. 8; Num. 3:10; 18:2–7). The Aaronites had the official priestly duties in the cultus, whereas the other clans of Levi (the Gershonites, the Kohathites, and the Merarites) served as assistants in that they were responsible for the tent of meeting and the other sacred items (Num. 3–4).

Elsewhere, particularly in Deuteronomy and the Deuteronomic History, *all* Levites appear to have had a priestly function (Deut. 18:1–8; 21:5; 33:8–11). Of particular interest is the story of Micah, his Levite, and the Danites in Judges 17–18. Micah, in need of a priest for his household shrine, hires a passing Levite from Bethlehem to serve in that role. Later, a group of Danites kidnap that same Levite to serve as their priest. Nowhere is this Levite said to be an Aaronite,[1] but neither Micah nor the Danites appear to regard this to be an important issue. On the other hand, it appears to be critical to both Micah and the Danites that their priest be a Levite.[2] Similarly, the characteristic term for the priests in Deuteronomy is "the priests, the Levites" (17:9, 18; 18:1; 24:8; Josh. 3:3), which implies that all Levites were priests.

The Documentary Solutions

The Wellhausen School

Documentary critics have made the problem of the Levites a matter of major significance in the reconstruction of the history of the Israelite priesthood. Although the various documentary interpretations differ greatly in particular details, all of them have three ideas in common. First, as one would expect, all documentary reconstructions divide the Bible among the sources of the Documentary Hypothesis and do their historical research accordingly. Second, all documentary approaches assert that some kind of rivalry among the Israelite priestly

1. In 18:30 the Levite is called Jonathan, son of Gershom, son of Moses (MT: Manasseh).

2. Micah had installed his son as a priest (Judg. 17:5), but he immediately seized the opportunity of taking a Levite as his priest when one appeared. See especially Judg. 17:13: "And Micah said, 'Now I know that Yahweh will be good to me, for this Levite has become my priest.'"

families stands behind many of the biblical narratives that relate to the history of the priesthood. This dialectical historical criticism is assumed to be valid by documentary critics even where the text itself neither states nor implies that a conflict among rival priests is in the background. Third, all the documentary approaches consider the biblical portrayal of the history of the priesthood to be hopelessly confused and in need of radical revision.

In the classic Wellhausen reconstruction, the fundamental point is that D makes all Levites to be priests, whereas P makes only Aaronites priests and the non-Aaronic Levites their subordinates. Other important elements of the theory are worth noting.

Levites originally had a secular role, there being no specialized priestly family in early Israel. Indeed, the tribe of Levi had been a warrior tribe, and these characteristics eventually disappeared from the scene. The early priesthoods (e.g., Ahimelech at Nob and that of Eli at Shiloh) were mantic, not cultic.

With the establishment of an official cult during the monarchy, the need for a cultic priesthood was felt. Kings began to appoint priests. David gave predominance to the Zadokite priests (2 Sam. 8:17), a position they held until the exile. Jeroboam elevated the shrines of Dan and Bethel, but the priests of the royal sanctuaries, especially in the more stable Jerusalem, became entrenched in their positions.

The priests then began to be associated with the tribe of Levi in the monarchy. By the time of the Josianic reform, all priests were called Levites, but considerable tension existed between the Jerusalem priesthood, which claimed to be Aaronic, and the dispersed Levites of Judah.

Josiah, under the influence of the Jerusalem priests, brought the Levites in from all the towns of Judah to Jerusalem (cf. Deut. 12), where the Aaronites could more easily control the situation. Ezekiel demanded that priestly functions be limited to the Zadokites, with the wider clan of Levi being permanently demoted to a more menial level of service (Ezek. 44:10–31). With the transition to the postexilic community, the idealized portrait of the Aaronite priesthood with their Levitical subordinates emerged in P.[3]

This interpretation, in various forms, continues to be the majority opinion among documentary scholars, although many now assert that Aaronites or Levites began to assume priestly duties considerably earlier than Wellhausen allowed. Scholars supporting the antiquity of the

3. Julius Wellhausen, *Prolegomena to the History of Ancient Israel,* preface by W. Robertson Smith (Cleveland: Meridian, 1957), 121–51.

Israelite priesthood would include Aelred Cody, A. H. J. Gunneweg, and Menahem Haran.

Haran, for example, has argued that a genuine Levitical priesthood goes well into Israelite antiquity, as is indicated by JE, D, and P. The major difference among these sources is that JE asserts that any Levite can serve at any shrine of Yahweh, D asserts that any Levite can serve at the central shrine, and P asserts that only Aaronites can serve as priests at the central sanctuary.

Haran questions, however, whether a secular tribe of Levi ever existed after the time of Moses. He also argues that Zadok was a Levite, and that most of the southern Levites were Aaronites. For Haran, the fundamental conflict of the Israelite priesthood was between the northern Levites (whose theological position is stated in E, a great deal of which was absorbed by D) and the Aaronites (P). The E documents (e.g., Exod. 32), therefore, have a tendency to be critical of Aaron.[4]

The Josianic reform had the de facto result of elevating the Jerusalem priesthood, although that was not its primary purpose. Ezekiel, reacting to the idolatry among some Levitical priests, demanded the subordination of the non-Zadokite Levites to the Zadokites, but this program was not carried out in the postexilic community. Instead, all southern priests (Aaronites), be they Zadokite or not, served as priests of the second temple, whereas the descendants of the northern priests served as their subordinates, the "Levites" of P.[5]

Cody, on the other hand, argues that Levi did exist first as a secular tribe but that the Levitical priests were genuine Levites until the exile, when the meaning of the term *Levite* was altered.[6] He argues that the Zadokites, however, were not Levites (they may have been Jebusite),[7] and that a rivalry developed between the Zadokites and the Levites.

The Zadokite-Levite conflict came to a head during the exile. In a compromise, the Zadokites artificially became members of the tribe of Levi as "Aaronites" (thus preserving a "Levitical" priesthood), but most genuine Levites had to assume a subordinate position in the second temple (thus assuring Zadokite primacy).[8]

4. *Temples and Temple Service in Ancient Israel* (Oxford: Oxford University Press, 1978), 73–92.

5. Ibid., 99–111.

6. *A History of Old Testament Priesthood* (Rome: Pontifical Biblical Institute, 1969), 29–38, 52–60, 125–74.

7. Ibid., 89–93.

8. Ibid., 156–74.

Other modifications and alternate positions have also been proposed.[9] It is clear that major differences exist among these scholars, but it is equally clear each has some kind of Levite-Aaronite conflict at the center of this reconstruction. The hypothetical conflict, in fact, is the pivot of each of these histories of the priesthood. Before this issue of conflict is considered, however, it is necessary to note two alternative historical reconstructions that move further away from Wellhausen and have had considerable influence.

Frank M. Cross

Frank M. Cross modifies the Wellhausen proposal in *Canaanite Myth and Hebrew Epic*. He asserts that behind the biblical narrative is an ancient controversy between the Mosaic (Mushite) priesthood of Dan, Shiloh, and various Negev shrines on one side and the Aaronite priesthood of Bethel and Jerusalem on the other.[10] This is, to say the least, a radical reconstruction of the history of the priesthood.[11]

Cross builds his case for a Mushite priesthood in conflict with the Aaronites especially on the following texts: Exodus 32; Leviticus 10:1–7; Numbers 12; 16; 25:6–15; Deuteronomy 33:8; Judges 18:30; 1 Samuel 2:27.

With Wellhausen, Cross sees a reference to the Mushite priesthood in Deuteronomy 33:8cd: "You tested him at Massah; / you contended with him at the waters of the Meribah." Cross notes that the incident at Rephidim (Exod. 17:1–7) is meant here and says that Moses' commendation raises the esteem of the Mushite priesthood.

9. E.g., Timothy Polk, "The Levites in the Davidic-Solomonic Empire," *StBib* 9 (1979): 3–22. In support of his thesis that Levites helped establish the monarchy and that non-Levites loyal to God and king could be adopted into the Levitical guild, Polk argues that the Korahites were a clan of great military prowess in the late period of the judges and the early monarchy, and that some were originally Benjamites with southern-Edomite connections. He also argues that the Korahites defected from Saul to David, and that they also supported the Aaronite Zadok against the Mushite Abiathar. The Korahites were thus given important functions in the Davidic sanctuary system. Polk cites Num. 16 as "indirect evidence" for his position, but this chapter is a significant problem for him, since the text presents the Korahites in an abortive rebellion against the joint authority of Moses and Aaron.

10. *Canaanite Myth and Hebrew Epic* (Cambridge: Harvard University Press, 1973), 195–215.

11. Cf. Brevard S. Childs, *Old Testament Theology in a Canonical Context* (Philadelphia: Fortress, 1986), 147–48.

Is it not equally possible that the intent is to show Moses as a representative of all Levites, including (not in contrast to) the Aaronites?[12] This interpretation is rendered all the more likely when it is recalled that there was a second incident, at Kadesh[13] (Num. 20:1–13), at which both Moses *and Aaron* played significant roles (vv. 2, 6, 10) but *Moses* failed. The incident at Kadesh is implied, in fact, in the harsher language of Deuteronomy 33:8d: "Yahweh *contended* with him at Meribah."

The Danite shrine (Judg. 18:14–31) did apparently have a Mushite priesthood.[14] In the text, the shrine is shown to be illicit because it had no divine sanction and was idolatrous (18:30–31). Most significantly, however, the legitimacy of the priest of that shrine, Jonathan, is not challenged. It is the shrine, not the priesthood of the shrine, that the narrative opposes. This contrasts with the condemnation of Jeroboam's Bethel shrine, which is attacked for having a non-Levitical priesthood (1 Kings 12:31–32).[15] It is unlikely, therefore, that Judges 18 is an anti-Mushite polemic and evidence for a Mushite-Aaronite rivalry.

Like other documentary critics, Cross tends to see conflict among rival priestly groups where none exists. He asserts, for example, that the incident of Baal of Peor (Num. 25) was meant to show the zeal of the Aaronites (Phineas) in the face of an acquiescent Moses. Apart from any other considerations, it is a perverse reading of the text to assert that verse 6 (in which an Israelite takes a cult prostitute right under Moses' nose) implies that Moses was unwilling to oppose the cult prostitution indicated in the story. The purpose of verse 6 is to show the enormity of the affront by the man with the prostitute; it is not an indictment of Moses. And an anti-Mushite interpretation is utterly impossible if the documentary division of the text between JE (vv. 1–5) and P (vv. 6–18) is disallowed.[16] It is equally unwarranted to see conflict among rival priesthoods behind Leviticus 10 or Numbers 12.

12. Cf. Peter C. Craigie, *The Book of Deuteronomy*, NICOT (Grand Rapids: Eerdmans, 1976), 395–96.

13. The "Meribah" of Deut. 33:8d probably refers to Kadesh (see Num. 20:13).

14. Reading "Moses" in 18:30 with a few Septuagint manuscripts and the Vulgate against the Masoretic Text "Manasseh." Note also the suspended *nun* in the Leningrad text.

15. Cross's assertion that Bethel claimed an Aaronite priesthood (*Canaanite Myth*, 199) is groundless.

16. Even a documentary reading does not establish Cross's reading. Cf. Philip J. Budd, *Numbers*, WBC (Waco: Word, 1984), 278: "There is no indication here that exclusive rights to some kind of priesthood are being claimed, or that the high priesthood is at stake."

One text, Numbers 16, does speak of a rival priestly group attempting to seize the priesthood of the central sanctuary, but this text is embarrassing for Cross's thesis. Here, a group of Levites, the sons of Korah, attempts to seize the duties of the central sanctuary from *both Moses and Aaron,* while Moses defends Aaron's right to the high priesthood! It is impossible to reconcile this with a hypothetical Mushite-Aaronite rivalry, and Cross can only assert that the conflict "stands far in the background."[17] This is hardly satisfactory. Two other significant texts in this regard are Exodus 32 and 1 Samuel 2:27ff., which will be discussed later.

It is worth noting that the burden of Cross's argument is to explain how it was that, instead of just one high priest, two priests, Zadok and Abiathar, were over the cult in David's reign. David was forced into this compromise, Cross argues, by the rival claims of the Mushites (Abiathar) and the Aaronites (Zadok). In fact, however, the text is fairly clear that Abiathar was the high priest in the reign of David, and that Solomon removed Abiathar for having supported Adonijah and installed Zadok in his place (1 Kings 2:26–27, 35). There was no dual high priesthood.

The real problem is the place of Ahimelech in 2 Samuel 8:17 and 1 Chronicles 24:3, 6, 21, where he, not Abiathar, is said to have served alongside Zadok.[18] The problem in 2 Samuel 8:17 could be resolved text-critically, as many have suggested, and Ahimelech and Abiathar could be transposed to read "Zadok son of Ahitub and Abiathar son of Ahimelech were priests."

The references in Chronicles to Ahimelech as Zadok's colleague are a problem too, unless it is assumed that the transposition took place early and the Chronicler followed the error.[19] This, however, is unsatisfactory; the Chronicler could not have been ignorant of the place of Abiathar in David's reign in the face of all that Samuel-Kings had to say about him.

The solution, as is often suggested, is that the Ahimelech of the Chronicler and 2 Samuel 8:17 was a son of Abiathar and grandson of Ahimelech the priest of Nob. The younger Ahimelech was apparently equal to Zadok in rank and with him oversaw the reorganization of the priesthood under David (1 Chron. 24). Zadok succeeded Abiathar

17. *Canaanite Myth,* 205.

18. Also see 1 Chron. 18:16, where Ahimelech should be read instead of Abimelech. Cf. NIV, RSV.

19. Thus E. W. Curtis and A. A. Madsen, *The Books of Chronicles,* ICC (Edinburgh: T. and T. Clark, 1910), 269–70.

to the high priesthood instead of Abiathar's son Ahimelech, however, because of the direct action of Solomon.

The Chronicler's understanding of the Solomonic temple as a type of the theocratic kingdom and his handling of the canonical literature are also critical. Abiathar is given little notice in Chronicles apparently because of the curse on the line of Eli in 1 Samuel 2 and because of Abiathar's support of Adonijah in 1 Kings 1–2. Despite the positive aspects of Abiathar's character, these two problems function canonically to disqualify him from being the priest of the ideal theocratic worship.

In addition, Chronicles deliberately sets up the relationship between Zadok and Ahimelech son of Abiathar in a way analogous to the nature of the priesthood after the death of Aaron. In Numbers 20:22–29, Eleazar was consecrated to be chief priest at Aaron's death. His brother Ithamar, however, continued to serve as a priest of the tent alongside him, according to 1 Chronicles 24:2. The full text of 1 Chronicles 24:2–3 is worth quoting: "But Nadab and Abihu died before their father did and had no sons. Eleazar and Ithamar then served as priests. David, along with Zadok, a descendant of Eleazar, and Ahimelech, a descendant of Ithamar, organized them into divisions for their order of service." The text then describes how the priestly divisions of Eleazar and Ithamar were given their assignments. The text implies, however, a primacy of position of Zadok over Ahimelech, just as Eleazar had primacy over Ithamar.[20]

The relationship of Zadok to Ahimelech was not that of Aaronite to Mushite but of descendant of Eleazar to descendant of Ithamar. The modus operandi the two had was comparable to that which their ancestors had. Chronicles thus looks back to the Davidic-Solomonic worship and beyond that to the Pentateuch as a type for the theocratic ideal.

Yehezkel Kaufmann

The renowned scholar Yehezkel Kaufmann used the documentary sources to formulate a history of the priesthood that was in many ways

---

20. It is not necessary to assume that the Ahitub, father of Zadok (2 Sam. 8:17), and Ahitub, grandfather of Abiathar (1 Sam. 22:20), were one and the same, and thereby regard the Chronicler's tracing of the line of Ahimelech to Ithamar as invalid, as does Jacob M. Myers, *1 Chronicles*, AB (New York: Doubleday, 1965), 164–65. Cf. Cross, *Canaanite Myth*, 214. Apparently the descendants of Aaron used a select number of names, including Phineas, Ahimelech, and Ahitub.

very unlike the classic Wellhausen position. Kaufmann was most concerned to establish an early date for P over against the postexilic date of the Graf-Wellhausen school. He argues that the fundamental conflict of the history of the priesthood was between the (non-Levitical) Aaronites and the Levites, the latter being under the leadership of the Zadokites. He considers this conflict to be very old, and separates it entirely from subsequent developments under Ezekiel and Ezra.[21] The passage 1 Samuel 2:27–36, to be discussed later, is a pivotal text in his theory also.

The Conservative Response

Conservatives have responded to the documentary-critical theories in a number of ways. They properly point out that Deuteronomy never implies that a central sanctuary should be installed in Jerusalem—if anything, it gives special attention to Mount Ebal (Deut. 27:1–8). Also, Gleason L. Archer, Jr., notes that much of P is ill-suited to a postexilic *Sitz im Leben*. In particular, it lacks any reference to the musical and scribal guilds that were of great importance in the postexilic temple.[22]

More importantly, however, the critical reconstruction is not really any more convincing or satisfying than the traditional view. Critical scholars have not been able to explain with any degree of unanimity when and why the Levites became the priestly tribe. The critical reconstruction is in fact more a statement of the problem than a solution to it. The Israelite priesthood, in the documentary model, is in terrible flux as it moves both toward and away from greater centralization almost at the same time. On the one hand, the specialized, family priesthood (Eli, Zadok) is an early phenomenon and antedates the more general association of the priesthood with the Levites.[23] On the other hand, a general (i.e., not necessarily Aaronic) Levitical priesthood exists through much of the monarchy until it is concentrated in Jerusalem in the priesthood of Zadok. The Aaronite-Zadokite priesthood cannot stand at both the head and the tail of the historical

---

21. Yehezkel Kaufmann, *The Religion of Israel, from Its Beginnings to the Babylonian Exile*, trans. Moshe Greenberg (reprint; New York: Schocken, 1972), 193–200.

22. Gleason L. Archer, Jr., *A Survey of Old Testament Introduction* (Chicago: Moody, 1974), 163.

23. A significant number of documentary critics accept the Aaronic (or at least Levitical) claims of the Elides or Zadokites (or both) as valid. See Cross, *Canaanite Myth*, 209–14; Cody, *History*, 70; Polk, "Levites," 19 n. 7; Haran, *Temples*, 76–78.

process. That is, it cannot be the precursor of the broader association of the priesthood with the Levites and also be the result of it.[24]

The widespread and early association of the priesthood with the Levites, a fact acknowledged by Wellhausen,[25] is also a major problem for the documentary theories. No persuasive explanation of this phenomenon has come forth. Similarly, according to the documentary reconstruction, the Deuteronomistic reform of Josiah establishes the exclusive privileges of the Jerusalemite priesthood, but it is Deuteronomy that most plainly asserts that all Levites are priests. The significance of this problem for the documentary reconstructions, in fact, has not been adequately addressed. If the Aaronic priests of Jerusalem were behind the production of D in the Josianic reform, why did they not suppress the pro-Levite material? If northern Levites were behind D, why did they support the reform directed against them and their theology?

This confused historical reconstruction tells us only what is very clear from the texts themselves: The Old Testament does not use the term *Levite* in a consistent way. The problem cannot be considered resolved, therefore, until the diverse and apparently contradictory meanings attached to the term *Levite* are explained in a way that is not dependent on historical anomalies.

A New Proposal

An alternative to both the critical and the traditional models exists, however, and it may be the key to the problem of the transmission and preservation of the Genesis source material during the Egyptian sojourn. This solution is as follows: The function of the Levites as scribes, teachers, and quasi-priests actually antedated the exodus and began in Egypt. During this time, for reasons unknown, members of the Levitical tribe began to take on the role of preserving the patriarchal traditions and teaching them to the community at large. Around

24. Wellhausen, *Prolegomena*, 148–51, makes a great deal of the supposed monarchical nature of the postexilic high priest as opposed to the preexilic high priest. This is, however, a distortion. Although the high priest was significant in the early postexilic, there being no king, he did not eclipse the secular ruler (cf. Zech. 3–4) until the intertestamental period. But even Eli was a man of considerable respect and power, as Wellhausen acknowledges (*Prolegomena*, 129), and he was clearly the high priest of the central shrine, since he possessed the ark.

25. Ibid., 146.

the same time, rudimentary priestly duties began to be assigned to them as well. By the time of the exodus, these roles were firmly established as Levitical—not by law but by tradition.

The position of a scribe among Egyptians was already an honored one long before Israel entered Egypt. The *Satire on the Trades,* a work describing the superiority of the scribal profession to all others, probably dates from the Middle Kingdom or earlier.[26] The need for trained scribes only increased with the growth of the empire, for with empire came the accompanying bureaucracy. Egyptian students would practice writing with word-lists, miscellaneous business letters, and instructional literature. One favorite work for practice from the time of Ramses II was the satirical letter of the scribe Hori to his colleague Amenemope.[27]

From the three major flowerings of ancient Egyptian culture—the Old, Middle, and New Kingdoms—comes a significant amount of literature. This includes hymns and religious texts, instructional material, tales, poems, and songs. For Israel in Egypt, the impetus to develop a scribal class of its own would have been strong. One may hypothesize that Israelite social structure, specifically its emphasis on the tribe as the fundamental component of organization, might have predisposed it to develop a clerical tradition in a single tribe rather than "democratically" spreading out this function within all the tribes. We might note also that high-priestly "dynasties" were not unknown in Egypt; the temple to Osiris at Abydos was governed by a succession of six high priests from a single family during the Ramasside period.[28]

The faithfulness of the Levites to Moses during the incident of the golden calf provided the impetus only for the installation of the Levites as stewards of the tent and its furnishings. The instructions on Sinai, in fact, did not concern the idea of the priesthood generally but only the function and maintenance of the central shrine of the tent. Especially during the wilderness wanderings, when the entire nation was concentrated in a small area and all worshiped at the tent of meeting, no need existed for a dispersed priesthood in the towns and villages of Israel. As such, all Levites ministered at the tent.

26. *ANET,* 432.

27. For a good picture of scribal student life, see K. A. Kitchen, *Pharaoh Triumphant: The Life and Times of Ramesses II* (Warminster, England: Aris and Phillips, 1982), 142–45. See also T. G. H. James, *An Introduction to Ancient Egypt* (New York: Harper and Row, 1979), 96.

28. Kitchen, *Pharaoh Triumphant,* 170.

Insomuch as the central shrine was of special significance, however, a special branch of Levi (the Aaronites) was given the task of performing the priestly duties, and no one else, not even a Levite, could officiate there. The unique importance of this shrine, a uniqueness founded on its possession of the ark of the covenant, was to be perpetuated throughout Israel's history, as was the Aaronite priesthood.

The generalized status of all Levites as local scribes and preservers of the Israelite traditions was not forbidden or terminated at Sinai. To the contrary, with the arrival of Israel in the land of Canaan, it was naturally understood that the Levites would disperse into the land and resume this role. Since the central shrine would no longer be continually moving, the need for a large staff of Levites to maintain and transport the tent and its furnishings would disappear.

After the conquest of Canaan, therefore, most of the Kohathites, Gerarites, and Merarites would naturally scatter throughout the land and take up their priestly responsibilities. No special legislation conferring this authority on them would be necessary since, in the memories of the people, that is what the Levites had always done.

In the Old Testament, two different concepts of the priesthood and the Levites existed contemporaneously and without conflict in the minds of the people. On the one hand, according to the Sinai legislation, only the specialized priesthood of the central sanctuary could serve there. Granted to the Aaronites, this function belonged for a time to the house of Eli, and later to that of Zadok. On the other hand, all Levites had a priestly role in the towns and villages of Israel.

The reforms of Josiah (and the shrinking of the state of Judah) later concentrated all Levites in the environs of Jerusalem, and with the passing of time, the "general" Levitical priesthood disappeared. During the exile and return, certainly, the general function of all Levites as local priests ceased entirely. The Danite sanctuary and the Bethel priesthood, however, were illegitimate from the beginning and were never recognized as valid by the Deuteronomic historian.

What evidence supports this theory? In no place does the Pentateuch explicitly assert that the Levites had a scribal role in the Egyptian sojourn. On the other hand, the Old Testament tells us almost nothing at all about this period. No reason exists for supposing that if the Levites did have a scribal role in Egypt, this particular bit of information should have been explicitly stated. Nevertheless, it is clear for a number of reasons that Levi held a special position among the Israelite tribes in Egypt prior to the exodus.

The Legislation at Sinai

Contrary to the common understanding, Levi was not given priestly privileges at the incident of the golden calf. The important passages are Exodus 32:29; Deuteronomy 10:8; 33:8–11; and Exodus 24:5.

Exodus 32:29

Exodus 32:29 reads, "You have been consecrated to Yahweh today, for each man was against his own sons and brothers, so that Yahweh has given you today his blessing." Moses says that the Levites were consecrated (literally, "your hands have been filled") and blessed because they did not refrain from killing their own family members who had fallen into idolatry. The filling of the hands can refer to the consecration of an individual to the priesthood of a particular shrine (cf. Exod. 29:9; Judg. 17:5; 1 Kings 13:33), but it can also refer to an individual's consecration to some other sacred (but not necessarily priestly) sanctuary duty, as in 1 Chronicles 29:5 and 2 Chronicles 29:31.

The consecration mentioned refers to the supportive role the Levites had at the tent of meeting. Their duties are described in detail in Numbers 4: They were to protect, transport, and maintain the holy utensils, the tent, and the ark. But Exodus 32 does not address the questions of whether the Levites already had served in a clerical position prior to this incident or of whether they had any sacred duties when away from the central sanctuary.

Also, the consecration, the "filling of the hands," does not imply that prior to that moment the individual concerned was simply a layman; the consecration is not to the office of priest (as is Christian ordination) but is to a specific function at a specific location. That is, one who is already of some kind of clerical class is "consecrated" to serve at a specific shrine (Judg. 17:12).[29]

Since "to fill the hands" does not mean "to ordain,"[30] it is impossible to maintain that Exodus 32:29 in any sense describes the "ordination" of the Levites. At any rate, it would be strange if so momentous an event as the transformation of Levi from laity to priesthood were given such a brief and elliptical notice in the literature. Exodus 32:29

29. Exod. 29 describes the consecration of Aaron to serve as high priest of the central shrine. However, this is not exceptional because Aaron was a priest before he was consecrated to serve at the tent of meeting.

30. See Roland de Vaux, *Ancient Israel,* 2 vols. (New York: McGraw-Hill, 1965), 2:346–47.

neither asserts that the general priestly privileges of Levi began here, nor does it refute the possibility that they had some kind of clerical duties prior to this time. It simply alludes proleptically to the supportive function they were to have at the central sanctuary.[31]

DEUTERONOMY 10:8

The function of Deuteronomy 10:8 in context is especially problematic. The verse reads, "At that time Yahweh separated the tribe of Levi to carry the ark of the covenant of Yahweh, to stand before Yahweh to minister, and to pronounce blessing in his name, as is still done today." As it stands, the verse not only does not associate the incident of the golden calf with the consecration of the Levites, it explicitly separates the two events and asserts that the consecration of the Levites to their sanctuary duties came much later than the worship of the golden calf. Indeed, as it now reads, the verse indicates that the Levites were consecrated to minister at the tent *after* the death of Aaron (v. 6)![32] This would appear to contradict previous indications (in Numbers) that Levites were maintaining the tent during the lifetime of Aaron.

At least two solutions, however, are possible. Deuteronomy 10:8 could refer to a second consecration of the Levites, of which we have no other record except for the record of the consecration of Eleazar (Num. 20:22–29). But this is an artificial, harmonizing solution and is not to be preferred.

A second solution is that Deuteronomy 10:6–9 represents a two-stage redactional addition to the text. The first redactional entry, verses 6–7, describes the movements of Israel after the episode at Kadesh-Barnea, Deuteronomy 9:23–29. The second entry, 10:8–9, is an explanatory note appended to the narrative of the golden calf, 9:7–21 and 10:1–5. This is the best solution, and it indeed asserts that a consecration of the Levites to their duties at the tent occurred some time after the sin of the golden calf. This is not a disputed or problematic point, however, since the Exodus narrative also explicitly indi-

31. The tendency of some to refer to the Levites of the tent of meeting as "hierodules" is misleading. The word *hierodule,* literally "temple-slave," is more appropriate to cult prostitutes and menials of pagan shrines than to the Israelite sanctuary. The duties of the Levites at the central shrine are presented in the texts as an honor, not a degradation or a demotion.

32. The question is what is the referent of "at that time" (v. 8a). It cannot be assumed that it refers to what immediately precedes.

cates that the tent of meeting was established and the priests and Levites consecrated after the incident of the calf (Exod. 36:8–40:38).

As a redactional insertion, Deuteronomy 10:8–9 reflects conditions after the conquest and settlement, as is plainly stated in the text itself ("as is still done today," v. 8). The passage has its origin late in the period of the judges or in the early monarchy. This is reflected in its exclusive concern with the ark, which was of course very mobile and played a major role in the history of that time (1 Sam. 4–7; 14:18; 2 Sam. 6; 7:2; 11:11; 15:24–29). Nothing is said of the Levitical duties toward the tent (which would indicate that it was either in a fixed location or destroyed) or the temple (which would demand a later *Sitz im Leben*).

Written from this perspective, the verse collapses and greatly simplifies the history and ministry of the Levites. As it stands, it asserts that some time after the worship of the golden calf, the "Levites" were set apart to carry the ark and to stand before Yahweh to minister and bless. The former is a part of the supportive sanctuary duty assigned to the Levites in the Sinai legislation, and the latter is a specific priestly function. According to the Sinai law, only the Aaronites could serve as priests at the central sanctuary. But all Levites could serve as priests in the local shrines in Israel on the basis of established tradition. The redactor has not differentiated between the Aaronite priestly function at the central shrine (the Aaronites, after all, were Levites) and the general priestly duties of the non-Aaronite Levites. He is, of course, only inserting a chronological note and not attempting to set forth the whole structure of the Israelite priesthood.

The text does not assert that prior to the incident of the golden calf Levites were laymen and that the priesthood fell to them because of what they had done on that occasion. The Aaronites, again, were Levites too, and the directive that they should officiate at the tent was given to Moses before the sin involving the golden calf (Exod. 29). In fact, Deuteronomy 10:8 does little more than give the chronological sequence that the incident of the calf preceded the consecration of the Levites to their duties. The valor of the Levites in Exodus 32 is significant, but it relates only to their consecration to serve as stewards of the central sanctuary—it has no wider relevance with regard to how and why the Levites, or the Aaronites, became priests.

DEUTERONOMY 33:8–11

The third passage, Deuteronomy 33:8–11, is part of the blessings of Moses. Here, the aged lawgiver mentions several incidents from the history of the Levites in a highly abbreviated and optimistic form. The text says that they received the Thummim and Urim (although only the Aaronites in fact received it), that the Levites were faithful in time of testing (verse 9 alludes to Exodus 32:29), that the Levites teach the Law to Israel (v. 10a, a general priestly function of the Levites), and that they fulfill priestly duties at the central sanctuary (v. 10b, an Aaronite function).

The text does not assert that all Levites fulfilled all the duties so described (and one should not expect careful delineation of separate duties in a liturgical passage such as this). Also, the text in no way asserts that the faithfulness of Levi at the golden calf was the reason they received the priesthood. To the contrary, that episode is merely mentioned as one of the positive moments in the history of Levi (all the tribes are presented in very favorable terms in this passage).

EXODUS 24:5

Exodus 24:5 states that, as part of the Sinai covenant ceremony, Moses sent the "young Israelite men" to offer sacrifices. This is often taken as, in one scholar's words, "a primitive touch, coming from before the time of a specialized priesthood (see Ex. 32:29 for Levi's later 'ordination')."[33]

This is not necessarily the case. As already indicated, Exodus 32:29 was by no means an "ordination" of Levi. Also, it is not certain that the "young men" were from all the tribes and not exclusively from Levi.[34] Even if it is conceded that the young men were from all the tribes, this does not mean that Levi had no special status at this time.

I have generally referred to pre-exodus Levi as the "scribal" or "clerical" tribe rather than the "priestly" tribe. In other words, I believe that Levi had the primary responsibility of preserving and transmitting the patriarchal religious traditions of Israel. In that sense, they were "clergy," but this is not to say that they were "priests" in the exclusive sense of being the only ones who had the right to offer sacrifice, pronounce benedictions, or perform other sacred duties.

To the contrary, the question of who might perform these duties must have been in a state of flux during the sojourn as Israel slowly moved from being a familial community to a national community. But as Levi took on scribal and clerical duties, the general understanding that Levites were the priests of the nation must have developed. By

---

33. R. Alan Cole, *Exodus,* TOTC (Downer's Grove: Inter-Varsity, 1973), 185.
34. Verse 4 is explicit that the pillars represent the twelve tribes, but nothing is said concerning the tribe(s) of the young men.

analogy, in modern religions that officially have no clergy, a de facto clergy develops among those who study and interpret the religion's sacred writings.

If the young men of Exodus 24:5 were in fact from all the tribes, this was probably because of the special significance of the ceremony—all the tribes had to be represented in the covenant confirmation (v. 4). It may also imply that the conceptual movement from "Levitical clergy" to "Levitical priest" had not yet fully taken place. It does not undermine the thesis that the Levites already had a special role prior to the exodus.

In summary, the Old Testament nowhere asserts that Levi's faithfulness at the sin of the golden calf was the reason they received general priestly duties among the tribes. Their faithfulness was a vindication of Levi and the approximate occasion, though not necessarily the reason, they were consecrated as support personnel at the tent of meeting.

The Golden Calf and the Aaronite Priesthood

The sin of the golden calf, in fact, provides strong indication that Levites were regarded as clerics by the Israelites at large, and that Aaron was recognized as chief of the Levites, prior to the making of that idol. In Exodus 32:1–6, the Israelites "gather around" Aaron and ask him to make gods (idols) to go before them. Aaron immediately tells them to give him their gold jewelry and makes the calf, and then builds an altar and proclaims a festival.

Why did the Israelites go to Aaron? The answer cannot be because he was associated with Moses, because the Israelites explicitly rejected Moses' authority over them (Exod. 32:1). The answer can only be that Aaron was recognized as having a kind of priestly leadership apart from his association with Moses. The text also indicates that Aaron directed the construction of an idol and a sanctuary, and also established a cultic holiday. This implies prior acquaintance with priestly objects and rituals on Aaron's part.

Further evidence is found in the manner God actually tells Moses to consecrate Aaron to the priesthood. The first explicit reference to the priestly duties of the Aaronites is in Exodus 27:20–28:5, where God tells Moses that the Aaronites are to keep the lamps burning in the tent of meeting and that the Aaronite priests are to have special garments made for them. In Exodus 29, the ritual of their consecration to the tent of meeting is set forth.

Conspicuously absent is a pronouncement that the Aaronites (and not some other family) should be the priests—it is simply assumed to be the case that the Aaronites are to be the priests. In fact, a public demonstration that God had chosen Aaron as the priest and the Levites as the assistants in the central sanctuary was not thought necessary until after Dathan, Abiram, and the sons of Korah had challenged Aaronite supremacy (Num. 16–18). The initial installation of the Aaronites as priests of the central sanctuary was therefore not a new and unanticipated heavenly fiat but the divine ratification of an already existent situation.

More than that, the evidence implies that Aaron was not the only priest in Israel prior to the exodus but that the Levites generally had scribal or clerical duties. Aaron's distinction was that he was their chief. This is seen in the way Aaron first appears to the reader in Exodus 4:14: "What about your brother, Aaron *the Levite*?" The specific reference to Aaron as a Levite is pointless if all that is meant is that Aaron is of the tribe of Levi. Moses himself was of the tribe of Levi, and he did not need to have his brother's tribe identified for him. The best understanding of the term *Levite,* then, is that it is not a mere genealogical reference (which would be "Aaron, son of Levi") but is indicative of the position Aaron held among the Israelites at that time.

This implies that *Levite* was already used as a common and semitechnical term for "priest." As Haran comments, "The simple truth is that this phrase is based upon the assumption that priesthood is in principle the privilege of the tribe of Levi, so much so that the appellation 'the Levite' becomes synonymous with a priest."[35] It is not quite accurate to say that "Levite" was completely synonymous with "priest," but rather there is here a semantic overlap between "Levite" and "priest."[36] Since Aaron was the leader of the Levites, the priests of Israel, Aaron was *the* Levite. Insomuch as the term for priest used here is indeed *Levite,* the implication is that clerical duty was by no means confined to the house of Aaron among the Levites.

Israel's Attitude toward Moses, Aaron, and the Levites

In the exodus generation, in fact, it was not the high priesthood of Aaron but the clerical function of the Levites that was regarded as fixed and inviolable. An important factor is that no protest against the

35. *Temples,* 68. Haran needlessly asserts that this appellation is anachronistic.
36. Cf. George Buchanan Gray, *Sacrifice in the Old Testament* (1925; reprint, New York: Ktav, 1971), 247.

Levitical priesthood appears in the narrative. Considering how bitterly the Israelites resisted Moses, and at times Aaron,[37] it is astonishing that they never spoke against the institution of the Levitical clergy. This can only be explained if this special Levitical role antedated the exodus.

Indeed, it is precisely at the greatest rebellion against Moses (that of Dathan, Abiram, and the sons of Korah) when the traditional and pre-exodus priesthood of Levi is established. In that incident, the sons of Korah tried to seize the specialized priesthood and received lay support from Dathan and Abiram (Num. 16). The rebellion itself was neither wholly religious nor wholly secular in character. The conspirators wanted to replace Moses as leader of the community and Aaron as high priest of the tent of meeting. The principal grievance of the lay opposition to Moses was that he had taken them out of Egypt into a wilderness and that he had taken too much authority to himself (vv. 3, 13).

The grievance of the sons of Korah was religious. They were themselves Kohathites (v. 1) and as non-Aaronic Levites had no right to minister as priests in the central sanctuary. But they had come to regard Aaron as no longer worthy to function as high priest, apparently because of his association with Moses (v. 11). They intended to replace him and assume control of the tent of meeting themselves. They were also motivated by simple greed for power and prestige (vv. 9–10).

What is most significant is that an alliance between lay leaders and Levites was necessary to mount this significant challenge to the authority of Moses and Aaron. The lay opposition to Moses, which had been fermenting from the very beginning of the exodus, was not sufficient alone (that is, without Levitical support) to force a confrontation. The conspirators apparently considered it essential that the tabernacle have a Levitical priesthood. This is indeed remarkable if the Levites had only been serving in a sacral capacity for a short time; one would expect that if the Levitical priesthood were a novelty, the laity would have rebelled against the entire Levitical institution as a fabrication of Aaron and Moses.

To the contrary, not only do the rebels not challenge a Levitical priesthood, they explicitly recognize it as valid. It was the sons of Korah, not the lay opposition, who stood before Yahweh with censers.

After the rebellion, the priestly function of the Aaronites and the supportive function of the rest of the Levites at the central sanctuary were again confirmed (Num. 17:1–18:7). The purpose of this

37. Exod. 16:2.

confirmation was to dissuade anyone from making another attempt at seizing the priesthood of Aaron. Here again, however, the passage is exclusively concerned with the central sanctuary, which at this stage of Israelite history was the tent of meeting. The text says nothing about the functions that the Levites are to have when they scatter and settle in Canaan, and it in no way discourages the Levites from assuming priestly duties in local communities after the settlement.

Similarly, the regulations for the offerings for the priests and Levites, Numbers 18:8–32, do not assert that non-Aaronic Levites would never have any priestly duties whatsoever. It only states that they do not have the priesthood of the central sanctuary (vv. 21–24).

The Levitical Priesthood in the Book of Deuteronomy

The description of the Levitical priesthood in Deuteronomy 18:1–8 does not contradict the rest of the Pentateuchal portrait of the role of the Levites. The critical part of the text, verses 6–8, reads:

> Now if a Levite comes from one of your towns anywhere in Israel in which he has resided, and comes with a sincere heart to the place Yahweh chooses, then he may minister in the name of Yahweh his God like all his brother Levites who stand there in the presence of Yahweh. He is to have an equal share of the food, in addition to what he has from the sale of family possessions.

Three questions must be asked:

1. Is the Levite described here an Aaronite or is any Levite, Aaronite or not, meant?
2. Does he serve as a priest or simply have a supportive, non-priestly role? To what does "minister in the name of Yahweh" refer?
3. Is "the place Yahweh your God will choose" the central sanctuary, that is, the tent of meeting?

Regarding the first question, it is difficult to deny that the Levite here is any Levite. A special Aaronic priesthood is not mentioned in context, and verse 1a, "The priests, the Levites, the whole tribe of Levi," is most naturally understood to mean that any Levite is at least potentially a priest. Rodney K. Duke has correctly argued that the phrase *the whole tribe of Levi* does not imply that every Levite was a priest.[38] On the other hand, it would be alien to this text to assert that some Levites cannot become priests. The most natural reading of the text is that while not all Levites are priests, all Levites *could be* priests. Wellhausen's observation that the Chronicler's formula ("the priests *and* the Levites") is distinct from the Deuteronomic formula is valid.[39]

In answer to the second question, the text is most naturally taken to mean that the Levites, as priests, offer sacrifices. This is implied in verses 3–5, which describe their share in the sacrifices. In ministering before Yahweh, the Levite did much more than just offer sacrifices, but that function cannot be excluded. On the other hand, "minister in the name of Yahweh" (v. 7) is a fairly general way of describing their function, and one need not assume that this ministry always necessarily included priestly duties at the altar. The ambiguity is deliberate and reflects the diverse roles of the Levites.

Finally, what is "the place Yahweh will choose"? The phrase obviously refers to the regulations for worship found in Deuteronomy 12, where the Israelites are told to destroy the Canaanite shrines (v. 2) and bring their sacrifices only to the place God chooses (vv. 13–14). Does this refer to the central sanctuary? The text seems distressingly obscure. The noun *place* is in the singular, which appears to imply that there can be only one sanctuary to Yahweh. On the other hand, neither the tent of meeting nor any central sanctuary is explicitly mentioned. One therefore cannot exclude the possibility that the text is not referring to one place but to any place that is legitimately a sanctuary to Yahweh.

Further indications that the latter is indeed the meaning of the phrase are found in the text. Deuteronomy 12:2–5 shows that the real concern of Deuteronomy is not that there be only one sanctuary but that no Canaanite shrine be used for worship. The phrase *make his name dwell there* (12:5), as J. A. Thompson says, simply denotes ownership.[40] Similarly, verse 13 does not say that sacrifice can take place in only one place in all of Israel but that the Israelites cannot sacrifice anywhere and everywhere. As R. K. Harrison says: "The real force of the contrast in Deuteronomy 12 is not between many altars

38. "The Portion of the Levite: Another Reading of Deuteronomy 18:6–8," *JBL* 106 (1987): 197–98.

39. *Prolegomena*, 147.

40. *Deuteronomy*, TOTC (London: Inter-Varsity, 1974), 41.

of God and one, but between those of the Canaanites dedicated to alien deities and the place where the name of God is to be revered."[41]

Concerning the singular noun *place,* it is best to follow M. H. Segal's conclusion:

> It may be added that the singular number in the expression "the place" in Deuteronomy denotes a single class to which the law applies and not one exclusively single locality. This accords with the regular use of the singular in the legal phraseology of the Pentateuch. Thus Deut. xii, 18: "thou and thy son and thy daughter and thy manservant" etc., does not mean one single son and one single daughter etc., but the whole class of sons and daughters etc., as it is stated explicitly before in v. 12. . . . If the law had meant to forbid a plurality of sanctuaries it would have said explicitly: the *one* place.[42]

Other texts also indicate this to be the case. In Deuteronomy 16:21–22, the Israelites are commanded not to set up an Asherah pole or sacred stone near "the altar" they build to Yahweh. This is not the single altar of the central sanctuary, for they already had the bronze altar that traveled with the tent of meeting. Here also, therefore, the singular refers to all altars in the land dedicated to Yahweh.[43] This understanding of the verse is supported by Exodus 20:24: "Make an earthen altar for me and sacrifice on it your burnt offerings and peace offerings, your sheep and goats and cattle. In whatever place I cause my name to be invoked, I will come to you and bless you." Here, unquestionably, more than one altar is in view, and there is no reason to doubt that these altars could function contemporaneously throughout Israel.

Several examples can also be cited where orthodox Yahwists made sacrifice away from the central sanctuary, be it the tent of meeting or the Solomonic temple. In Judges 6:24–26, Yahweh explicitly commands Gideon to build an altar and make sacrifice. Also, 1 Samuel 7:17 states that Samuel built an altar to Yahweh at his home in Ramah, and in 1 Samuel 16, he sacrificed at Bethlehem. These examples are significant because Samuel was himself the successor of Eli. He, more than anyone else, had reason to preserve the status of the central sanctuary.

41. *Introduction to the Old Testament* (Grand Rapids: Eerdmans, 1969), 642.
42. *The Pentateuch: Its Composition and Authorship* (Jerusalem: Magnes, 1967), 88.
43. Cf. Harrison, *Introduction,* 643.

First Kings 18:30 mentions an ancient altar to Yahweh on Mount Carmel. Elijah repaired this altar and worshiped there in his confrontation with the priests of Baal. Insomuch as the text mentions that the altar antedated the conflict between Elijah and Jezebel's priests, it cannot have been an ad hoc altar strictly built for that occasion. See also Judges 2:5 and 1 Samuel 15:21; 20:6.

One text might seem to indicate that sacrifices could be given only at the tent of meeting. In Joshua 22, the tribes of Reuben and Gad and the half-tribe of Manasseh built an altar on the west side of the Jordan at Geliloth prior to their return to the east side. The altar was evidently quite large (v. 10), and the rest of Israel, thinking that the tribes of the transjordan had set up a rival central sanctuary and that they had abandoned the covenant God of the tent of meeting, was alarmed (v. 19). The transjordan tribes then responded that what they had established was not to be an altar for sacrifices but was a witness and a memorial to the fact that they too belonged to Israel.

This account, however, does not mean that the Israelites believed that sacrifice could be given only at the tent of meeting. The altar at Geliloth was of such significance that, if it had possessed a priestly cult, it would have immediately rivaled the tent of meeting. To preclude this danger, the transjordan tribes explicitly prohibited the making of sacrifices on this altar. The altars of Jeroboam, however, were prophetically condemned not because sacrifice was offered on them but because they were both rivals to the central sanctuary and did not use Levitical priests (1 Kings 12:31–13:5).

On the other hand, the Old Testament never indicates that the Israelites ever had a large number of legitimate, functioning altars. The Deuteronomic formula is that a legitimate altar was one that Yahweh had chosen for his name. This implies that a genuine altar of Yahweh had to be established with prophetic support. This would, of course, greatly limit the number of licit altars in the land.

It is probably illegitimate, in fact, to phrase the question in such a way as to presume that Deuteronomy 12 *either* refers to the one central sanctuary *or* to many legitimate sanctuaries, as though the two concepts were mutually exclusive. Although, as this study indicates, Deuteronomy allows for a plurality of legitimate altars, the central sanctuary where the ark rested was the *quintessential* "place where Yahweh made his name dwell." In this light, Deuteronomy implicitly warns against depreciating the central sanctuary.

The critical text, Deuteronomy 18:1–8, addresses an ambiguous situation with equally fluid language. The general Levitical priesthood and the freedom of the Levites to minister in various places in the nation are not opposed. It is assumed that any Levite could serve in a local shrine that is genuinely Yahwist, and so "minister in the name of Yahweh" in that way. Nevertheless, the central sanctuary and its specialized priesthood is not diminished. On the basis of the already established Sinai laws, it is understood that a Levite who "ministers in the name of Yahweh" at the central sanctuary does so in a supportive and not a priestly role.

Deuteronomy exclusively supports neither a central sanctuary and priesthood nor a dispersed priesthood at multiple sites. It addresses an approaching situation, the religious life of Israel after the conquest, and it does so with a goal not of regulating precisely the number of sanctuaries but of protecting the people from idolatry.

An Extra-Pentateuchal Text: 1 Samuel 2:27–28

A significant text outside the Pentateuch on the history of Israel's priesthood is 1 Samuel 2:27–28:

> And a man of God came to Eli and said to him, "Thus says Yahweh: 'Did I not reveal myself to your father's house when they were in Egypt, in Pharaoh's house? I chose him from all the tribes of Israel to be my priest, to go up to my altar, to burn incense, and to wear an ephod before me. And I gave your father's house all of the Israelite food offerings.'"

Several problems immediately emerge. First, to whom does "your father's house" refer? Is it the Aaronites (Kaufmann), the Mushites (Cross), or simply the Levites? Second, do these two verses mean that God chose this house for the priesthood while they were still in Egypt, or are the exodus and the Sinai revelation understood to have occurred between verse 27 and verse 28?

It is clear, first of all, that Eli was not a Mushite priest and that the "house" is not the line of Moses. The strongest argument in favor of a Mushite interpretation is the statement that God revealed himself to Eli's father's house while they were in Egypt. The only Israelite to whom God spoke in Egypt, as far as we know, was Moses. It is possible, of course, that the passage contains an ancient Levitical tradition of a revelation given to their fathers while they sojourned in Egypt. Even if the text alludes to the revelation to Moses, however, that does not mean that Eli was a Mushite. To the contrary, both Eli and Moses were part of a larger house, that of Levi, and God's revelation to Moses was in effect a bestowal of favor on the whole Levitical tribe. Eli, as the head of the Levites of his day, stood in that tradition.

Equally important, the biblical data demonstrate that the house of Eli was not Mushite but Aaronite, through the line of Ithamar. In comparing 1 Kings 2:27 (which asserts that the priest Abiathar was of the house of Eli) to 1 Chronicles 24:3, 6 (which says that Abiathar was of the line of Ithamar), it is evident that the house of Eli was descended from Ithamar, youngest son of Aaron.

The fact that the data are indirect and come from two such distinct sources as Kings and Chronicles strengthens rather than weakens the case. If, after all, a text had plainly stated that Eli was of the line of Aaron, one might argue that this was contrived in order to show that the high priesthood had not been in non-Aaronic hands. On the other hand, one could argue to the contrary that the Aaronites may have had reason to want to obscure Eli's Aaronic descent since his career ended in disgrace. As it is, however, the Bible simply indicates, with no evident motive behind it, that Eli was Aaronic.[44] The thesis of a rival Mushite priesthood at Shiloh is not sustained.

One must now ask whether the "house of your father" was the Aaronic line exclusively or the whole house of Levi. Kaufmann takes the former position.[45] Although he was at many points very critical of the Documentary Hypothesis, Kaufmann is too much influenced by documentary critical reasoning and therefore argues that P and D preserve the history of a conflict between the Aaronites on one side and the Zadokites and Levites on the other.

Kaufmann asserts that in P the Aaronites "demand the exclusive privilege of serving the altar and consent to Levi's being only hierodules."[46] He further argues that Exodus 32 and Deuteronomy 9–10 are anti-Aaronite Levitical propaganda and that Numbers 16–17 is an Aaronite condemnation of Levi. Kaufmann also maintains on the basis of 1 Samuel 2:27–36 that the Zadokites considered themselves to be Levites but not Aaronites.[47]

In fact, the Bible neither asserts nor implies that Aaron was at conflict with the Levites as a whole. Contrary to the Documentary Hypothesis, Exodus 32 is not a JE insertion into a P narrative but is

44. Cf. Haran, *Temples*, 87, 97.
45. *Religion*, 197–98.
46. Ibid., 198.
47. Ibid., 197.

integrally related to the whole.[48] Also, as has already been noted and as Kaufmann himself admits, the story of the golden calf relates only to the tabernacle duties of the Levites, not to their general priestly duties.[49] It is difficult to see why the Levites would propagate a story which left them, in Kaufmann's term, as mere hierodules in the central sanctuary.

The story of the rebellion of the sons of Korah, similarly, cannot be anti-Levitical Aaronite propaganda for the simple reason that the text explicitly links Aaron to the Levites. The rebellion, Numbers 16, was immediately followed by the budding of Aaron's rod, Numbers 17, as a demonstration of God's choice of Aaron. The story does not set Aaron against the Levites—to the contrary, Aaron's rod "represented the house of Levi" (v. 8).

As noted (p. 216), the preexodus designation *Aaron the Levite* (rather than "Aaron the priest") implies that the special status of Levi was already a fact of Israelite life and links Aaron to the Levites at a very early stage. Aaron was chief priest not in contrast to the Levites but because he was head of the Levites. He was, in effect, the chief Levite.

48. Source critics have disagreed regarding the sources and redactions responsible for this narrative, although they have generally assigned the bulk of the narrative to either J or E. For a good review of the literature, see John I. Durham, *Exodus*, WBC (Waco: Word, 1986), 417–21. In fact, it is very difficult to say what objective means could separate J or E from P here (the divine names are not relevant this late in Exodus). Martin Noth, *Exodus*, trans. J. S. Bowden, OTL (Philadelphia: Westminster, 1962), 243–45, asserts that Exodus 32 is part of the "old Pentateuchal narrative" and that the references to Aaron are inserted by an anti-Aaronite group. His assertion only indicates the circular nature of documentary analysis. The narrative is earlier than the priestly legislation because the legislation is known to be late, and the references to Aaron are polemical because they are known to be so. Regarding the allegations of internal contradictions in the narrative, see Brevard S. Childs, *The Book of Exodus*, OTL (Philadelphia: Westminster, 1974), 558–59. Childs himself, however, gratuitously assumes a J source for the chapter. The meaning and purpose of the narrative also becomes hopelessly pliable under the Documentary Hypothesis. Noth, *Exodus*, 245–46, says Exod. 32 is a later insertion into J meant to condemn the Jeroboam sanctuaries. If that were the case, however, surely the reference to Aaron (which Noth regards as secondary anyway) would have been expunged in the final P redaction—his name would seem to add legitimacy to Jeroboam's calf shrines. In fact, earlier documentary critics argued that the story was originally meant to add legitimacy to the old Aaronic sanctuary at Bethel, where a bull shrine, they argued, existed well before Jeroboam. Kaufmann, *History*, 197, on the other hand, says the real purpose of the story is to condemn Aaron. Here again, the exegetical chaos wrought by the Documentary Hypothesis is evident.

49. *Religion*, 198.

The text of 1 Samuel 2:27ff., similarly, is not anti-Aaronite polemic from the Zadokites. To the contrary, Zadok was himself Aaronite (1 Chron. 6:50–53; 24:3).[50] Nor is it proper to assert that the oracle is anti-Elide propaganda from the Zadokites.[51] The fact that the Zadokites in some sense fulfilled the prophecy of verse 35 does not mean that the text was written by them or for their advantage. One wonders why the passage cannot be exactly what it purports to be: A message from a man of God given well before the elevation of the Zadokites under David, a message meant not to set one priestly house against another but to rebuke Eli for his neglect of God's honor.

Historicizing exegesis tends to obscure the broader canonical functions of the text. The "faithful priest" promised in verse 35 is indeed Zadok, and before him, Samuel, who is the archetype of a faithful priest. More important than either of these observations, however, is that the promise functions typologically and canonically as a pointer to the eschatological kingdom. This is certainly something other than priestly political polemic.

The "house of your father" in 1 Samuel 2:27, therefore, refers neither to the Mushite line, of which Eli was not a member, nor even to the Aaronic line, but more generally to the house of Levi and, to the degree that it is specific at all, to Eli's family.[52] This is an oracle, however, not a history, and its language should not be pressed for a precise history of the priesthood. The curse of verse 31 is not directed against the house of Moses, Aaron, or even Levi, but against the house of Eli. He is condemned for having substituted his rich ancestral heritage for obedience to Yahweh. This is not a text about the conflicting claims of rival priestly houses but a condemnation of Eli and his sons.

We must now turn to the question of whether verses 27–28 imply the establishment of a Levitical priesthood prior to the exodus. It is beyond question, first of all, that verse 28 alludes to stipulations of the Sinaitic code of the priesthood of the central sanctuary, as indicated in the reference to the ephod (cf. Exod. 28:4ff.; 39:2ff.). The verse

---

50. One can always argue that the Chronicler's genealogy of Zadok is an attempt to establish the legitimacy of both the Aaronic and Zadokite lines by artificially joining the two together. But the Chronicler's genealogy receives some support from 2 Sam. 8:17. Most important here, however, is the arbitrary manner in which material from Chronicles is disregarded. One can hardly investigate the history of the priesthood in a meaningful way by discarding data at will.

51. See, e.g., P. Kyle McCarter, Jr., 1 Samuel, AB (New York: Doubleday, 1980), 92–93; H. W. Hertzberg, I and II Samuel, OTL (Philadelphia: Westminster, 1974), 37–39; Henry Preserved Smith, Samuel, ICC (Edinburgh: T. and T. Clark, 1898), 23.

52. Cf. Smith, Samuel, 22.

plainly has the Sinai code in view and cannot be treated as a reference to preexodus priestly practices.

On the other hand, it is curious that the oracle explicitly speaks of a revelation to Eli's ancestors while they were in Egypt. It could be that the prophet alludes to the revelations given to Moses, as previously described. But it is hard to see why that would be the case, since no known revelation to Moses while he was in Egypt concerns the establishment of the priesthood. It is possible, therefore, that 2:27 alludes to the establishment of the Levites as the clerical tribe while they were in Egypt and thus attests to an ancient Levitical tradition to that effect. If so, the prophet has telescoped the two events, the ancient revelation to the Levites, verse 27, and the Sinai legislation, verse 28, in his brief summary of the ancient origins of the priestly privileges of Eli's line.

This would mean that the preexodus tradition of a Levitical priesthood originated in an early oracle, which is alluded to only in 2:27. But we would hasten to add that our position that the Levitical clergy antedated the exodus in no way is contingent on a special reading of this passage.

In summary, 1 Samuel 2:27–36 has nothing to do with conflicts among Elide, Mushite, Aaronite, or Zadokite priests. It is exactly what it looks like, a prophetic condemnation of Eli and his sons for their sin. Verses 27–28 *may* allude to an old tradition that the Levites were set apart for ministry during the sojourn in Egypt.

The Josianic Reform

2 KINGS 23

In the Wellhausen reconstruction of the history of the priesthood, the centralization of the priesthood under Josiah is the key to the entire problem. Behind the reform, according to Wellhausen, was the political power of the Zadokite priesthood, a priesthood locked in a struggle with the Levites. The destruction of the various local shrines was thus the beginning of the end of the general priestly function of the Levites. It also marked the beginning of the process whereby the high-priestly Zadokites (later idealized as Aaronites in P) came to dominate the Levites and reduce them to the function of hierodules.

Several observations, however, greatly weaken the force of the Wellhausen hypothesis. First, in stark contrast to Deuteronomy, which allows for the peaceful migration of the Levitical priests, Josiah brought the priests into Jerusalem by force.[53] Second, the Josianic reform was never an anti-Levitical movement but was a rejection of the syncretism that had developed both in the Jerusalem temple and in the local shrines (v. 4ff.). Also, the term *Levite* is never used in 2 Kings 23—those forced to come in from the surrounding communities are simply called "priests." This does not mean that these local priests were not Levites, but it does indicate that neither their status as Levitical priests nor the mere fact that they functioned outside Jerusalem was considered offensive. They were recognized as priests.

As a reasonable solution to this historical problem, one may assume that by the time of Josiah the Levitical priests in the local communities had greatly apostasized. Indeed, not only in the smaller shrines but in the Jerusalem temple itself, idolatrous worship was well established (vv. 4–7). Josiah destroyed all the idols and concentrated worship in Jerusalem neither because of rivalry among priestly groups nor because of a supposed Deuteronomic "law of the central sanctuary" but for administrative reasons: It would be far easier to check the return to idolatry if worship were concentrated under the eye of the king in one location—the Jerusalem temple—and not scattered throughout the countryside.

In concentrating the priesthood in this way, Josiah was not following any Deuteronomic stipulation that Jerusalem should be the central sanctuary or that there could only be one altar to Yahweh in the land. He was introducing an entirely new concept in order to fulfill the Sinaitic and Deuteronomic mandate against idolatry.

Once the Levites were brought to the Jerusalem temple, however, the Levitical priests could no longer serve at the altar (v. 9). This was not because of a rivalry between the Zadokites and Levites but because of the long established *Sinaitic* (not Deuteronomic) law of the central sanctuary, which stipulated that only Aaronites could serve there. In short, the Josianic reform was not in principle nor in purpose a movement away from a generalized Levitical priesthood but was an administrative plan to control the nation's tendency to wander into idolatry. Its result, however, was to put an end to the Levitical priesthood of the local shrines.

Ezekiel 44

In his vision of the restored temple, Ezekiel gives a brief description of the role of the priesthood (Ezek. 44:5–31). In interpreting this

53. See John Gray, *I and II Kings*, 2d ed., OTL (Philadelphia: Westminster, 1970), 734.

text, it is most important to bear in mind that the language is symbolic to the degree that it may be called apocalyptic. Ezekiel is not attempting to describe a temple that he expects to be built in any fully literal sense—whether in a millennial kingdom (dispensationalism) or as part of a Zadokite program for reconstructing the historical priesthood and continuing the suppression of the Levites (Wellhausen).

Instead, Ezekiel 40–48 presents, in highly idealized, sacramental terms, the hope for the salvation of the nation and the establishment of the kingdom of God in the face of the terrible trauma of the Babylonian conquest. It is also consciously canonical in outlook.

Seen in this light, the stipulations of Ezekiel 44 perfectly accord with prior history and theology. The assertion that idols and foreigners would not be allowed in the new temple (vv. 5–9) reflects a sad history of apostasy epitomized by the admission of foreign cults to the Jerusalem temple in the reign of Manasseh (2 Kings 21:1–9)[54] and demonstrated to Ezekiel in his vision (Ezek. 8). Similarly, the assertion that the Levites who fell into idolatry in the various shrines could work at the temple but not serve as priests of the holy things (vv. 13–14) is not part of an anti-Levitical movement among the Jerusalem priests. It is a deliberate reflection on the conditions that prevailed prior to Josiah's reformation and a bestowal of approval on his attempt to halt the spread of idolatry (2 Kings 23). Apparently non-Aaronic Levites and foreigners had served as priests of the temple during the Manassite apostasy.

Ezekiel's purpose, however, is not to establish regulations for the priestly orders but to oppose the apostasy. Insomuch as the Zadokites themselves are called Levites in this very text (v. 15), it is hard to see this as part of an anti-Levitical program. In the context of Ezekiel's vision, these verses represent the hope for a pure and unified worship of Yahweh in the eschatological theocracy.

The role of the Zadokites and the praise they receive (v. 15ff.) function canonically. This section has been a particular difficulty for interpreters. Walther Eichrodt, for example, says that it would be astonishing if these words had come from Ezekiel and that Ezekiel 7:26 and 22:26 are better indications of what the prophet thought of the Jerusalem priesthood. He therefore considers this section to be from a legislator of the Jerusalem priesthood.[55] Walther

---

54. Cf. Haran's study of Ezekiel's indictment of the priestly idolatry (*Temples*, 103–7). As he observes on p. 106, "There is no doubt that the shadow of Manasseh's period hovers over this accusation, just as the impressions of Manasseh's activities are discernible throughout Ezekiel's prophecy as a whole."

55. *Ezekiel*, trans. Cosslett Quin, OTL (Philadelphia: Westminster, 1970), 565.

Zimmerli, who sees in this text evidence of a complex, multilayered history behind Ezekiel 40–48, also argues that this commendation of Zadok cannot have come from Ezekiel.[56] He flatly states that the "slogan which can be heard here, 'Zadokites versus Levites,' and its historico-theological underpinning have no basis in the preaching of the prophet Ezekiel. . . ."[57]

This conclusion, however, fails to recognize Ezekiel's conscious reflection on the canonical history of the priesthood. The Zadokites are remembered favorably not because Ezekiel was unaware of any apostasy among the Jerusalem priests but because of the positive description of them in the canonical record, particularly in the history of the reign of David and Solomon (e.g., 2 Sam. 15:24). Indeed, the Davidic monarchy is the theological backdrop for Ezekiel's vision of the renewed kingdom of God (37:15–28). The biblical portrayal of the various figures and institutions of the Davidic theocracy informs and directs his portrayal of the future kingdom. This would include the Davidic monarch, the Solomonic temple, the Zadokite priesthood, the Josianic reforms, and, negatively, the Manassite apostasy, all of which are alluded to in Ezekiel's theocratic vision. This is not, therefore, an assertion that all Zadokite priests had been faithful and good (Ezek. 8!) but is a reflection on the fact that in the canonical history nothing bad is said concerning Zadok and his priesthood.[58]

In conclusion, Ezekiel 44 has nothing to do with any hypothetical conflict between the Levites and the Jerusalem hierarchy. It is a vision of an eschatological theocracy conceived in canonical terms. The Levites are condemned not because they were necessarily worse than the Zadokites but as a deliberate affirmation of the Josianic reform. The Zadokites are praised not because they were free from sin but as part of an eschatological vision of pure worship. Nothing Ezekiel says, moreover, contradicts our basic thesis that the general Levitical clergy was an ancient institution, which existed contemporaneously with the

56. *Ezekiel,* trans. James D. Martin, 2 vols. (Philadelphia: Fortress, 1983), 452–64.

57. Ibid., 464.

58. A simple analogy to this is in the use of the figure of Melchizedek as a Christological model in Heb. 7:1–3. When the text says that Melchizedek was "without father or mother . . . or end of life," he does not imply that Melchizedek literally had no parents or that he never died. Instead, the fact that the Bible does not say explicitly that he had a father or mother or that he experienced death is made a canonical model for the eternal priesthood of Christ.

worship at the central sanctuary under the direction of the Aaronites until the Josianic reform and the exile.

Postexilic Texts

In the postexilic period, the historical forces at work came to their natural conclusion. With the Josianic suppression of the local sanctuaries and gathering of all Levites to Jerusalem, their traditional role as priests of the extended community began to be forgotten. This process came to its conclusion with the experience of the exile. In the minds of the exiles, only one sanctuary had any meaning: the Jerusalem temple.

After the exile, the Israelites who rebuilt their community were determined to follow the letter of the law in establishing sanctuary worship (Ezra 6:18). The danger of falling into idolatry was keenly felt, and provision was made for no altar besides that of the central sanctuary. The shrunken postexilic community had no need for a general priesthood outside Jerusalem anyway.

The postexilic community in effect followed the principles of the Josianic reform with the result that non-Aaronic Levites were permanently relegated to a support role, and they were carefully differentiated from the priests.[59] This had always been the place of the Levites in the central sanctuary, and it was in no sense an innovation.

This being the case, it is not surprising that the Levites are portrayed exclusively in a supportive role in the Chronicles (e.g., 1 Chron. 23). This is not because of a desire on the part of the Chronicler to suppress the previous history of the Levites; rather, it is simply an indication of his exclusive concern with the Jerusalem sanctuary. He does not deny that the Levites had other roles outside Jerusalem; he merely has nothing to say about that aspect of Israelite history. It is not a matter of political conflict but of theological interests. He is, in the tradition of Ezekiel, looking toward a new theocracy founded on a Davidic model.

Extrabiblical Evidence

Finally, we must note that one piece of extrabiblical evidence *may* support the contention that the Levitical priesthood is a preexodus institution. In 1899, D. H. Muller published some Minaean inscriptions

---

59. E.g., Ezra 3:8–12; 6:16–20; 8:15–33.

found at El-'Ela in Arabia. Three of these may describe certain persons with the term *lawi'a,* which some have regarded as meaning "priest." Insomuch as these inscriptions were dated by some as early as 1500 B.C., a number of scholars wondered if the term *Levite* (= *lawi'a?*) may have been used as a term for priests prior to the exodus.[60]

This accords very well with the present argument that Levites functioned as priests at this time, and one can imagine that either the term *Levite* or the Levites themselves spread to the regions of Sinai and Arabia prior to the exodus.

Nevertheless, one must use the evidence of the Minaean inscriptions with great caution. First, the date of the inscriptions is not established. Second, and more significant, the texts are obscure and *lawi'a* may not mean "priest" at all, but, as Jamme translates it, "pledge, loan."[61] It is unwise, therefore, to make too much of these inscriptions.

To summarize, one can make a number of conclusions regarding the Levites. First, the term *Levite* has a double sense in the Old Testament narratives. On the one hand, any Levite was of clerical stock, and *Levite* was even used as a loose synonym for *priest.* The Levites all had a traditional priestly role in the nation at large. On the other hand, only the specialized priesthood (originally the Aaronites) could serve at the central sanctuary. In the context of a discussion of the tent of meeting, therefore, *Levite* generally refers to a non-Aaronic descendant of Levi (of the Kohathites, Merarites, or Gershonites) who had a supportive role. Failure to take into account these two uses of the term *Levite* has resulted in much confusion.[62]

Second, although the central sanctuary was always important, it was of greatest importance very early and very late in the history of Israel. During the wilderness wanderings, the tent of meeting was the only sanctuary for the Israelites; immediately prior to and after the exile, the Jewish state was so small that outlying altars and a scattered Levitical priesthood were no longer needed and were a threat to orthodoxy.

But in the period after the conquest, when the Israelites were scattered all over the land, exclusive use of the central sanctuary was no longer possible and other local altars were used. This situation is not

---

60. Cf. Fritz Hommel, *The Ancient Hebrew Tradition as Illustrated by the Monuments* (London: SPCK, 1897), 278–79; Gray, *Sacrifice,* 242–47.

61. *ANET,* 665. De Vaux, *Ancient Israel,* 2:369, also rejects the translation *priest.*

62. A parallel to the dual use of *Levite* is the dual use of the term *Chaldean* in Daniel. There, the term *Chaldean* is used both in an ethnic sense, for the Chaldee race (5:30), and technically, for the priests and astrologers. See Harrison, *Introduction,* 1113–14.

forbidden in Deuteronomy. Nevertheless, unfettered proliferation of altars was discouraged and the use of Canaanite shrines was forbidden. The Levites ministered in various ways at this time throughout Israel.

This interpretation of the history of the Levites is intelligible only if the Levites were regarded as clerics by the people prior to the exodus. The Book of Exodus itself supports this conclusion. It was not de jure, from Sinai, but de facto. For this reason, the general role of Levites as priests continued somewhat independently of the legislated system of the central sanctuary.

This brings us back to the original question: How were the sources of Genesis transmitted during the Egyptian sojourn? The Levites, during the Egyptian sojourn and for reasons unknown, adopted the roles of scribe and teacher, and in those roles preserved the traditions of the patriarchs. This does not, of course, tell us everything about how the traditions were maintained. Nevertheless, it gives us a basis for thinking that there was a channel through which the traditions were handed down in a reliable, organized fashion.

It also tells us how it is that Moses possessed these records. As a Levite himself, and a brother of Aaron, the records would have been immediately accessible to him. Urgenesis is therefore the Mosaic redaction of the Levitical records of the history of the patriarchs.

12

Memories
of a Wandering People

Formal analysis implies that the sources to Genesis included ancestor epics, negotiation tales, a migration epic, and other material such as the gospel of Abraham. I have suggested what may have been the setting and intention of these sources. In every case except Genesis 1, the most reasonable setting for the material is the sojourn in Egypt.

This conclusion contrasts with previous studies, which have attempted to place Genesis in a setting of the late monarchy or the exile. Nevertheless, analysis of not only the sources but of the whole of Genesis indicates that the Egyptian sojourn is the best setting for the book.

Alienation as the Theme of Genesis

A theme of alienation pervades the entire text of Genesis. It begins with the expulsion of Adam and Eve from Eden. Humanity is driven from its home, and the world itself is now an alien place. Sin and guilt lead to estrangement of every kind, and the cry of Cain is the cry of all: I am cast out from the presence of both God and the rest of humanity (4:14). Although of a common family, the human race is divided and scattered. Languages are divided, people are dispersed, and all bonds of unity are lost.

Abraham, at the very beginning of his story, is told to separate himself from homeland and family (12:1). He is forever an alien in a strange land and must resort to stratagem to save his skin as he moves among peoples he does not know (12:10–20). In this, he is followed by his son Isaac, who also must frequently retreat in the face of local opposition (26:19–22). Only God's promise that someday the whole land will belong to his offspring sustains Abraham. When his wife dies, he must negotiate even to have enough land to bury his dead.

Lot, though he tries to assimilate into the local culture of Sodom, cannot do so. He cannot accept the Sodomites' behavior, and in turn they despise him (19:9). He flees Sodom for Zoar, but even that place, a "very small" village (19:20), gives him no safe haven. He leaves it because "he was afraid to stay in Zoar" (19:30). At the end, Lot is the ultimate outcast. He is physically removed from society, in that he is living in a cave, and he is socially outcast, in that he has broken the universal taboo against incest.

Jacob is an alien wherever he goes. His own home is too dangerous for him and he must flee to Haran (27:41–46). There, his superficial acceptance by relatives does not alter his status as an outsider. He is cheated in the most intimate of all matters, the choice of a wife (29:15–30). When he prospers, his fate is that of every prosperous alien; he is looked upon as a threat and forced to flee (31:1–55). He returns to the land of his birth again as an outsider and must face the danger of confronting his brother, Esau, who has become assimilated to his environment. Even though he survives that encounter, Jacob must ever be on his guard, for he knows how precarious his position is. He must beware lest he become a "stench" to the native population (34:30).

The sons of Jacob are also aliens. Famine forces them to go to Egypt to stand as suppliants before a foreign official. That this official is in fact their brother does not alter their awkward position. He is, after all, the brother they almost murdered, and they go through an ordeal in which they, on more than one occasion, look like fools.

Joseph is ever the alien. He is hated by his brothers and by their hand is sold as a slave. Even though he quickly prospers in Potiphar's house, his precarious status as a slave is evident. When he resists the harassment of a woman who would make him her sexual toy, she easily disposes of him. He is a man without rights. Even his rise to power does not alter his alien status. He still depends on the good will of Pharaoh just as all Israel depends on him. When Joseph dies, his body lies strangely out of place in a coffin in Egypt. And it becomes clear how precarious Israel's position is when a new pharaoh, who does not remember Joseph, comes to power.

The full text of Genesis, an ancestor epic, stresses above all that Israel is the most alien of peoples in an alienated world. The sense of estrangement and homelessness is mitigated only by the promises of God. In that, there is hope of finally finding a home.

Because of its profound concern with alienation, only two possibilities exist for the setting of the composition of Genesis: Either it is the product of the period of the sojourn and the exodus, or it is the product of the Babylonian exile. This is because a work that addresses the problem of alienation is most likely to have a setting in a community that was itself alienated. In no other periods of Israel's history were the problems of alienation and homelessness so severe. The question, therefore, is which of the two settings provides the more reasonable backdrop for the composition of Genesis.

An Exilic Setting for Genesis?

Neither the complete text of Genesis nor any individual source relates well to the Babylonian captivity. Apart from the fact that nothing in the text alludes to or relates in any way to the captivity,[1] the stories are ill-suited to address that crisis.

The stories of Joseph are a good test case. I have already argued that this material is a migration epic and serves the purpose of telling how Israel came to find itself in Egypt. The most reasonable assumption is that the tradents of this material were themselves in Egypt and addressed an audience in Egypt to answer the question of how they came to be living there. Here, however, I want to draw attention to the matter of how poorly this material is suited to a setting in the exile.

First, Joseph is himself identified with Ephraim and Manasseh rather than Judah, and it is difficult to see how the central figure of a story meant to address the crisis of the captivity could be other than Judah. Also, although Joseph goes to Egypt as a slave, this is not the

---

1. There is of course reference to Babel in Gen. 11:1–9, but it is difficult to read this as polemic against the neo-Babylonian empire. It cannot be regarded as a veiled assault on sixth-century Babylon because the reference to Babel is explicit rather than veiled (as in apocalyptic). On the other hand, there is no explicit attack on anything that can be identified as sixth-century Babylon. Certainly there is no hint that the original readers were themselves in Babylon.

result of hostile actions by an alien power but by the brothers themselves (including Judah).

Furthermore, it is hard to see how the particular events of the Joseph narrative have anything to do with the situation of the Israelites in Babylon. What, for example, could one make of Joseph's rise to power? Was this an exhortation to the Israelites in Babylon to work hard and rise to the top in Babylonian government circles? That hardly makes sense. In contrast, as the story of how Joseph came to be in a position to provide a place for the children of Jacob in Egypt, the Joseph material makes very good sense.

Finally, there is really no explanation for composing a story that recounts why Israel came to be in Egypt for a community nowhere near Egypt. One may of course postulate that the entire Pentateuch has been composed as a theological analogue for the deliverance of the Israelites from Babylon, but this, too, is problematic.

Another aspect of Genesis, which illustrates the difficulty of associating the composition of the book with the captivity, is its many promises of the land of Canaan as the inheritance of Abraham, Isaac, and Jacob. As a work that has its setting in Egypt, these promises are the hope of an alien people; in the setting of the captivity, however, they are mockery.

For the exiles in Babylon, the covenants would have been only cruel reminders that they had been promised the land, had received the promises, and then had forfeited their inheritance. If this is the case, then Genesis and indeed the entire Pentateuch is a book not of comfort but of condemnation. But it is impossible to read Genesis as having that purpose. The text everywhere looks forward to the fulfillment of the promises, not backward to their fulfillment and forfeiture.

It is for this reason that the Pentateuch cannot be regarded as looking back to the exodus as an analogue for release from Babylon. In light of the warnings contained in Deuteronomy (28:15–68; 31:14–22), it could only be read as grim condemnation by the exiles. This reading contradicts the theme of looking toward the future, which is present throughout the books.

In summary, Genesis is the book of the memories of an alien community. In it, members of this community recall that they have been strangers and outsiders from the very beginning. At the same time, it is the book that gives them the anticipation that someday they will have their own land and be strangers no more. Only the Egyptian sojourn can be the setting of material that has this purpose.

The Use of the Sources in the Sojourn and After

Although the Israelites of this time had no Bible and the boundary between canonical and noncanonical story was not yet set, the various traditions of the fathers must have played a protocanonical role in informing the growing community of its identity, of the identity of its God, and of the inheritance awaiting them. In particular, the Genesis stories told the Israelites that they were the heirs of the covenant given to Abraham, Isaac, and Jacob.

The redaction of the sources into Urgenesis during the time of the exodus is also reasonable. As an ancestor epic, Genesis speaks of danger and alienation, but it also recites stories of survival. For Israel in the wilderness, a nation without a land, this would have been a meaningful expression of encouragement.

Conclusion: The Date of the Composition of Genesis

It is clear that the traditional understanding of Genesis as the product of the exodus period is still the best solution to the problem of the origin of the book. Drawn from sources that explained to Israel in Egypt its historical origins and the causes of the sojourn, Genesis expresses hope for the future and lays the foundation for the new work of God, the exodus.

The Question
of Inspiration

E vangelical scholars, perhaps more than their colleagues, will be interested in how the concept of inspiration relates to the source history of Genesis proposed in this book. This is a legitimate question but it is theological, not historical or literary, in nature. As such, it stands outside the main focus of this book and is best addressed as an appendix to this presentation.

Evangelical scholars have always known that the question of how a book in the Bible can be said to have both human and divine authorship is highly complex. Few if any evangelicals ascribe to the "dictation" theory, as they are so often accused. Rather, most evangelicals believe that the Spirit of God guided the human authors in such a way that, although their personalities and historical circumstances were in no way obscured or obliterated, their canonical writings contain an authority and a veracity that may rightly demand that they be received as the Word of God.[1]

---

1. For a good presentation of an evangelical position on inspiration, one with which I fully concur, see David S. Dockery, "The Divine-Human Authorship of Inspired Scripture," in *Authority and Interpretation: A Baptist Perspective,* ed. Duane A. Garrett and Richard R. Melick (Grand Rapids: Baker, 1987), 13–43.

Still, evangelicals have not fully explored one aspect of inspiration due to their adherence to the "great writer" understanding of the origin of the Bible. By "great writer," I refer to the fact that when evangelicals speak of the authorship of Scripture, they almost always mean the great, original authors such as Moses, Isaiah, Jeremiah, John, or Paul. Any questions about sources the biblical authors may have used are set aside.

Nevertheless, even a conservative view of the origin of the Bible must allow that some of the books may have gone through three stages. These are the promulgation of source materials prior to the great writer, the collection of the source materials and the use of them by a great writer in putting together a single work, and subsequent revision of that work. The prologue to Luke's Gospel states that it went through at least the first two stages. Evidence for the third stage, editorial revision, has been presented for Genesis and Deuteronomy in this book. The question to be raised, therefore, is this: Apart from the inspiration of the great writer, how might one speak of the inspiration of those who first compiled the source stories or who later edited complete books?

Regarding the "inspiration" of those who first compiled the source material, a minimal view would be that at least part of what they compiled was true and trustworthy, and that the inspired great writer was then able to separate the wheat from the chaff and use only valid material in his book. Luke, in his prologue, to some degree implies this very thing. His careful investigation of his sources (Luke 1:3) indicates more than just setting down his source material in a pleasing order.

On the other hand, many of the original compilers of the sources themselves were surely as inspired by God as the great writers who followed them. In the case of Luke's Gospel, the tradents who stood between Jesus and Luke notwithstanding, much of the material (e.g., the parables) came directly from Jesus himself, and he was surely inspired! For this reason, I believe that in the case of Genesis there was genuine divine inspiration not only in the person of Moses but in the persons who compiled the stories long before him.

With regard to editorial revision subsequent to the work of the great writer, I have already argued that this was for the most part limited to revising vocabulary, especially place names, which might have lost their meanings to subsequent generations. The place name *Dan*, in Genesis 14:14, is a case in point. If there were in fact even greater, more significant revisions, this in and of itself is not startling (the account of Moses' death in Deuteronomy 34 is certainly a significant addition to the book). The perspective of "canonical criticism" may be helpful here. When and by whom modifications may have been made I do not know, but one can assume that they were made by men of sufficient authority to make them. As such, the finished product (Genesis as it now stands) may be regarded as the canonical Word of God and any attempt to get behind it to the Mosaic original on the presumption that the latter would have more authority is misguided. There is no reason to believe that subsequent revisions in any way contradicted the original.

Having said all that, the importance of the great writers of Scripture should not be regarded as diminished. Luke is no less a great evangelist for having admitted to the use of sources, and Moses is no less the "author" of Genesis on the grounds that he used sources or that what came from his hand has undergone revision. Genesis is still "the First Book of Moses."

𝔹

A Critique
of Three Recent Hypotheses
# of Pentateuchal Origins

In chapter 3, having given reasons for abandoning the Documentary Hypothesis and the traditio-historical approach, I dealt with R. N. Whybray's theory of the origin of the Pentateuch. I focused upon Whybray because, as a scholar who rejects the older solutions of biblical scholarship, he may be regarded as on the leading edge of contemporary research in seeking a new answer to the challenge of Pentateuchal origins. Also, his own solution is both simple and straightforward, which makes it a good candidate for the consideration of alternative solutions.

Nevertheless, Whybray is not the only modern scholar seeking a new approach to the Pentateuch. His analysis draws upon the groundbreaking work of Rolf Rendtorff. Also, Thomas L. Thompson and John Van Seters, two scholars whose works I have cited extensively, have each developed new hypotheses regarding the origin of the Pentateuch. In light of the significance of these contributions to the cur-

rent search for a new consensus, a few words on these alternative theories are in order.

Rolf Rendtorff

In *Das überlieferungsgeschichtliche Problem des Pentateuchs* (English:
The Problem of the Process of Transmission in the Pentateuch),[1] Rolf
Rendtorff builds upon the traditio-historical work of Hermann
Gunkel, Gerhard von Rad, and Martin Noth. Unlike these scholars,
however, he severs the impossible bond between form-criticism and
the Documentary Hypothesis. In order to do this, he devotes a considerable amount of space to criticizing the Documentary Hypothesis,
and in particular attacks the idea that J and P form continuous strands
that can be traced through the Pentateuch.

Against the Documentary Hypothesis, Rendtorff repeatedly demonstrates that adherents of the hypothesis have nothing that can be
meaningfully called a consensus in their analyses of the Pentateuch.[2]
He also points out that efforts to buttress the hypothesis with pieces
of hard evidence, such as assigning particular Hebrew words and
idioms to particular documents, collapse under investigation.[3] Most
importantly, he shows that the notion of the "theology of the Yahwist"
is illusory.[4]

Rendtorff does not develop an alternative theory in great detail (his
concern is more with the process of transmission than with a specific
delineation of sources). Nevertheless, he does give us an outline of
such a theory.

The starting point for Rendtorff's analysis is that investigations hith-
erto have focused on either the very smallest units of text from the traditio-historical point of view or the latest, literary stage in the development of the Pentateuch. He wants to turn attention to the larger units
of text that make up the intermediate stage between these two. These

1. Rolf Rendtorff, *Das überlieferungsgeschichtliche Problem des Pentateuchs*, BZAW 17
(Berlin: W. de Gruyter, 1977); English: *The Problem of the Process of Transmission in the
Pentateuch*, trans. John J. Scullion, JSOTSS 89 (Sheffield: JSOT Press, 1990). The fol-
lowing citations are from the English text.

2. Ibid., 28–29; 101–17; etc.

3. E.g., ibid., 147–50.

4. Ibid., 119–36. On the "theology of P," see 163–70. Rendtorff does allow for a theological reworking of certain texts from a priestly perspective, but he does not admit to
any priestly document as it has been traditionally understood.

larger units would include the primeval history; the individual narratives of Abraham, of Isaac, of Jacob, and of Joseph; and the (separate and distinct) exodus, Sinai, and wilderness traditions. As an example of his method, he evaluates the patriarchal stories in some detail.

Rendtorff's analysis does not run through Genesis but across it;[5] there is no individual source, such as J, which contains a history of Israel from creation through to the exodus and beyond. Instead, individual stories about Abraham (for example) first grew up in isolation from stories about Jacob. Although Rendtorff prefers not to speak of "sources" or an all-embracing theory of the origin of Genesis, it is probably a legitimate inference that the "process" he envisages implies separate Abraham, Jacob, or Joseph "sources"[6] (as opposed to sources that run through the entire Pentateuch).

At this point, the divine promises to the patriarchs become very important in Rendtorff's analysis. It is these promises which first hold together collections of traditions about individual patriarchs, and then bind the patriarchs to one another.[7] Rendtorff argues on form-critical grounds that the patriarchal narratives contain three separate types of promises. These are the promise of offspring, the promise of a land, and the promise of guidance.[8] He also notes that there is a promise of "blessing" but contends that this is not an independent promise theme.[9] These promise addresses have themselves "gone through a varied and many-layered process of development" and have also been part of a "reworking and theological interpretation of the patriarchal stories."[10]

The theological reworking on the basis of the promises to the patriarchs is a distinctive aspect of the patriarchal narratives; it does not carry over into Exodus.[11] A subsequent priestly reworking of some material added that distinctive theological point of view, and a Deuteronomistic redaction helped to unify the whole of the Pentateuch.[12] In this manner, the Pentateuch grew from the smallest and

5. Cf. Gordon J. Wenham, "The Religion of the Patriarchs," in *Essays on the Patriarchal Narratives,* ed. A. R. Millard and D. J. Wiseman (Winona Lake, Ind.: Eisenbrauns, 1980), 161–95, p. 184.

6. By "sources" I do not mean a written document but a complex of traditions in dynamic growth.

7. Rendtorff, *Problem,* 83.

8. Ibid., 55–68.

9. Ibid., 64–65.

10. Ibid., 82–83.

11. Ibid., 84–89.

12. Ibid., 94–100; 169–70; 189–203.

earliest traditions, through to the larger units of narrative, and finally to the unification of the whole. Throughout the process, theological reworking and redaction served to demarcate and unify various units.

Rendtorff's thesis is open to a number of questions. First, his methodology is based on assumptions that are now widely challenged, some by Rendtorff himself. In light of how thoroughly he shreds linguistic arguments for the Documentary Hypothesis, it is surprising to see him using similar arguments in his own analysis. For example, he divides the promises of many descendants into two groups on the basis of the presence or absence of the word *seed* and the verbs *to increase* and *be fruitful*.[13]

His whole analysis of the promises, by the way, strikes one who is not already convinced of the validity of his method as very strange. For example, in the promises of the land, he considers it significant that in some texts the promise is given only "to you" (e.g., Gen. 15:7) but others add "and to your seed" (e.g., Gen. 28:13). Finally, some texts have only "to your seed" and not "to you" (e.g., Gen. 15:18). For Rendtorff, this is nothing less than evidence of historical development in the evolution of the promise.[14] One wonders, however, if formulaic language is as rigid as Rendtorff imagines; if there is any reason for a specific variation in the wording of a formula, it is far more likely to be driven by context and the narrator's intent than to be evidence of a tradition history behind the formula.[15]

In addition, Rendtorff appears to accept without question the axiom that smaller equals earlier; that is, that the traditions all began as small, self-contained units. As has already been noted, narratives frequently contain literary asides, background information, and the like. No narrator, ancient or modern, operates within the kind of constraints that the traditio-historical approach demands.

Aspects of Rendtorff's conclusions are unrealistic. It is difficult to see, for example, how the traditions about Abraham could have survived in isolation from the traditions about Jacob, and it is especially strange that so many promises from God would be attributed to

13. Ibid., 61–64. Cf. Bernhard W. Anderson, review of Rolf Rendtorff, *Das überlieferungsgeschichtliche Problem des Pentateuchs*, *CBQ* 40 (1978): 100–103, and R. E. Clements, Review of Rolf Rendtorff, *Das überlieferungsgeschichtliche Problem des Pentateuchs*, *JSOT* 3 (1977): 46–56.

14. Rendtorff, *Problem*, 57–61.

15. For example, the promise that the land would be given "to your descendants" in Gen. 15:18 is in the context of a divine prophecy about the future of Abram's offspring; it would be out of place here for the promise to be related to Abram personally.

Abraham if originally he had no connection to Jacob. Throughout the literature, Israelites speak of themselves as sons of Jacob (Israel), not of Abraham. Similarly, it is hard to imagine how the exodus tradition could have existed separately from its larger narrative frame. Finally, as R. E. Clements notes, Rendtorff's conclusions depend heavily on a rigid distinction between a redactor and an editor.[16]

Thomas L. Thompson

Thompson, like Whybray and Rendtorff, rejects the Documentary Hypothesis. He also dismisses all attempts to describe Genesis as a historical or theological work, and insists that Genesis be read as a literary work, that is, as narrative. In disavowing all attempts to historicize or theologize Genesis, Thompson seems to feel that he has achieved a more pristine reading of the text than his predecessors and colleagues.[17] The motivation he most frequently assigns to the stories of Genesis is that they are aetiological.

Thompson contends that Genesis, along with Exodus 1–23, is the origin tradition of Israel. He sees Genesis as the final product of a five-stage literary development. These five stages are (1) smaller units and tales, (2) larger, compound tales, (3) traditional complex-chain narratives, (4) the *toledoth* structure, and (5) a post-*toledoth* redaction. In contrast to tradition historians, he believes that the transition from one stage to the next was very short. The fourth stage, the *toledoth* structure, served to unify the whole narrative of Genesis as a preface for the exodus narrative. The last stage was a final revision of the fourth.[18]

In asserting all of Genesis to be under a *toledoth* structure, he contends that it is prehistory (and nonhistorical). More than that, it is an attempt to describe the origin of the Israelite people in the context of the origin of all the nations of the earth (again, the aetiological motif dominates). For this reason, Genesis 5:1a is both the structural linchpin of Genesis and its intended title (Gen. 1–4 is in effect a preface).[19]

Therefore, working with Genesis as a narrative held together by a *toledoth* structure, he is able to discern the purpose of Genesis as an

16. Clements, review, 51.
17. Cf. Thompson, *Origin,* 196, 206.
18. Ibid., 62–65.
19. See ibid., 170, for a schematic diagram of Thompson's understanding of the structure of the book.

origin tradition: *"According to the origin tradition of Genesis and Exodus, in the received form of Toledoth, Israel is autochthonous and indigenous to Palestine."*[20]

There are points made by Thompson with which I can agree since I independently came to some similar solutions.[21] My four-stage theory for the background of Genesis (chap. 4) is somewhat similar to his five-stage development. Like him, I see the *toledoth* passages as crucial to understanding the structure of Genesis, although my understanding of the book's structure differs markedly from his (I am particularly unpersuaded by the significance he attaches to Gen. 5:1a). I also agree that Genesis tells the Israelites that they belong in Canaan, but I reject his use of terms like "autochthonous" and "indigenous." Apart from these qualified points of agreement, however, I find Thompson's presentation unacceptable for several reasons.

First of all, he gives no evidence at all to support his notion of "traditional complex-chain narratives" in Genesis. This is no small problem, since the concept is at the very heart of his analysis of Genesis. As Burke O. Long states, "We are asked to accept a key component of his theory, the . . . 'complex chain narrative,' not on the basis of public evidence but on Thompson's word."[22]

Also, Thompson is consistently fragmenting unified biblical narratives into smaller, isolated units. He sees variants "A" and "B" in the composition of the flood narrative,[23] describes three simpler, variant tales in the story of Jacob's return to Canaan (Gen. 32),[24] and attempts to isolate two simpler variants in the story of Joseph's abduction (37:12–35).[25]

Thompson frequently points out what he believes to be secondary additions. For example, in his discussion of Genesis 14, he contends that the capture of Lot is a secondary.[26] He also argues that 15:7–21 is separate from the "mainline narrative" (Gen. 15:1–6) since it is "written from the perspective of the final pentateuchal historiography."[27] In Genesis 19, verses 27–28 and verse 30 are both redactional

20. Ibid., 80.

21. I had reached my major conclusions before reading his book.

22. Burke O. Long, review of *The Origin Tradition of Ancient Israel*, *JBL* 108 (1989): 330.

23. Thompson, *Origin*, 77.

24. Ibid., 110–11. Thompson also argues that 32:24–32 was originally independent of its present context" (p. 110).

25. Ibid., 119–21.

26. Ibid., 87.

and verse 29 is a theological gloss.[28] Finally, the putting of money in the sacks of the brothers in Genesis 44 is argued to be secondary on the grounds that it is inconsistent with the placement of a silver cup in Benjamin's sack.[29]

The reasoning behind Thompson's source criticism amounts to little more than aesthetic judgments. A writer is free to put in details which may strike a later reader as inconsistent, irrelevant, or needless theologizing. That a reader may find some of this disturbing is not grounds for treating certain portions or texts as secondary. The significant point here is that Thompson is using older methods of source criticism, although it is clear that original stories can and do contain digressions, suspension of action, and even apparent contradiction. (Indeed, modern novelists have made the disorientation of the reader something of an art form.) In Thompson's analysis, however, smaller is earlier, often even the appearance of contradiction is evidence of interpolation, and the suspension of one storyline for another is evidence that the separate plot lines come from separate sources.[30] These criteria are simply the demons of the older source criticism come back in one of their most determined exorcists.

Also, one must wonder how it is that Thompson can detect theologically motivated redactional texts in light of his own assertion that the five stages of development covered a very short time and were even *"unquestionably contemporaneous with the final redaction."*[31] If the perspective of the theological texts was contemporary with the texts that develop the main story lines, how can one meaningfully contend that they were not in fact all written by the same person at the same time? No significant ideological contradiction is present in any of these passages.

Perhaps most troubling in Thompson's thesis is his notion that the *toledoth* structure is meant to show that Israel is autochthonous to the land of Canaan. Such a notion is peculiar from the very outset—it is as

27. Ibid., 88.

28. Ibid., 94.

29. Ibid., 127.

30. For example, Thompson argues that in Gen. 26, "Isaac and Rebecca certainly know nothing of Jacob and Esau, their children" (p. 102). He also considers the absence of Lot from Gen. 12:10–20 to be highly significant (p. 85). While I agree that the texts in question here come from different sources (for reasons described in chap. 6), the fact that Esau, Jacob and Lot are not mentioned in these texts has no evidential significance. From the standpoint of the storyline of the book of Genesis, it is merely a case of suspension of action.

31. Ibid., 62.

though one were to take the American stories of the Pilgrims and Plymouth Rock and conclude that Caucasian Americans believed themselves to be indigenous to North America. Both Genesis and Exodus are insistent on the point that the Israelites, even from the time of their earliest ancestors, are aliens.

Even so, the whole notion that Genesis describes the origin tradition of an autochthonous people collapses when comparison is made to legends of other nations, something which Thompson does not do. The Koreans, for example, have a myth which describes their autochthonous origin in their peninsula. It states that a celestial being, Hwanung, descended from heaven to Mount Paektu (in northern Korea) with three thousand followers and established a divine city. One day, a tiger and a bear on the mountain asked Hwanung to transform them into humans. He gave each a bundle of mugwort and garlic and told them to avoid the sunlight for a hundred days. The tiger was not able to follow his instructions but the bear persevered and was transformed into a woman. Hwanung then married the woman and they had a son, Tangun. Tangun became the ancestor of the Korean people and established the capital at Asadal (now Pyongyang) in 2333 B.C.[32]

The Athenians believed that the first king and founder of their city was Cecrops, sometimes said to have been a son of Hephaestus. "As an indication of his autochthonous origin Cecrops is often represented as of serpent shape below the waist."[33] He is said to have been the judge between Athena and Poseidon in their contest for dominion over Athens.

Rome, in addition to the migration story of Aeneas, has the equally famous story of the brothers Romulus and Remus. The brothers were said to be the sons of Mars by the Vestal Rhea Silvia, whom he had raped. The twins were set adrift on the Tiber and came to rest in the grotto Lupercal, where they were nursed by the she-wolf and reared by the shepherd Faustulus. Romulus then founded the city of Rome (and in a fit of anger killed his brother) and populated his city by the abduction of the Sabine women.

This brief survey is meant only to point out that legends of the autochthonous origins of peoples and Genesis have little in common. In the myths described, one notes several features. First, the ancestor of the race is often described as the son of a divine father and human mother. Second, the ancestor is often related to some animal in story

32. Andrew C. Nahm, *A Panorama of Five Thousand Years: Korean History* (Seoul: Hollym, 1983), 14.
33. *Oxford Classical Dictionary*, s.v. "Cecrops."

or presentation, whether it be the Korean bear, the serpentine shape of Cecrops, or the Roman she-wolf. Third, the ancestor founds the capital city of his people, be it Pyongyang, Athens, or Rome.

Genesis contains none of this. The fact that Genesis does not in any way relate the patriarchs to Jerusalem is especially noteworthy in light of Thompson's suggestion that the Josianic reformation is the most likely provenance for the book.[34] It is difficult to think of a period in Israel's history when concern about the centrality of Jerusalem would have been more pronounced. All in all, it is very difficult to see how Genesis can have the purpose and background Thompson attaches to it.

John Van Seters

Van Seters argues that the Deuteronomistic historian was the first significant writer in the corpus of Genesis to Kings. He believes that J and P then composed the Tetrateuch in order to complete the canonical history of Israel. This was done in two stages, with J first telling the stories of the patriarchs[35] and P then making his distinctive contributions.[36] The structure of the patriarchal narrative is thus primarily the work of the Yahwist.

I have already given reasons for rejecting both Van Seters's source analysis of the patriarchal stories (chap. 2) and his understanding of the Deuteronomistic history (chap. 3). At this point, I only want to observe that Van Seters's proposition is essentially a revision, albeit a radical one, of the Documentary Hypothesis. Insomuch as the Documentary Hypothesis is without any substantial evidential support (as I have described in chap. 1), a theory which remains within that framework can hardly be sustained. Van Seters himself notes that the Documentary Hypothesis "is largely viewed as obsolete."[37] Continued talk about J, D, and P in any form is fruitless; an entirely new approach is needed.

---

34. Thompson, *Origin*, 195–96.

35. Cf. Van Seters, *Abraham*, 313, for a presentation of his ideas on the growth of the Abraham narrative.

36. Van Seters, *Search*, 323.

37. Ibid., 16.

Select Bibliography

Books and Monographs

Aharoni, Yohanan. *The Archaeology of the Land of Israel*. Translated by Anson F. Rainey. Philadelphia: Westminster, 1982.

Albright, William F. *From Stone Age to Christianity*. 2d edition. New York: Doubleday, Anchor Books, 1957.

Andersen, Francis I. *The Sentence in Biblical Hebrew*. The Hague: Mouton, 1974.

Archer, Gleason L., Jr. *A Survey of Old Testament Introduction*. Chicago: Moody, 1973.

Brueggemann, Walter, and Hans Walter Wolff. *The Vitality of Old Testament Traditions*. Atlanta: John Knox, 1975.

Budd, Philip J. *Numbers*. WBC. Waco: Word, 1984.

Cassuto, Umberto. *The Documentary Hypothesis and the Composition of the Pentateuch*. Translated by Israel Abrahams. Jerusalem: Magnes, 1941.

Childs, Brevard S. *Introduction to the Old Testament as Scripture*. Philadelphia: Fortress, 1979.

———. *Old Testament Theology in a Canonical Context*. Philadelphia: Fortress, 1986.

———. *The Book of Exodus*. OTL. Philadelphia: Westminster, 1974.

Clarke, Howard. *Homer's Readers*. London and Toronto: Associated University Presses, 1981.

Coats, George W. *From Canaan to Egypt*. Washington, D.C.: Catholic Bible Association, 1976.

———. *Genesis: With an Introduction to Narrative Literature*. FOTL. Grand Rapids: Eerdmans, 1984.

———. ed. *Saga, Legend, Tale, Novella, Fable*. JSOTSS 35. Sheffield: JSOT Press, 1985.

Cody, Aelred. *A History of Old Testament Priesthood*. Rome: Pontifical Biblical Institute, 1969.

Cole, R. Alan. *Exodus*. Downer's Grove: Inter-Varsity, 1973.

Craigie, Peter C. *The Book of Deuteronomy*. NICOT. Grand Rapids: Eerdmans, 1976.

Cross, Frank M. *Canaanite Myth and Hebrew Epic*. Cambridge: Harvard University Press, 1973.

Curtis, E. W., and A. A. Madsen. *The Books of Chronicles*. ICC. Edinburgh: T. and T. Clark, 1910.

Doukhan, Jacques B. *The Genesis Creation Story*. Berrien Springs, Mich.: Andrews University Press, 1978.

Driver, S. R. *An Introduction to the Literature of the Old Testament*. 1897. Reprint. Gloucester, Mass.: Peter Smith, 1972.

Durham, John I. *Exodus*. WBC. Waco: Word, 1986.

Eichrodt, Walther. *Ezekiel*. Translated by Cosslett Quin. OTL. Philadelphia: Westminster, 1970.

Eissfeldt, Otto. *The Old Testament: An Introduction*. Translated by Peter Ackroyd. New York: Harper and Row, 1965.

Evans, J. A. S. *Herodotus*. Boston: Twayne, 1982.

Fehling, Detlev. *Herodotus and His 'Sources'*. Translated by J. G. Howie. Leeds: Francis Cairns, 1989.

Fishbane, Michael. *Text and Texture*. New York: Schocken, 1975.

Flory, Stewart. *The Archaic Smile of Herodotus*. Detroit: Wayne State University, 1987.

Fohrer, Georg. *Introduction to the Old Testament*. Translated by David E. Green. Nashville: Abingdon, 1968.

Gray, George Buchanan. *Sacrifice in the Old Testament*. 1925. Reprint. New York: Ktav, 1971.

Gray, John. *I and II Kings*. 2d ed. OTL. Philadelphia: Westminster, 1970.

Green, William Henry. *The Higher Criticism of the Pentateuch*. 1895. Reprint. Grand Rapids: Baker, 1978.

Gunkel, Hermann. *The Folktale in the Old Testament*. Translated by Michael D. Rutter. Sheffield: Almond, 1987.

Guthrie, Donald. *New Testament Introduction*. Downer's Grove: Inter-Varsity, 1970.

Hammond, N. G. L., and H. H. Scullard. *Oxford Classical Dictionary*. 2d ed. Oxford: Oxford University Press.

Haran, Menahem. *Temples and Temple Service in Ancient Israel*. Oxford: Oxford University Press, 1978.

Harrison, R. K. *Introduction to the Old Testament*. Grand Rapids: Eerdmans, 1969.

Hart, John. *Herodotus and Greek History*. London: Croom Helm, 1982.

Hertzberg, H. W. *I and II Samuel*. OTL. Philadelphia: Westminster, 1974.

Hommel, Fritz. *The Ancient Hebrew Tradition as Illustrated by the Monuments*. London: SPCK, 1897.

How, W. W., and J. Wells, eds. *A Commentary on Herodotus.* London: Oxford University Press, 1912.

Immerwahr, Henry R. *Form and Thought in Herodotus.* Cleveland: Case Western Reserve University, 1966.

James, T. G. H. *An Introduction to Ancient Egypt.* New York: Harper and Row, 1979.

Kaiser, Walter C., Jr. *Toward an Old Testament Theology.* Grand Rapids: Zondervan, 1978.

Kaufmann, Yehezkel. *The Religion of Israel, from Its Beginnings to the Babylonian Exile.* Translated by Moshe Greenberg. Reprint. New York: Schocken, 1972.

Keil, C. F. *Hosea.* Translated by James Martin. Reprint. Grand Rapids: Eerdmans, 1954.

Kidner, Derek. *Genesis.* TOTC. Downer's Grove: Inter-Varsity, 1967.

Kikiwada, Isaac M., and Arthur Quinn. *Before Abraham Was: A Provocative Challenge to the Documentary Hypothesis.* Nashville: Abingdon, 1985.

Kirkpatrick, Patricia G. *The Old Testament and Folklore Study.* JSOTSS 62. Sheffield: JSOT Press, 1988.

Kitchen, K. A. *Ancient Orient and Old Testament.* Chicago: Inter-Varsity, 1966.
———. *Pharaoh Triumphant: The Life and Times of Ramesses II.* Warminster, England: Aris and Phillips, 1982.

Knight, Douglas A., ed. *The Hebrew Bible and Its Modern Interpreters.* Chico, Calif.: Scholar's Press, 1985.

Kuhn, Thomas S. *The Structure of Scientific Revolutions,* 2d ed. Chicago: University of Chicago Press, 1970.

Leaf, Walter, and M. A. Bayfield. *The Iliad of Homer.* 2 vols. 1898. Reprint. London: Macmillan, 1968.

Lichtheim, Miriam. *Ancient Egyptian Literature.* 3 vols. Berkeley: University of California Press, 1973.

Lister, R. P. *The Travels of Herodotus.* London: Gordon and Cremonesi, 1979.

Long, Burke O. *The Problem of Etiological Narrative in the Old Testament.* BZAW 108. Berlin: Verlag Alfred Töpelmann, 1968.

Longacre, Robert E. *Joseph: A Story of Divine Providence.* Winona Lake, Ind.: Eisenbrauns, 1989.

Lord, Albert B. *The Singer of Tales.* Cambridge: Harvard University Press, 1960.

McCarter, P. Kyle, Jr. *1 Samuel.* AB. New York: Doubleday, 1980.

Michalopoulos, Andre. *Homer.* New York: Twayne, 1966.

Millard, A. R., and D. J. Wiseman, eds. *Essays on the Patriarchal Narratives.* Winona Lake, Ind.: Eisenbrauns, 1983.

Motyer, J. A. *The Revelation of the Divine Name.* London: Tyndale, 1959.

Myers, Jacob M. *1 Chronicles.* AB. New York: Doubleday, 1965.

Nahm, Andrew C. *A Panorama of Five Thousand Years: Korean History.* Seoul: Hollym, 1983.

Noth, Martin. *A History of Pentateuchal Traditions.* Translated by Bernhard W. Anderson. Englewood Cliffs, N.J.: Prentice-Hall, 1972.

———. *The History of Israel.* London: SCM, 1958.

Pfeiffer, Robert H. *Introduction to the Old Testament.* New York: Harper and Brothers, 1941.

Rad, Gerhard von. *Genesis.* Translated by John H. Marks. Philadelphia: Westminster, 1961.

Radday, Yehuda T., and Haim Shore. *Genesis: An Authorship Study.* Rome: Pontifical Biblical Institute, 1985.

Redford, Donald B. *A Study of the Biblical Story of Joseph (Genesis 37–50).* Leiden: Brill, 1970.

Rendtorff, Rolf. *The Problem of the Process of the Transmission of the Pentateuch.* Translated by John J. Scullion. JSOTSS 89. Sheffield: JSOT Press, 1990.

Schmidt, Werner H. *Introduction to the Old Testament.* Translated by Matthew J. O'Connell. London: SCM, 1984.

Scott, John A. *The Unity of Homer.* New York: Biblo and Tannen, 1965.

Segal, M. H. *The Pentateuch: Its Composition and Authorship.* Jerusalem: Magnes, 1967.

Seow, C. L. *A Grammar for Biblical Hebrew.* Nashville: Abingdon, 1987.

Shimron, Binyamin. *Politics and Belief in Herodotus. Historia* 58. Stuttgart: Franz Steiner, 1989.

Skinner, John. *A Critical and Exegetical Commentary on Genesis.* 2d ed. ICC. Edinburgh: T. and T. Clark, 1930.

Smith, Henry Preserved. *Samuel.* ICC. Edinburgh: T. and T. Clark, 1898.

Soggin, J. Alberto. *Introduction to the Old Testament.* OTL. Philadelphia: Westminster, 1976.

Soulen, Richard N. *Handbook of Biblical Criticism,* 2d ed. Atlanta: John Knox, 1981.

Speiser, E. A. *Genesis.* AB. New York: Doubleday, 1964.

Stanford, W. B. *The Odyssey of Homer.* 2d ed. 2 vols. New York: St. Martin's, 1959.

Stigers, Harold G. *A Commentary on Genesis.* Grand Rapids: Zondervan, 1975.

Thompson, J. A. *Deuteronomy.* TOTC. London: Inter-Varsity, 1974.

Thompson, R. J. *Moses and the Law in a Century of Criticism Since Graf.* Leiden: Brill, 1970.

Thompson, Thomas L. *The Historicity of the Patriarchal Narratives. BZAW* 133. Berlin: de Gruyter, 1974.

———. *The Origin Tradition in Ancient Israel.* JSOTSS 55. Sheffield: JSOT Press, 1987.

Tsumura, David Toshio. *The Earth and the Waters in Genesis 1 and 2: A Linguistic Investigation.* JSOTSS 83. Sheffield: JSOT Press, 1989.

Van Seters, John. *Abraham in History and Tradition.* New Haven: Yale University Press, 1975.

———. *In Search of History.* New Haven: Yale University Press, 1983.

Vaux, Roland de. *Ancient Israel.* 2 vols. New York: McGraw-Hill, 1965.

Waters, K. H. *Herodotus the Historian*. London: Croom Helm, 1985.

Weiser, Artur. *The Psalms*. Translated by Herbert Hartwell. OTL. Philadelphia: Westminster, 1962.

Wellhausen, Julius. *Prolegomena to the History of Ancient Israel*. Preface by W. Robertson Smith. Cleveland: Meridian, 1957.

Wenham, Gordon J. *Genesis 1–15*. WBC. Waco: Word, 1987.

Westermann, Claus. *Genesis 1–11*. Translated by John J. Scullion. Minneapolis: Augsburg, 1984.

Whybray, R. N. *The Making of the Pentateuch*. Sheffield: JSOT Press, 1987.

Williams, R. D., ed. *The Aeneid of Virgil*. Glasgow: St. Martins, 1973.

Wiseman, P. J. *Clues to Creation in Genesis*. Edited by D. J. Wiseman. London: Marshall, Morgan and Scott, 1977.

Wolf, F. A. *Prolegomena to Homer*. 1795. Translated by Anthony Grafton, with an introduction by James E. G. Zetzel. Princeton: Princeton University Press, 1985.

Zimmerli, Walther. *Ezekiel*. Translated by James D. Martin. 2 vols. Philadelphia: Fortress, 1983.

Articles and Essays

Aitken, Kenneth T. "The Wooing of Rebekah." *JSOT* 30 (1984): 3–23.

Alexander, T. Desmond. "Genesis 22 and the Covenant of Circumcision." *JSOT* 25 (1983): 17–22.

———. "Lot's Hospitality: A Clue to his Righteousness." *JBL* 104 (1985): 289–91.

Alt, Albrecht. "The God of the Fathers." In *Essays on Old Testament History and Religion,* translated and edited by R. A. Wilson, 3–77. Oxford, 1966.

Anderson, Bernhard W. "From Analysis to Synthesis: The Interpretation of Genesis 1–11." *JBL* 97.1 (1978): 23–39.

———. Review of R. Rendtorff, *Das überlieferungsgeschichtliche Problem des Pentateuchs*. *CBQ* 40 (1978): 100–103.

Boyd III, Jesse L. "An Example of the Influence of Egyptian on the Development of the Hebrew Language During the Second Millennium B.C." In *A Tribute to Gleason Archer,* edited by Walter C. Kaiser, Jr., and Ronald F. Youngblood, 191–95. Chicago: Moody, 1986.

Brueggemann, Walter. "David and his Theologian." *CBQ* 30 (1968): 156–81.

Carmichael, Calum M. "Some Sayings in Genesis 49." *JBL* 88 (1969): 435–44.

Cassuto, Umberto. "The Prophet Hosea and the Books of the Pentateuch." In *Biblical and Oriental Studies,* translated by Israel Abrahams, 2 vols., 1:79–100. Jerusalem: Magnes, 1973.

Childs, Brevard S. "A Study of the Formula, 'Until This Day.'" *JBL* 82 (1963): 279–92.

Clark, W. M. "The Flood and the Structure of Pre-patriarchal History." *ZAW* 83 (1971): 184–211.

Clements, R. E. Review of R. Rendtorff, *Das überlieferungsgeschichtliche Problem des Pentateuchs. JSOT* 3 (1977): 46–56.

Coats, George W. "Abraham's Sacrifice of Faith." *Interp* 27 (1973): 389–400.

———. "The Joseph Story and Ancient Wisdom: A Reappraisal." *CBQ* 35 (1973): 285–97.

———. "The Yahwist as Theologian? A Critical Reflection." *JSOT* 3 (1977): 28–32.

Cody, Aelred. Review of *The Historicity of the Patriarchal Narratives,* by Thomas L. Thompson. *Bib* 57 (1976): 263.

Cohn, Robert L. "Narrative Structure and Canonical Perspective in Genesis." *JSOT* 25 (1983): 3–16.

Davis, John J. "The Camel in Biblical Narratives." In *A Tribute to Gleason Archer,* edited by Walter C. Kaiser, Jr., and Ronald F. Youngblood, 141–52. Chicago: Moody, 1986.

DeWitt, Dale S. "The Generations of Genesis." *EvQ* 48 (1976): 196–211.

———. "The Historical Background of Genesis 11:1–9: Babel or Ur." *JETS* 22 (1979): 15–26.

Duke, Rodney K. "The Portion of the Levite: Another Reading of Deuteronomy 18:6–8." *JBL* 106 (1987): 197–98.

Emerton, J. A. "Some False Clues to the Study of Genesis XIV." *VT* 21 (1971): 24–47.

———. "The Origin of the Promises to the Patriarchs in the Older Sources of the Book of Genesis." *VT* 32 (1982): 14–32.

———. "The Riddle of Genesis XIV." *VT* 21 (1971): 403–39.

———. "An Examination of Some Attempts to Defend the Unity of the Flood Narrative in Genesis. Part I," *VT* 37 (1987): 401–20; and "Part II," *VT* 38 (1988): 1–22.

Fishbane, Michael. "Composition and Structure in the Jacob Cycle (Gen. 25:19–35:22)." *JJS* 26 (1975): 15–38.

Goldin, Judah. "The Youngest Son or Where Does Genesis 38 Belong." *JBL* 96 (1977): 27–44.

Good, Edwin M. "The Blessing on Judah, Gen 49:8–12." *JBL* 82 (1963): 427–32.

Hasel, Gerhard F. "The Genealogies of Gen. 5 and 11 and their Alleged Babylonian Background." *AUSS* 16 (1978): 361–74.

Hauser, Alan J. "Linguistic and Thematic Links between Genesis 4:1–16 and Genesis 2–3." *JETS* 23 (1980): 297–305.

Helyer, Larry R. "The Separation of Abram and Lot." *JSOT* 26 (1983): 77–88.

Kessler, Martin. "Genesis 34—An Interpretation." *RefR* 19 (1965): 3–8.

Lambert, W. G. "A New Look at the Babylonian Background of Genesis." *JTS* n.s. 16 (1965): 287–300.

Long, Burke O. Review of *The Origin Tradition of Ancient Israel. JBL* 108 (1989): 330.

McKenzie, Brian Alexander. "Jacob's Blessing on Pharaoh: An Interpretation of Gen 46:31–47:26." *WTJ* 45 (1983): 386–99.

Miscall, Peter D. "The Jacob and Joseph Stories as Analogies." *JSOT* 6 (1978): 28–40.

Morrison, Martha A. "The Jacob and Laban Narrative in Light of Near Eastern Sources." *BA* (Summer 1983): 155–64.

Paradise, Jonathan. "Marriage Contracts of Free Persons at Nuzi." *JCS* 39 (1987): 1–36.

Polk, Timothy. "The Levites in the Davidic-Solomonic Empire." *StBib* 9 (1979): 3–22.

Prewitt, Terry J. "Kinship Structures and the Genesis Genealogies." *JNES* 40 (1981): 87–98.

Rad, Gerhard von. "The Form-Critical Problem of the Hexateuch." In *The Problem of the Hexateuch and Other Essays*. Translated by E. W. Trueman Dicken, 1–78. London: SCM, 1966.

Radday, Yehuda T. "Chiasmus in Hebrew Biblical Narrative." In *Chiasmus in Antiquity*, edited by John W. Welch, 99–100. Gerstenberg Verlag, 1981.

Rendtorff, Rolf. "Pentateuchal Studies on the Move." *JSOT* 3 (1977): 43–45.

———. "The Yahwist as Theologian? The Dilemma of Pentateuchal Criticism." *JSOT* 3 (1977): 2–10.

Roberts, J. J. M. Review of *Abraham in History and Tradition*, by John Van Seters. *JBL* 96 (1977): 109.

Schmid, H. H. "In Search of New Approaches in Pentateuchal Research." *JSOT* 3 (1977): 33–42.

Smith, Robert Houston. "Abram and Melchizedek (Gen 14:18–20)." *ZAW* 77 (1965): 129–53.

Speiser, E. A. "The Wife-Sister Motif in the Patriarchal Narratives." In *Biblical and Other Studies*, edited by Alexander Altman, 15–28. Cambridge: Harvard University Press, 1963.

Tucker, Gene M. "The Legal Background of Genesis 23." *JBL* 85 (1966): 77–84.

Van Seters, John. "The Problem of Childlessness in Near Eastern Law and the Patriarchs of Israel." *JBL* 87 (1968): 401–8.

———. "The Yahwist as Theologian? A Response." *JSOT* 3 (1977): 15–19.

Wagner, Norman E. "A Response to Professor Rolf Rendtorff." *JSOT* 3 (1977): 20–27.

Waltke, Bruce K. "Oral Tradition." In *A Tribute to Gleason Archer*, edited by Walter C. Kaiser, Jr., and Ronald F. Youngblood, 17–34. Chicago: Moody, 1986.

Weisman, Z. "National Consciousness in the Patriarchal Promises." *JSOT* 31 (1985): 55–73.

Wenham, Gordon J. "The Coherence of the Flood Narrative." *VT* 28 (1978): 336–48.

———. Review of H. H. Schmid, *Der sogennante Jahwist*. *JSOT* 3 (1977): 57–60.

White, Hugh C. "The Divine Oath in Genesis." *JBL* 92 (1973): 165–79.

Whybray, R. N. "Response to Professor Rendtorff." *JSOT* 3 (1977): 11–14.

Williams, James G. "The Beautiful and the Barren: Conventions in Biblical Type-Scenes." *JSOT* 17 (1980): 107–19.

Wilson, Robert R. "The Old Testament Genealogies in Recent Research." *JBL* 94 (1975): 169–89.

Woudstra, M. H. "The *toledoth* of the Book of Genesis and their Redemptive-Historical Significance." *CalThJ* 5 (1970): 184–89.

Younger, Lawson. Review of *In Search of History*, by John Van Seters. *JSOT* 40 (1988): 110–14.

Index of Authors and Subjects

261

Index of Scripture